THE ARCTIC

WHAT EVERYONE NEEDS TO KNOW®

THE ARCTIC

WHAT EVERYONE NEEDS TO KNOW®

KLAUS DODDS AND MARK NUTTALL

OXFORD
UNIVERSITY PRESS

OXFORD
UNIVERSITY PRESS

Oxford University Press is a department of the University of Oxford. It furthers the University's objective of excellence in research, scholarship, and education by publishing worldwide. Oxford is a registered trade mark of Oxford University Press in the UK and certain other countries.

"What Everyone Needs to Know" is a registered trademark of Oxford University Press.

Published in the United States of America by Oxford University Press 198 Madison Avenue, New York, NY 10016, United States of America.

Library of Congress Cataloging-in-Publication Data
Names: Dodds, Klaus, author. | Nuttall, Mark, author.
Title: The Arctic : what everyone needs to know /
Klaus Dodds and Mark Nuttall.
Description: New York, NY : Oxford University Press, 2019. |
Includes bibliographical references.
Identifiers: LCCN 2018055473| ISBN 9780190649814 (hardback : alk. paper) |
ISBN 9780190649807 (paperback : alk. paper)
Subjects: LCSH: Arctic regions. | Arctic peoples. |
Arctic regions—Environmental conditions. |
Environmental degradation—Arctic regions. |
Conservation of natural resources—Arctic regions. |
BISAC: HISTORY / Historical Geography. | HISTORY / Polar Regions. |
SCIENCE / History.
Classification: LCC G606 .D64 2019 | DDC 998—dc23
LC record available at https://lccn.loc.gov/2018055473

1 3 5 7 9 8 6 4 2

Paperback printed by Sheridan Books, Inc., United States of America
Hardback printed by Bridgeport National Bindery, Inc., United States of America

CONTENTS

5. Warming Arctic   160

6. Resourceful Arctic   178

FOREWORD

Now when I was a little chap I had a passion for maps. I would look for hours at South America, or Africa, or Australia, and lose myself in all the glories of exploration. At that time there were many blank spaces on the earth, and when I saw one that looked particularly inviting on a map (but they all look that) I would put my finger on it and say, "When I grow up I will go there." The North Pole was one of these places, I remember. Well, I haven't been there yet, and shall not try now. The glamour's off. Other places were scattered about the hemispheres. I have been in some of them, and . . . well, we won't talk about that. But there was one yet — the biggest, the most blank, so to speak — that I had a hankering after.

—Joseph Conrad, *The Heart of Darkness*

Everything—our culture is based on the cold, the snow, and the ice.

—Sheila Watt-Cloutier, "Climate Change Is a Human Rights Issue: An Interview with Sheila Watt-Cloutier," March 4, 2016

The Arctic occupies a contradictory space in the popular imagination—remote and uninhabitable yet also fantastical and alluring. It is also understood to be under threat from rapid climate change; the future of its peoples, wildlife, and environments imperiled by a warming trend that is affecting the region twice as fast as the rest of the world. The Arctic is in trouble.

For those who have never visited the Arctic, it is a region of ice and polar bears. Children can and do imagine a magical world where Santa Claus and his reindeer live somewhere near the North Pole. The northern reaches of the world are, of course, replete with fairy tales, sagas, and adventures in volcanic, wind-swept, and ice-filled kingdoms. The dramatic, mysterious, and heroic are the stuff of adult storytelling as well—a litany of explorers, sailors, and aviators have encountered fame, misfortune, and disaster in the Arctic. There is no shortage of candidates: from Sir Hugh Willoughby and his crew, who disappeared on the coast of Russia's Kola Peninsula in the mid-sixteenth century, to the unknown fate of Henry Hudson in the bay that bears his name in 1611, to Sir John Franklin's doomed Northwest Passage expedition in the mid-nineteenth century and the disappearance of Roald Amundsen on his way to Spitsbergen in the late 1920s and Gino Watkins in East Greenland in the early 1930s.

But the impact of outsiders on the Arctic has been more than an occasional expeditionary foray. From exploration, trapping, whaling, sealing, and fishing to coal mining, oil and gas exploration, and marine insurance, and scientific research, the footprint of others is various and varied. In Britain, a legion of whalers and traders started their Arctic adventures in cities such as Aberdeen, Bristol, Cambridge, and London. Elizabethan explorers such as Martin Frobisher voyaged to what is now known as the Canadian Arctic in the 1570s, and persuaded the Anglo-Russian Muscovy Company to sponsor exploratory work. Sailing into the bay he named for himself in the southeastern part of Baffin Island (naming other parts of the island after his political and commercial sponsors, e.g., Cape Walsingham after Sir Francis Walsingham), Frobisher hoped to find a northern maritime passage to Asia—in essence, a shorter trade route—as well as assess the potential for gold discoveries along the way. Material he found on the southern coast of Baffin Island turned out to be iron pyrite—fool's gold rather than gold—but Frobisher did not arrive home empty-handed. On their return from a second voyage in 1577, the crew forcibly brought three Inuit with them from Baffin Island. They died shortly after their arrival in England.

The Northwest Passage was thought to be a strait that separated Baffin Island from another stretch of land. However, it remained undiscovered by Frobisher. Later, the Hudson's Bay Company was active in the area Frobisher had traveled in, setting up a trading post in 1914 and, at the head of Frobisher Bay, the US Air Force established the beginnings of what is now the community of Iqaluit in 1942. At the time, this was the largest air base in the North American Arctic. The runway (which is over 2,700 meters long) serves as an emergency landing site for transatlantic flights and was an alternative NASA landing site for the Space Shuttle. The town of Frobisher Bay was renamed Iqaluit by the community in 1986 (it was formalized the following year), and it became the capital of the newly established Canadian territory of Nunavut in 1999.

The search for the Northwest Passage remained an obsession. Franklin and his men set off in 1845 to navigate through the last unknown section of the passage in the central Canadian Arctic. Their two ships became icebound near Victoria Strait and all 129 crew disappeared. "The lost men's bodies, waiting, drift and freeze," wrote the American poet Helen Hunt Jackson in *An Arctic Quest*. After multiple search expeditions from the mid-nineteenth century onward, Franklin's two vessels, HMS *Erebus* and HMS *Terror*, were finally found in northern Canadian waters in 2014 and 2016 respectively. Inuit knowledge contributed to determining where the wrecks lay on the seabed off King William Island, though previously Inuit oral testimony had been largely ignored. The ships have been designated national Canadian historic sites and are under the jurisdiction of Environment Canada. In October 2017, it was announced that the United Kingdom was gifting the wrecks to

Canada; Parks Canada has hired a number of Inuit guardians to watch over the sites. An extraordinary ending for vessels that were used initially by the Royal Navy as warships, including service in patrolling the Mediterranean, and which were then refitted for Antarctic and Arctic adventures.

In northern British cities, such as Dundee and Hull, the Arctic whaling and fishing trades respectively were pathways to wealth. Orkney was a major recruitment ground for the Hudson's Bay Company from the early eighteenth century onward. By the late eighteenth century, the Hudson's Bay Company workforce in Canada was overwhelmingly sourced from the small farms and fishing villages of many of the Orkney islands. The relationship between the company and the archipelago lasted until the early twentieth century.

Connections between the British Isles and the Arctic continued to be reinforced by disaster. The sinking of the British trawler *Gaul* in mysterious circumstances in February 1974 while fishing in northern Norwegian waters was headline news. Stories abounded that the trawler was a spy vessel and might have been sunk by a Soviet submarine. Fame and fortune in the Arctic were always counterbalanced by disaster and loss.

The vast majority of humanity will never visit the Arctic, although the growth of polar tourism does mean more people are heading north, many of them on cruise ships to the Northwest Passage, to Greenland, Iceland, and Svalbard. They are venturing into areas, though, that are being increasingly affected by human activities. But it is important to remember the Arctic has been a zone of human interaction for centuries, and social and ecological relationships have been profoundly disrupted in the past. For example, colonial powers and commercial expeditions made their presence felt on indigenous peoples and hunted and extracted fish, seals, minerals, and fur pelts. What has changed in the intervening period is the scale and intensity of human and climatological forces.

Climate change and ongoing resource extraction bring different kinds of threats and challenges—in the Arctic we face the ultimate paradox of human existence. How can we learn to live sustainably with our planet? Will Arctic resources be left in the ground and below the subsea floor as part of a global climate change mitigation strategy? There is an urgent need to understand the Arctic and more and more people are responding to this. In some cases, they do this by simply wanting to visit the Arctic and experience what they can of a region punctuated with ice, water, mountains, and extreme weather. Or else they visit in considerable numbers as part of Arctic exhibitions organized by august institutions such as the British Library and National Maritime Museum in London.

The task of this book is to make sure that Arctic fairy tales don't obscure other stories that can and should be told about this part of the world. The Arctic is in motion.

ACKNOWLEDGMENTS

As ever, we have accumulated a reservoir of debts to people and organizations who sponsor and support our research in the Arctic/High North. Our thanks to Tim Bent at Oxford University Press who commissioned us to write the book in the first place and to the proposal reviewers for their supportive comments. Klaus Dodds is thankful to the Leverhulme Trust for the award of a Major Research Fellowship (2017–2020), which gave time and space for completing this book. He thanks the British Academy for an International Partnership and Mobility Award (2016–2018), which also supported his Arctic-related research. Mark Nuttall thanks the Department of Anthropology at the University of Alberta as well as Ilisimatusarfik/University of Greenland and the Greenland Climate Research Centre for research funding and institutional support. We owe a debt of gratitude to our polar networks of physical/natural and social scientists, artists and filmmakers, policy officials, journalists, and many people from northern communities; colleagues and friends who have contributed to conversations about the Arctic—past, present, and future. None of the above bear any responsibility for our analysis, observation, and judgment about Arctic affairs. Above all, however, we thank our respective families, who continue to be immensely supportive of our endeavors, which often take us away from our homes to various northern places.

THE ARCTIC

WHAT EVERYONE NEEDS TO KNOW®

INTRODUCTION

ONE ARCTIC, MANY ARCTICS

Every week, stories about the Arctic, usually addressing the state of sea ice extent and thickness, diminishing glaciers, rapidly thawing permafrost, acidification of the Arctic Ocean, the resource potential of the region, the opening of new shipping routes, and possible geopolitical tensions, appear in the media. The headlines and accompanying reports are often grounded in the experiences of the five coastal Arctic states—Canada, Norway, Denmark/Greenland, Russia, and the United States— or linger on the Arctic-focused aspirations of countries such as China, India, Singapore, South Korea, and Japan. Asian states are noticeably investing in polar infrastructure, science, and resource-development projects.

As sea ice recedes, there is a widespread suggestion that Arctic countries are determined to secure ever-more territory in the Far North, while non-Arctic states seek greater access to it. The ownership of the continental shelves of the maritime Arctic will determine who has sovereign rights to exploit natural resources. Canada, Denmark/Greenland, and Russia are in pole-position due to their geographical proximity to the North Pole.

Much of this discussion is framed within a context of climate change and the rapid melting of Arctic ice, which, it is often suggested, might then facilitate further commercial extraction of resources, as well as pose a threat to the region's indigenous cultures and to its wildlife. It provides plenty of raw material for intrigue and speculation. The media is fond of pointing out that there are some big numbers in the mix. The hydrocarbon potential of the Arctic region, according to some assessments and estimates, including those of the US Geological Survey, may amount to 13% of the world's undiscovered oil and 30% of its undiscovered natural gas.

These stories draw from and simplify the work of Arctic social scientists and natural and physical scientists. They trivialize the geographies of the Arctic, simplify its geopolitics, and are knowingly selective of what may make for eye-catching news—there is more attention on diminishing ice in the Arctic Ocean and starving polar bears, or on ships attempting to transect the Northwest Passage, than on the sensitivity of Finland's boreal forests to changing temperatures, for example, the decline of Iceland's fox population, or the health and well-being of the Arctic's indigenous peoples. Some scientists write popular books with titles that indicate dramatic change and an uncertain future for the Arctic as ecosystems approach tipping points—*A Farewell to Ice* by noted Cambridge oceanographer and polar scientist Peter Wadhams being one example, while Danish journalist Martin Breum's recent book *Cold Rush* is one of the latest additions to a literature concerned with threats to Arctic security and potential conflicts over territory and resources as the region warms. When indigenous peoples are mentioned in these accounts, they are written about as trying to maintain traditions under threat from globalization, global warming, and resource development, or struggling with issues of self-determination.

These are, of course, critical issues. And, true, hunting, fishing, and reindeer herding remain vitally important activities for the livelihoods of many indigenous peoples; but human life in the Arctic is diverse and increasingly so. The vast majority of Arctic residents live in towns and cities—some of them small, but still predominantly urban in character—and sometimes, on the surface at least, their daily lives are not often dissimilar to their counterparts in more southerly parts of North America, Nordic Europe, and Russia. In Greenland's capital, Nuuk, a city of 17,000 people, commuters have to contend with an often frustrating morning rush hour on their way to drop their children at school or headed to their jobs in offices, retail, or fish-processing plants; Tromsø in Arctic Norway has a population of almost 72,000 who have access to large shopping malls and the same kind of retail experience one can find in Oslo; and Oulu in northern Finland, with a population of some 200,000, is a hub for research and innovation in technology and has recently branded itself as a smart city. And across the Arctic today, there are many indigenous communities actively involved in extractive industries and engaged in businesses with an international reach.

A point we reinforce in this book is that the Arctic is not disconnected from the rest of the world and has long been affected and shaped by global influences. However, this history is often little understood. There seems to be greater interest in the Arctic than perhaps ever before, and this raises a series of questions, some of which we consider and answer in the following chapters. But where and what is the Arctic? Where does it begin, and where does it end? Attempting to answer this seems a good place to start.

Where does the Arctic begin and end?

Defining places and regions is rarely free from controversy. As we will show in the next chapter, definitions of the Arctic vary and diverge considerably, according to any number of scientific, environmental, geographical, political, and cultural perspectives and biases. And to complicate this further, climate change is contributing to shifting many physical boundaries that had been drawn as fixed points and zones and marked ecosystems on maps and charts.

The Arctic is also synonymous with the "North" and the "circumpolar North." We also use these terms, although many high latitude places defined as "northern" in this sense are not necessarily "Arctic." If anything, we show in this book that the Arctic is a dynamic, complex, diverse, and integral part of the world, a place with rich histories and disagreements about its nature and about its future, rather than an empty, remote, distant, and forbidding region at the top of the globe. It is also a place in motion.

So, an initial answer to our first question is that locating and defining the Arctic is not so straightforward. And like any definition, it can reveal and obscure the multiple ways we divide the world into places and regions. Canadians refer to "the North," "mid-North," and the "provincial Norths," while Norwegians talks about the "High North." In Russia, they get around that issue by not only identifying a "Far North" but also use the term "areas equivalent to it," which allows slippage southward depending on the criteria used.

What makes this question a lot harder to answer than it should be is unrelenting change. Once we might have thought the Arctic could and should be defined by lines on maps such as the Arctic Circle. Coupled with that latitudinal definition, we might also point to adjectives like cold, ice, and snow as material, sensory, and elemental markers of the Arctic. We contend that the scale and scope of change scrambles a common-sensical perception and understanding of the Arctic.

In January 2017, it was reported that 2016 had been the warmest year on record for the globe as a whole, and that warming ocean waters off Alaska were bringing widespread ecological changes; that Norway's Statoil was optimistic its Korpfjell license area in the Barents Sea could contain 10 billion barrels of oil; and that Russian president Vladimir Putin was pushing to strengthen national interests in the Arctic by bolstering Russia's military presence in its northern regions.

Responding to the news that Russia was investing in more nuclear icebreakers and equipping its Northern Fleet (based near Murmansk on the Kola Peninsula) with ice-capable corvettes carrying cruise missiles, US Defense Secretary James Mattis commented that Moscow was taking "aggressive steps" in the Arctic. It was a news-filled month for an increasingly globally significant region.

A couple of months later, at the end of March 2017, scientists from the National Snow and Ice Data Center (NSIDC) in Boulder, Colorado, published the results of research that suggested a new record for low levels of winter ice in the Arctic Ocean had been set. A number of scientists were quoted in various media as saying the findings were "disturbing" and that the Arctic was now in a "deep hole."

In April, a paper published in *Science* reported on research carried out in the eastern Eurasian basin—north of the Laptev and East Siberian Seas—that found that warm Atlantic water is increasingly pushing to the surface and melting floating sea ice. This mixing, the authors said, has not only contributed to thinner ice and to larger areas of previously ice-covered open water, but it is also changing the state of Arctic waters in a process they termed "Atlantification"—and they warned this could soon spread across more of the Arctic Ocean, transforming it fundamentally. Other scientists speak of "Pacification" and report farther movements of warmer and denser waters into the previously frozen ocean. Heat, nutrients, lower latitude species, pollutants, and microplastics are following in their collective wake.

So, in that one year, 2017, we can point to reports of Arctic change on many different fronts—biological, geophysical, and resourceful. Move forward to summer 2018, forest fires raged north of the Arctic Circle in Sweden, and research published by scientists working for NASA, who had constructed a sixty-year overview of Arctic sea ice thickness beginning in 1958, concluded, since scientists began observing and recording it, that the Arctic Ocean's ice cover is now younger and thinner.

Meanwhile, in August 2018 it was reported that sea ice off the north coast of Greenland, which is the oldest and thickest in the Arctic Ocean, and compacted by the Transpolar Drift, had started to break up. Scientists from the Danish Meteorological Institute expressed alarm that this ice was becoming more mobile in waters where ice is, on average four meters thick and not easily moved. The following month, Danish shipping company Maersk announced that its container vessel *Venta Maersk* had completed a trial passage of Russia's Northern Sea Route (NSR), from Vladivostok to St. Petersburg, while at the end of October Sovcomflot's oil tanker *Lomonosov Prospect*, which is powered by liquified natural gas (LNG), voyaged over 2,000 nautical miles in under eight days through the NSR carrying petroleum products from South Korea to northern Europe. *Lomonosov Prospect* only required nuclear icebreaker assistance in the region of the Ayon ice massif in the East Siberian Sea. These trends, movements, and mobilities are set to continue.

Who lives in the Arctic, and is that changing?

So much of what we are told about the Arctic is partial, out of date, and simply wrong. Many children grow up imagining the Arctic as populated by native peoples (simplified as "Eskimos") living in igloos. Indigenous cultures are diverse, and many indigenous peoples live below the Arctic Circle. In most parts of the circumpolar North, non-indigenous residents far outnumber indigenous Arctic peoples, largely because of the legacies of colonialism and settlement, but also because of recent trends in immigration, rural-urban migration, and the global processes of demographic change. The communities living in the Arctic are not unchanging. Arctic regions are also cosmopolitan places, with indigenous writers such as Greenland's Niviaq Korneliussen charting their social, cultural, and sexual—and urban—complexities.

In chapter 3 we will explore the ways in which indigenous peoples think about their Arctic surroundings as homelands and how this is central to land claims, self-determination, and self-government. In some parts of the Arctic, however, everyone is a migrant, an incomer, or a settler who nurtures their own relationships and senses of place with their surroundings— and the composition of Arctic towns and communities is far more diversified than many people imagine. In Longyearbyen, the administrative center of Svalbard (Norway's Arctic Ocean archipelago, which has a population of around 2,600), a Thai community has grown there since the early 1980s. Working mainly in the hotel sector, Thais make up the second-biggest community, after Norwegians, but the town's international character is also defined by many other foreign long-term and seasonal residents. Longyearbyen may have its origins in a set-tlement established by the Boston-based Arctic Coal Company in 1906, but now you are far more likely to meet people working there who are from Malaysia, Armenia, and Argentina, and see Asian tourists rather than coal miners. Longyearbyen is also a busy place throughout the year, not just when a large number of cruise ships visit during summer—international students study changing Arctic ecosystems at UNIS, the University Centre in Svalbard, while the town is host to a number of festivals, even during the coldest winter months. Svalbard has been branded the "the cultural capital of the High Arctic" by the archipelago's official tourist board. Longyearbyen plays host to the world's most northerly Oktoberfest, the annual Polarjazz festival at the end of each January, and the annual Dark Season Blues festival, among many others.

In Greenland, people from Thailand and the Philippines work in low-wage service sectors, especially in hotels, restaurants, and housekeeping, but they also run their own successful businesses. Many have families—some have mar-ried Greenlanders and Danes—and their children learn Greenlandic and Danish in school; an earlier generation born in Greenland, and now in their early twenties, are making their own careers and homes in places such as Nuuk and Ilulissat. One of the newer restaurants to have opened in Nuuk specializes in Greenlandic-Filipino fusion cuisine. Tourists arriving at Ilulissat airport will be greeted in the baggage claim area by a sign advertising a Chinese and Thai fast food café, alongside an advertisement for muskox trophy-hunting adventures. In Alaska, Filipinos have been working and living on Kodiak Island for more than 150 years, mainly employed in the fishing and salmon-canning industries. Over 30% of the community is Filipino or Filipino-American by heritage. Many other ethnic communities live in Alaska—for example, there are around 11,500 Mexicans in Anchorage (a city of just over 298,000 people), many of whom retain their links with Mexico and spend time there and in Alaska, while a Vietnamese-American community has grown since the 1970s and 1980s in Nome, a town of some 3,800 people on the Seward Peninsula on Alaska's Norton Sound, an inlet of the Bering Sea.

A traveler arriving at Iqaluit's airport would very likely take a cab to their hotel driven by a migrant to Canada from Syria or Somalia, just as they would from airports in Montreal, Toronto, or Edmonton. Nunavut's capital is home to around one hundred Muslims, who work as doctors, engineers, and government officials, as well as in service industries; and the Islamic Society of Nunavut opened a building in February 2016 that acts as a mosque and community space. The most northerly mosque in Canada opened in Inuvik, in the Mackenzie Delta region of the Northwest Territories (NWT) in November 2010.

In the Russian North and in Siberia the mix of ethnic groups is similarly cosmopolitan—the city of Yakutsk in the Sakha Republic, for instance, is home to Yakuts, Russians, Ukrainians, and Tatars, as well as to people from a number of Siberian indigenous groups, including Yukaghir, Dolgans, Evens, Evenks, and Chukchis. Non-indigenous settlers from other parts of the Russian Federation also make their homes in many other parts of the Russian North and Russian Far East.

So, the Arctic is made up of a series of multiethnic and multicultural homelands—and as we shall see later in this book, there is diversity within indigenous populations themselves. And those homelands are changing and changeable. Asian, European, and American communities are integral to Arctic economies and societies and have been for decades if not centuries.

What effect is climate change having on those who live in the Arctic?

Climate change dominates contemporary discussion of the Arctic. Warming brings with it profound consequences for people, animals, and ecosystems. The impact of warming is uneven; the loss of sea ice and the thawing of permafrost mean risks and vulnerabilities, but also allow opportunities and possibilities.

For some involved in extractive industries, further resource development in the Arctic is thought of as being made easier by climate change, as remote places become more accessible. It is assumed by many that as the frozen Arctic Ocean becomes less so, it becomes more navigable to shipping. For others, the loss of sea ice is disastrous because it affects a way of life dependent on moving across that very substance that is melting and less secure. Canadian Inuit activist Sheila Watt-Cloutier, a former international chair of the Inuit Circumpolar Council (ICC), an indigenous peoples' organization that represents Inuit throughout the Arctic, wrote in her memoir, *The Right to Be Cold* which was published in 2015, that a warming Arctic poses an existential threat to a people and a culture predicated on a semipermanent state of cold, snow, and ice. For her and others, the presence of snow and ice is necessary for the survival of Inuit culture and livelihoods. A melting Arctic means indigenous homelands are in danger of being changed dramatically. Thinning sea ice makes travel and hunting more precarious. Travel is more expensive if one is using more fuel to battle through ice-clogged waters in boats during winter and spring instead of moving across the frozen surface of the sea by snowmobile or dogsled. Traditional indigenous knowledge becomes less reliable than it once was, making it difficult to anticipate what lies ahead on a journey, and this in turn means there is increased potential for stranding, accidents, and even drowning while out hunting. Sea ice is akin to critical infrastructure to Inuit.

Russian leaders might take a more benign view about the loss of sea ice in the Arctic. A northern port such as Sabetta, on the Yamal Peninsula, could develop as a major hub for shipping oil and LNG through the NSR. The Yamal Peninsula is a breathtaking prospect for Russia with total reserves and resources in the fields estimated to be 26.5 trillion cubic meters of gas, 1.6 billion tons of gas condensate, and 300 million tons of oil. President Putin and his government detect economic opportunities in a changing Arctic, which may enhance prospects for the country's future as an Arctic energy superpower. Russians do worry about environmental change in the Arctic, but they also recognize that there is too much resource potential in the north of their country to ignore. Less sea ice means that LNG shipping could be easier to operate.

If Putin senses opportunities to develop the Russian North further (and one must remember that it was industrialized heavily during the Stalin era), elsewhere other senior politicians, such as Donald Tusk, president of the European Council, and former UN Secretary-General Ban Ki-moon, have been warning of the dangers of unrelenting environmental change. These warnings have often been made during visits to Greenland's Ilulissat Icefjord, a UNESCO World Heritage Site in Disko Bay, which has become an iconic place for world leaders to travel to and ponder the situation we find ourselves in. Standing as close as they can manage to the edge of the glacial ice of Sermeq Kujalleq (also known as the Jakobshavn Glacier) or moving on tourist boats through iceberg-studded waters, distinguished visitors to the icefjord appear to express astonishment at how climate change is happening before their eyes as icebergs calve and collapse from the glacier's front. Calving is sometimes termed "ice ablation or ice disruption" by glaciologists and occurs when a glacier expands and produces icebergs of varying shapes and sizes. This happens when a glacier front moves closer to warmer waters. While it is not caused by climate change per se, more dramatic calving events occurring in the Arctic—especially in Greenland—are entirely consistent with it. Sermeq Kujalleq is the fastest-moving glacier in the world and produces around 10% of all the icebergs in Greenland's waters. In the last decade or so, it has doubled its speed (moving some forty meters or around 130 feet every twenty-four hours), and its front has receded significantly.

Ice that cracks, tumbles, and crashes into the sea acts as a visceral expression of rising temperatures and a melting world. But environmental change also generates enticing opportunities for communities and businesses in the Arctic to benefit and profit from an expansion of the tourist, mining, and commercial sectors. So, determining and understanding the effects of climate change on those who live in the Arctic is not straightforward. Some communities will face an existential threat to their ways of life, while others will seek to capitalize on opportunities. Disappearing ice may mean indigenous Inuit hunters face difficulties with travel by boat and dog-sled, but it allows other visitors access. Tourism in the Arctic is a growing industry—every time senior political figures visit Greenland to express concern about the state of the island's ice sheet or glaciers, they help promote it as an alluring last-chance tourist destination. Ice is marketed as disappearing, and tour operators appeal to people to visit and experience the Arctic before it is too late.

What are the competing visions of and for the Arctic?

Political leaders, north and south, are not alone in mobilizing their agendas for the Arctic. Change, however dramatic, even disastrous, creates opportunities. Environmental organizations enlist activists, actors, musicians, and an array of celebrities (as well as images of charismatic animals, such as polar bears) in campaigns to draw attention to the plight of a region framed as fragile, vulnerable, unstable, and increasingly accessible. In June 2016, an online video was released of a performance by Italian pianist Ludovico Einaudi of his composition *Elegy for the Arctic*. Einaudi played his piece, written specifically for the video, on a grand piano positioned on an artificial iceberg platform constructed of wood and floating on the sea near Svalbard's Wahlenbergbreen Glacier. The event was organized and staged by Greenpeace, whose ship *Arctic Sunrise* had transported the musician, his piano, and the two-ton platform to this High Arctic Norwegian territory.

Elegy for the Arctic is an evocative composition, and the video's release was timed to coincide with a meeting in Spain of the OSPAR (Convention for the Protection of the Marine Environment of the North-East Atlantic) Commission, where nations of the northeast North Atlantic were deliberating plans to protect parts of the Arctic Ocean from oil drilling and overfishing. As Einaudi plays, glacial ice tumbles into the water—a natural climax to the piece.

Images of the Arctic's melting glaciers and vanishing sea ice, and the region's wildlife supposedly under threat, such as the polar bear, the seal, the whale, and the Arctic fox, are often used to radicalize global attention. They demand our attention and warn those who might be complacent about a laundry list of worries: climate change; habitat loss; threats to animals; the exploitation of oil, gas, and minerals; and increased commercial and military shipping. They work to drum up public and political support for international campaigns as the Arctic itself is consumed by a "hostile environment" created by human intervention.

Environmental groups such as Greenpeace and the World Wide Fund for Nature (WWF) also use the voices and views of celebrities and well-known personalities to garner public interest and heighten awareness of threats to the Arctic. Actors such as Emma Thompson and Leonardo DiCaprio have been in the vanguard of the most recent campaigns urging boycotts of oil and gas companies operating in the northern latitudes. In 2016, for example, Thompson visited the Baffin Island community of Clyde River with a Greenpeace delegation focused on highlighting the effects of climate change, but also to campaign with Inuit hunters against offshore seismic testing and bring national and global attention to local anxieties about the potential impacts on narwhals and other marine mammals.

Environmental campaigners demand the designation and protection of eco-regions such as the North Water polynya (Pikialasorsuaq in Greenlandic, which means "the great up-welling"), a large area of ice-free open sea between the High Arctic coasts of Greenland and Canada, and what WWF has termed the Last Ice Area, a region encompassing parts of northern Greenland, the Canadian High Arctic archipelago, and parts of the Arctic Ocean. In November 2011, WWF also teamed up with Coca-Cola, which first used the imagery of polar bears in its advertising in 1922, to launch the Arctic Home campaign to raise funds needed in support of WWF's efforts to protect polar bear habitat. Coca-Cola redesigned its can, changing the color from red to white, complete with an image of a mother polar bear and her two cubs roaming across Arctic ice and snow, at the start of the campaign, which raised over USD$2 million.

Environmental campaigning is not without its critics. For Arctic community members, it often reflects "southern" biases and conceits and says little about how indigenous peoples struggle for their rights to determine how and why animals should be hunted and where resources should be either conserved or exploited. The economic needs and cultural rights of Inuit and other northern residents appear trumped by the popular appeal of polar bears and other charismatic species.

The Arctic Home campaign depicted the polar bear in a pristine, yet threatened, wilderness—WWF uses the term "iconic species of the Arctic Ocean"— while ignoring that some Inuit communities in Alaska, Canada, and Greenland hunt it, eat its meat, and utilize its fur for clothing. Fundraising would hardly be successful if it displayed images of polar bear pelts stretched on frames outside homes in north Greenland settlements. Imagery and iconography are important. It would be interesting to see how successful a global public campaign to save the Greenland shark would be. Like the polar bear, the Greenland shark is a top predator in the Arctic. It is known to live not just in deep waters but also at the ice edge and at the surface of the sea. A rare animal that can reach an age of 400 years, some scientists worry that it may be endangered. Few people would describe the Greenland shark as charismatic, however, let alone iconic, or would necessarily worry about its future. So, the tough message here is—if you want to assemble a conservationist vision for the Arctic, then choose the right animal with the right kind of global public appeal.

But while indigenous hunters and fishers are concerned over the loss of sea ice, and threats to traditional hunting and fishing, we should not presume northern communities are anti-development. Attitudes toward industrialization, urbanization, resource extraction, and commercial shipping are diverse. The indigenous and wider human history of the Arctic involves multiple entanglements with overseas investors, companies, states, and immigrant communities. When northern communities put forward their visions for the Arctic, they are as complex and contradictory as anywhere else in the world. Few people living in the Arctic would say they wouldn't want Internet connectivity, or that they are flatly against any kind of resource development. Both are integral to many northern communities. Traditional and modern beliefs and lifestyles can and do coexist with one another.

Northern communities are also well aware that their visions for the Arctic involve trade-offs. The second-largest island in the United States (after Hawai'i), Kodiak, was once the center of Russian fur trading with Alaska Natives in the late eighteenth and early nineteenth centuries. In recent decades, resource-related development, such as mining and fish processing, has brought with it opportunities for employment and investment in infrastructure including health and education. It has also carried with it consequences ranging from pollution to the social and cultural disruption that often accompanies the influx of migrant "fly in, fly out" workers.

So, there are competing visions of and for the Arctic, and often they boil down to a struggle to determine how to conserve a region that some wish to see as a "wilderness," and others regard as a homeland that has to sustain communities. All of which means that there is controversy aplenty.

Why is it important to resist Arctic stereotypes?

The struggle between conservation and development encapsulates what is at stake when we think about and discuss the Arctic. In a nutshell, our visions regarding the Arctic often rest on unstated assumptions and prejudices about the region and its peoples.

It is far too easy to stereotype indigenous Arctic livelihoods and cultures as traditional, vulnerable, and under threat from global forces. Inuit and other indigenous and northern peoples are perfectly capable of reconciling a desire for high-speed Internet connectivity; to train for a range of careers; to travel to other parts of the world for education, employment, or vacations; or to seek the development of local and regional economies based on mining and oil extraction in some cases, with a strong sociocultural connection to subsistence hunting for polar bears, seals, whales, or reindeer herding. Indigenous peoples in the Arctic are also adept at representing themselves and their communities, and many have embraced social media alongside novels, radio, film, and video production. And yet it is still not uncommon to read and hear stories that depict indigenous peoples as disconnected from modern living, exoticize their cultures, or ignore the legacies of colonization and rapid and abrupt social change and dislocation.

Northern residents are also significant players in Arctic geopolitics. Land claims settlements in Alaska and Canada and self-government arrangements for Greenland have given indigenous peoples some control (considerably so in the case of Greenland) over the political institutions and bureaucracies that affect their lives, as well as resource rights, and many are active participants in the development of businesses such as commercial fisheries and extractive industries. The Arctic Slope Regional Corporation (ASRC), for instance, was established, pursuant to the Alaska Native Claims Settlement Act (ANCSA) of 1971, and represents the interests of 13,000 Iñupiat shareholders in northern Alaska. ASRC operates a number of companies concerned with resource development, petroleum refining, and marketing, and owns title to almost 5 million acres of land on Alaska's North Slope. Under this land there are potential riches in the form of oil, gas, and coal as well as minerals. ASRC has been involved with oil and energy projects since the 1970s (oil was discovered at Prudhoe Bay on Alaska's northern coast in 1968) and, as a private for-profit corporation, is committed to developing more resources.

For Iñupiat from North Slope communities, working at the Prudhoe Bay oil complex and participating in spring bowhead whale hunts do not seem incompatible activities. Earning much of one's income from employment on drilling rigs or oilfield supply services while harvesting and preparing the meat from marine mammals are both part of contemporary life in northern coastal Alaska. In recent decades, some environmentalists and animal rights groups have argued that because of social change and the introduction of new technologies, such as rifles and outboard engines, Inuit were no longer "traditional" hunters. In the eighteenth and nineteenth centuries, and even up to the mid-twentieth, British and American companies and customers had no such qualms about burning whale oil, wearing seal pelts, or using whale-bone in corsets.

What frustrates many northern residents in the Arctic is the perception that decisions about the future of the region are negotiated and made elsewhere, and often involve external stakeholders with little visible presence in those communities. Paradoxically, energy companies and environmental groups can also be accused of too much presence. Striking the right balance is not easy, but often the word "consultation" is cited as pivotal to how local communities judge their relationships with external stakeholders.

If economic decision-making affecting local communities in the Arctic is given less media attention, global warming is often framed as a matter of cultural survival for all indigenous communities. But this is misleading. Its effects are experienced in different ways, depending on how people are situated geographically, politically, and economically. For example, in Greenland, where the climate is changing particularly rapidly and is having noticeable impacts on environment and society, some of the residents of Nuuk see changes in the weather as an inconvenience rather than disruptive. In the far north of this vast island, many hundreds of miles away from Nuuk, hunters express concern about thinning sea ice, poor dogsledding conditions, and increasing difficulties in hunting seals and other marine mammals. In the sheep-farming areas of the south, however, farmers are extending the grazing range for their animals and are experiencing bumper harvests of potatoes, beets, parsnip, turnips, cauliflower, and strawberries that are then sold in the country's supermarkets. Experimental forest plantations are also doing well in south Greenland because of a warmer climate. This illustrates the regional context to climate change, as well as its challenges and opportunities. Not everyone thinks and feels the same about climate change in the Arctic. Climate change may be an issue of cultural and economic survival for some; for others it also holds the promise of economic prosperity. Many Greenlandic political leaders think of climate change as enabling oil and gas exploration and mining development, which could lead to greater autonomy and possible independence from Denmark.

A warmer climate means Greenland will be able to produce more foods and offset the high cost of imports. For some politicians in Nuuk, Greenland's melting inland ice and glaciers, disappearing sea ice, and more productive soil are also seen as empowering efforts toward greater self-determination. If we want to understand why people in the Arctic can think and act quite differently on issues such as climate change and resource development, then we need to be aware of and understand a medley of interests and wishes. There are multiple Arctics.

What are the main drivers for these multiple Arctics?

Five key drivers inform and underwrite our understanding of the multiple Arctics we will return to throughout the chapters in our book

First, the region is on the frontline of debates about climate change and environmental transformation. The world's cryosphere (the frozen water parts of the earth) is pivotal to the scale and pace of climate change and how we cope with sea-level change. By the end of the twenty-first century, there will be 10 billion people sharing our planet, and many of them will live in mega-cities and in coastal and low-lying regions. A melting Greenlandic ice sheet (combined with a melting Antarctic ice sheet) is bad news for cities such as Miami and Shanghai, and for low-lying Pacific island countries such as Tuvalu and Kiribati, as well as Indian Ocean states, and may be more of a concern for people there than for some residents of Greenland.

The Arctic is integral to global consciousness about climate change. Rising temperatures are having profound effects on permafrost; ocean temperatures and salinity; air currents; and land, marine, and ice ecologies. The Arctic is "greening" in the summer as snow and ice cover diminish (while the boreal forest is "browning" because of drier, hotter weather). Given that the Arctic climate plays a major role in the regulation of global climate, there will be considerable effects on weather systems worldwide, as well as other environmental reconfigurations, including coastal erosion and sea-level rise. There are multiple stressors at play, with short- and long-term consequences that we cannot always anticipate in terms of their scale, impact, and timing. But we know that change is coming; jet streams are altering, polar vortexes are affecting North American winters, and the Greenland ice sheet is melting. Arctic climate change is multifaceted and its effects are multilocational.

In the Arctic, human and non-human inhabitants are affected by climate change. The extent and stability of sea ice has an impact on the livelihoods of Inuit hunters and the habitat of polar bears and seals. Sámi reindeer herders in northern Fennoscandia (i.e., Norway, Sweden, and Finland) and in Russia, such as those from Evenki and Nenets communities, face the loss of grazing land. They are also confronted with challenges to winter and spring travel, as ice paths across frozen lakes and rivers become more dangerous for their herds, altering traditional migration routes. Even for those Arctic residents not engaged in hunting, fishing, or reindeer herding, continued sea ice loss, thawing permafrost, and "strange weather" extracts a price. Communities are exposed to more severe flooding and storm damage, leading in some cases to forced relocation. Responding to its effects and risks, as well as the opportunities climate change can bring, will require concrete action at both national and international levels. The Arctic is ground zero for climate change.

A second driver is globalization. The world is becoming increasingly more integrated and networked (and, ironically, perhaps, more uncertain and insecure). Few parts of the world are not connected with other regions, and not affected or influenced in some way by these entanglements. It is now commonplace to speak of a "global Arctic" and to hear leaders around the world describe the Arctic as a "global concern." Annual meetings, such as the Arctic Circle assembly held in Iceland, which bring together scientists, policymakers, industry and business, trade positively on the globalization of the Arctic.

Globalization involves processes, institutions, and regimes that intensify a multiplicity of connections across the globe. The Arctic has a long history of being affected by, but also contributing to, global processes and governance. The circumpolar North has rich histories of human movement and has long been the focal point of human imagination and ambition. It has been the object of exploration and scientific research, the results of which been commemorated on maps and in books. Indigenous peoples have lived in Arctic regions for millennia and have left their imprints on the land, but so have more recent commercial whaling and mining activities, or the search for trade routes. Arctic environments and communities bear the scars of colonialism, with governments introducing resettlement and residential schooling policies for indigenous peoples.

The northern reaches of the world have much to contribute to our current understandings of the histories of human movement across and around the planet and of global connections and global processes. They are where international law, multilateral organizations, political devolution, indigenous autonomy, environmentalism, and adaptable governance systems all intersect. The global Arctic brings to the fore how governance and geopolitics are adapting to widespread and substantive environmental and social change.

There has been a shift since the 1990s from considering the Arctic as a Cold War geopolitical frontline of sorts to a part of the world ever-more integrated with economic, political, and cultural markets, actors, and interests. One brief example would be the growing involvement of China, India, Japan, South Korea, and Singapore in Arctic shipping, science, resource development, and trade investment. The emergence of a new global Arctic is a work in progress, drawing together new and old stakeholders and interests alike.

A third driver is global geopolitics. The Arctic is attracting more global political attention. In August 2007 a Russian mini-submersible descended to the Lomonosov Ridge on the Arctic Ocean seabed and deposited a titanium-constructed (corrosion resistant) Russian flagpole. The image of the flag went viral and unleashed a hailstorm of commentary. European and North American newspapers reported that Russia had kick-started a new scramble for Arctic territory and resources. The reaction to the Russian expedition revealed, at the very least, some disagreement about how to make sense of it. Was it a subaquatic land grab or a scientific achievement or both? What kind of Arctic was at stake here? The Arctic, and specifically the Arctic Ocean, is imagined as integral to the concerns of Canada, Denmark/Greenland, Norway, Russia, and the United States (often referred to as the Arctic 5, or A5). Political leaders in these five Arctic countries are perfectly capable of warning their domestic constituencies about the perfidious actions of others. Overall, the reaction of both the Russian and Canadian media reinforced the idea of the Arctic Ocean as being an integral part of their respective countries. Both sides want to stake their claim to it.

Canadian government officials were reported as being furious that such a thing could have happened. Peter MacKay, the then foreign minister, offered the most memorable assessment. He opined, "This isn't the fifteenth century. You can't go around the world and just plant flags and say, 'we're claiming this territory.' [Russia] is posturing. This is the true north strong and free, and they are fooling themselves if they think dropping a flag on the ocean floor is going to change anything." And, for good measure, he added, "We established a long time ago that these are Canadian waters and this is Canadian property."

In a press conference, the Russian foreign minister, Sergei Lavrov, linked the flag-planting encounter to the ongoing endeavors of the Russian scientific community to map and survey the Lomonosov Ridge. The Arktika expedition, as part of the 2007–2008 International Polar Year, was to ascertain whether this ridge was actually a territorial extension of the Siberian continental shelf. Russian scientists and political figures alike hoped that this would reinforce a new submission to the UN's Commission on the Limits of the Continental Shelf (CLCS) relating to an extension of sovereign rights over the central Arctic Ocean seabed. While planting a Russian flag was unlikely to sway the professional judgment of those scientific experts attached to the CLCS, most people around the world would have little understanding of the work of the commission. The CLCS asked Russia to go away and reconsider its technical submission. No one country will ever enjoy full sovereignty over the North Pole and central Arctic Ocean. Still, the flag-planting incident touched a raw nerve. There was no doubt that others were worried that Russia was intent on claiming and extracting resources well beyond its northern national exclusive economic zone.

This illustrates that Arctic geopolitics are prone to both alarmism—about dramatic environmental change in a fragile and vulnerable region, and the claiming of territory and resources—and a reassuring gloss that the Arctic is a place from which new ways of thinking about human-environment relations, sustainability, and international cooperation can emerge. A tension exists between the territorial grip of Arctic states and the interests and investments of non-Arctic states, corporations, and international bodies such as the UN International Maritime Organization. Reactions to the Russian flag planting in the Arctic intensified following Russia's annexation of Crimea, the crisis in eastern Ukraine, and involvement in Syria. Was this a sign of things to follow? Western sanctions against Russia, paradoxically, allowed Chinese corporations to become more involved in Russian Arctic–based energy and infrastructural projects. Russia needs investment in order to develop its oil and gas potential, and it turned to the one country happy to provide it. Evidence, if any were needed, that the geopolitics of the Arctic is intimately linked to affairs elsewhere.

The fourth driver is technology. Historically, the Arctic has been a space for industrial-scale experimentation. The development and introduction of the steam-driven ship and the explosive gun transformed mid-nineteenth-century whaling, allowing vessels to deplete whale populations by the end of the century. During the Cold War, what was termed "cold weather engineering and technology" continued pre-1945 experimentation and testing with materials designed to help infrastructure withstand low temperatures and seasonal variability. As technological gains were secured, human interference in the region intensified as military and civilian communities extended their reach on Arctic landscapes, waters, and ecologies.

Drone technology, including underwater submersibles, aerial and sail drones, will be increasingly important to scientific monitoring and observation alongside a new generation of icebreakers and satellites, environmental auditing, security planning, and search and rescue/surveillance operations. For some, drones and automated icebreakers represent the latest iteration of human ingenuity—making it safer and cost-effective to operate in the Arctic and gather high-resolution data from large expanses of ocean (which can be delivered to a desktop computer or mobile phone). Underwater drones were used in the search for the Franklin vessels in the central Canadian Arctic as well as to hunt for new scientific clues about the state of sea ice in the central Arctic Ocean. Digital infrastructures enhance and improve broadband connectivity, and advances in areas, such as telemedicine, improve the access northern residents have to healthcare services and medical professionals.

The fifth driver is northern autonomy—of indigenous peoples and northern communities. With a broader definition of the circumpolar North, it would stretch along and occasionally meander below 60°N latitude, and the population would be around 13 million (we explore the different ways of defining the Arctic in the next chapter), which is less than 1% of the world's population. A narrower definition of the Arctic (as opposed to the circumpolar North) would mean a population of 4 million, with the indigenous population constituting about 10% of that figure. Every part of the Arctic has its own complex social history and geography, and the relationship between indigenous and non-indigenous peoples and societies varies, with Greenland and the Canadian territory of Nunavut having the highest levels of indigenous political representation, in the Greenlandic parliament and Nunavut legislature respectively. Often, however, parts of the Arctic, mostly notably the central Arctic Ocean, are represented as remote and unoccupied, and these representations spark the interests of those five Arctic Ocean coastal states to consolidate their hold on it. The interests and wishes of indigenous peoples are usually downplayed and even ignored entirely because Arctic coastal states and other nations imagine these remoter parts of the ocean and the seabed to be beyond indigenous purview. Little surprise, then, that indigenous communities are swift to argue that they are essential to any future discussions of the Arctic and that international legal regimes, such as the Law of the Sea, should not be used to cut them out of future discussions.

The Arctic covers a vast part of the northern reaches of the globe. This book does not pretend to provide comprehensive coverage of the Arctic, nor is it a compendium of wildlife, an ethnographic account of circumpolar cultures, an audit of the state of the geopolitics of the region, or a summary of the latest science about northern environments and climate change. Rather, in the spirit of this series, we set out to discuss a range of issues that everyone should need to know when they seek to understand the contemporary Arctic.

The five drivers we have outlined—climate change, geopolitics, globalization, technology, and northern autonomy—are responsible for making the Arctic a more complex region. Different experiences, ideas, and interests intersect with one another. There is no one Arctic. Instead multiple Arctics collide, coexist, and conflict with one another. In order to deepen our appreciation of these multiple Arctics, we need to return to something that haunts any interrogation of the Arctic—lines, boundaries, and definitions. They matter, they remain stubbornly persistent, and yet they are being scrambled by climatic and geopolitical change. Our next chapter enters this geographical thicket.

1

LOCATING TRUE NORTH

It is common to point to the Arctic Circle (66°N) as indicative of the start of the Arctic and "true north." If you land at Rovaniemi airport in Finnish Lapland, you are told you have arrived at the home of Santa Claus. The town lies on the Arctic Circle. Lines are integral human cultures, and the Arctic bears the imprint of that desire to define and order.

Sometimes how we define and delimit the earth is like being caught in freezing fog or a whiteout. Each time we think we can express some confidence in a definitional construct that allows us to see our way out of it, along comes a fog of complexity or a blurring of the world before us that messes with our sense of perceivable distance, disorienting us, and restricting our vertical and horizontal vision. Lines, as anthropologist Tim Ingold reminds us, can and do fray, crease, crack, and disappear.

When it comes to defining the Arctic, there is plenty of freezing fog or reduction of visibility and contrast to contend with. In their 1997 book *The Myth of Continents*, the geographers Martin Lewis and Kären Wigen consider how once we start drawing lines on maps and postulating this is where one region (or a continent like Europe) begins and ends has implications for how we gather and organize our knowledge and understanding of the physical structures and properties and classification of the world. The politics of inclusion and exclusion is not just an academic matter. For Arctic states such as Canada, Denmark/Greenland, Norway, and Russia, being "Arctic"—not just "northern"—is integral to their national selves.

One implication that follows from that self-identification is that those countries and communities have a strong interest in promoting, protecting, and policing their Arctic interests and regions. In Russia, northern residents take great pride in living and working "furthest north" in some of the coldest places in the world. Travel to Norway, and you will soon be introduced to a term "High North," which the unwary might assume refers only to the northern portion of the country and the archipelago of Svalbard. In Norwegian political documents, though, the High North is often better thought of as a "Wider North." It stretches from east Greenland and Iceland to Scandinavia and western Russia, and drops southward to include the Faroe Islands and Shetland Islands. So care is needed not to assume everyone knows what they are talking about when terms like Arctic, High North, Furthest North, and even Wider North are deployed.

Why does anyone care what is and what is not "true north"?

The "North" does get used interchangeably with the "circumpolar North," and both in turn are often seen as synonymous with the "Arctic." Definitional fog is confusing, but it also suits others eager to impress their stakeholders about their extensive portfolios and significance to national governments and global constituencies.

A prime example of an agency reveling in the stretchable nature of "North" is Natural Resources Canada (NRC), the Canadian government's department of natural resources. It has isolated the presence of permafrost as the most useful way of defining a northern boundary. NRC states that the line "provides a natural boundary between northern and southern Canada." The decision might seem innocuous. A geographical feature (soil, rock, or sediment that is frozen for more than two consecutive years) is their chosen point of departure for "northern Canada."

But there is nothing natural about it. Permafrost can be sporadic, and with warming in the Canadian North, the boundary between permafrost and non-permafrost is mobile. Every year that "line" moves, but we suspect the maps NRC uses probably don't reflect the reality of a moveable border. Canadian agencies might like the linear approach to northerness because they can point to a map and reassure their political masters that Canada is a "northern nation."

To muddle things further, NRC's map of northern Canada depicts Canadian geography north of 50° latitude as the northern reaches. So, it does more than simply point to the presence of permafrost. However, its map of the world's "Northern Circumpolar Region" defines it as the area above 55°N and uses this line to wrap around the globe. While this excludes some of the northern parts of Canada's provinces, it includes part of northern England, most of Scotland, practically all of Denmark, all of Estonia, Latvia, and much of Lithuania. In this definition, or at least hinted at on the map, Copenhagen and Edinburgh are in the circumpolar region, and both cities are not built on permafrost. Some Danish and Scottish politicians may, however, be quite happy for their respective capitals to be located in this northern circumpolar region, especially as the Kingdom of Denmark is increasingly asserting an identity as an Arctic state, and as Scotland is moving forward with its own strategy for how it relates to the Arctic. So lines on the map are often arbitrary, but they might suit the purposes of some to maintain them.

The way in which we map the world reveals the identity politics at stake (e.g., including Denmark as part of that wider northern circumpolar region or Canada as a huge northern nation), and in turn helps promote, circulate, and sustain an emotive economy. The hopes, fears, and desires of governments, corporations, and peoples so often pivot on whether they are inside or outside the "North" and the "Arctic."

Canada is a great example of a country that has defined itself as a northern nation. For a good deal of the nineteenth century, a majority of the land we now know as Canada was made up of Rupert's Land and the North-Western Territory. In July 1870, the Hudson's Bay Company transferred these regions to the British Crown, which then transferred them to the government of Canada, and they were renamed the North-West Territories. Hudson's Bay Company trade routes centered on Fort Edmonton were major travel arteries in the Canadian northwest, and, in the early decades of the twentieth century, Edmonton and northern Alberta were settled by pioneers who arrived from many different places seeking a new life, encouraged by the slogan "The North is the new West." In 1905, Alberta and Saskatchewan were hived off from the North-West Territories.

With the absorption of other parts of the North-West Territories by Manitoba, Ontario, and Québec in 1912, the districts that remained north of 60° were renamed the Northwest Territories (dropping the hyphen) by the Canadian Parliament—and it was not to change again until 1999 when the creation of the territory of Nunavut (with its majority Inuit population) led to further shrinkage in area. Over the last one hundred years or so, then, the "north" in Canada has moved further north, and the twentieth century saw a redefinition and a reconfiguration of what constitutes the Canadian North.

Canada is a northern nation, as politicians have repeatedly stated in recent years, but internally it has its own gradients of northern-ness. Today, the Canadian North is generally recognized by government departments (notwithstanding NRC's various cartographic depictions) as comprising the three territories north of 60° (Yukon Territory, Northwest Territories, and Nunavut) and is often talked about as a place one goes to and which one enters from the south. Immigrants to Canada from all over the world send their children to school, and one of the first things they learn is to sing the Canadian national anthem and that their new country is "the True North Strong and Free." It is easy to forget how recent the "true north" really is. The north in Canada is synonymous with so many different things; undeveloped, wilderness, resource frontier, and it is integral to national identity. The vast majority of Canadians will sing about it, but they will never get to experience the "true north" of their own country. Many Canadians prefer to travel south for their vacations and seek out the warmer weather of the Caribbean and Mexico.

How have we defined the Arctic?

Canada's "true north" might be a nineteenth- and twentieth-century affair, but that should not be allowed to obscure a longer-lasting fascination with finding the "true north." In *The Histories*, the ancient Greek philosopher Herodotus remarked, "I cannot but laugh when I see numbers of persons drawing maps of the world without having any reason to guide them." For thousands of years, there have been astronomers, cartographers, explorers, and geographers intrigued to discover the furthest point north.

Ancient Greeks, however, looked to the heavens for inspiration. The word "Arctic" is derived from the Greek *arktikós*, meaning "of the Bear" (*arktos* being Greek for bear), referring to the constellations Ursa Major and Ursa Minor, both of which are visible in the northern night sky. Beyond the Arctic Circle, the sun shines continuously for twenty-four hours at least once in the year during summer. The sun will disappear from the horizon at least once a year for twenty-four hours during winter. In practice, it means that a long period of darkness prevails for large parts of the winter while the summer is characterized by long stints of light. Despite what maps might suggest, the Arctic Circle is not a static line, and its precise latitude varies with the axial tilt of the planet: it is best thought of as a zig-zag circular pattern.

While prone to a little northerly drift of some ten meters a year, the Arctic Circle encompasses 20 million square kilometers of land, ice, and sea. North of the line lies the Arctic Ocean and much of the northern landmass areas of seven out of the eight Arctic countries of Canada, Greenland (Denmark), United States (Alaska), Russia, Finland, Norway, and Sweden. The other Arctic state, Iceland, lies just below the Arctic Circle, and only the small island of Grímsey, due north of the mainland, straddles it. The percentage of national territory lying north of the Arctic Circle, therefore, varies greatly between each Arctic state. If we use the Arctic Circle as a primary indicator, Canada (25%) and Russia (30%) are the two largest Arctic states and Iceland would be minuscule. Some 15% of Sweden's national territory lies above the Arctic Circle, whereas the figure is closer to 25% in Finland's case.

Imaginary or not, the Arctic Circle continues to fascinate. "Crossing the Arctic Circle is a significant event," says the website of Finnish Lapland's Arctic Circle information office (based at the Santa Claus Village near Rovaniemi). Like many other tourism promoters in Arctic countries, the information office encourages visitors to purchase a certificate that authenticates and proclaims that they have crossed the threshold of the Arctic Circle and have entered the Arctic. It captures precisely the idea that the Arctic is a place apart and venturing into it is something adventurous, worthwhile—extraordinary almost—and to be commemorated. From a Finnish perspective, crossing the Arctic Circle perhaps underscores the feeling that Helsinki, while being a northern city, is not in the Arctic parts of the country. And while frostbite, scurvy, and death on the ice and on the tundra may have been markers of earlier heroic attempts to reach into and explore the Arctic, most tourists are likely to feel content with a certificate.

Physical geographers have in the past used other biogeographical indicators to define the Arctic, such as the northern limit of tree growth; in effect, the line or, more accurately, the border zone between tundra and the boreal forest, or taiga—the biome of coniferous forest. Tundra is defined as the coldest biome, where tree growth is virtually impossible because of extremely low temperatures, low precipitation, simple vegetation structures, and very short growing seasons. The etymology of the term likely comes from a Finnish word, *tunturi*, used to describe a treeless hill or plain (although the derivation may also lie in the Sámi word *tundar* and the Russian *tundra*, from where we get the word used in English).

In summer, Arctic tundra is swampy in parts and is carpeted with mosses, low shrubs, and lichens—and below the surface the subsoil is often frozen and characterized by permafrost. Groundwater seeps to the surface from thawing permafrost during summer, helping the growth of tundra plants, and although lakes and ponds abound, it is a land with scant ice-free water and little precipitation. Surface melting in the spring provides some moisture for plants, shrubs, and even dwarf trees, but root systems will be shallow because of the frozen ground. Strong winds, heavy snow, temperature extremes, unreliable levels of moisture, and soil disturbance means that the plants, and the animals that they support, have to be capable of enduring long winters and short summers.

The tundra attracts huge numbers of shorebirds, waterfowl, and other birds that nest there in summer, while caribou, Arctic fox, wolves, muskox, and polar bears, as well as the occasional grizzly bear roam this vast, treeless environment. Polar bears do not hibernate during winter, which is an important hunting season, unlike black bears and grizzly bears, although pregnant females do need to spend the winter in a den in a form of hibernation. Species of birds that spend the summer on tundra, such as snow geese, Arctic terns, and tundra swans, migrate south in the winter season. Indeed, few bird species remain throughout the winter—you may see, fleetingly, a snowy owl or a ptarmigan, but you are sure to hear, and see, a raven—*tulugaq* in Inuktitut (the language spoken by the Inuit of the central and eastern Canadian Arctic)—an extraordinary bird that survives the winter through a combination of predation and scavenging, often following polar bears around in the hope of picking up scraps of meat. The raven is a central figure in the mythologies of all indigenous peoples of the Arctic. In the oral histories of many Inuit groups, Tulugaq is a primeval ancestor who brought daylight for the people. In some Siberian and Alaskan stories, Raven created the earth and taught people how to make clothes from animal furs, how to make boats, and how to weave nets for fishing. It often appears as a trickster figure. Winter is the raven's season, when it is almost alone in plying the northern skies; courtship begins in January, and females lay their eggs between mid-February and late May.

Further south, the boreal, or taiga, forest is to be found around the 50° to 60° latitude and covers vast swathes of Eurasia and North America where the growing season is around 120–130 days rather than 50–60 days. This is a sub-arctic ecosystem—after the oceans it is the world's largest biome—comprising dark coniferous forests of cedars, firs, pines, larches, and spruces, interspersed with birches. In Canada, the boreal forest covers almost 60% of the land area of the country, while in Russia the taiga stretches for 5,800 kilometers. Between the boreal forest and the tundra lies a transitional zone in which trees are sparse and short, such as dwarf willows, dwarf birches, and alders.

While the distinction between the tundra and boreal biomes is real, the boundary is not clear-cut, and the respective coverage of each biome varies all over the Arctic. In Greenland, for example, there is no boreal forest (although there are five species of trees or large hardy shrubs) and only tundra on the edges of an island dominated by an immense ice sheet and mountains in the coastal interior. In Siberia, the boreal, or taiga, forests cover an enormous area, and the Siberian zone accounts for over 60% of the world total. As you travel in a vast country like Canada or Russia or in the state of Alaska, the treeline is not circular or straight but is jagged, depending on local climate, human–non-human interactions, and underlying geology. Recent research suggests that the treeline is moving north due to the warming trend in the Arctic, but progress is slow (perhaps no more than 100 meters per year in places in terms of northward drift) and highly variable, depending on local and regional circumstances. But any change is not trivial. If the tundra recedes and the boreal forest advances further northward, then more sunlight is absorbed rather than reflected back into the atmosphere. Trees and shrubs also alter hydrological cycles because of great transpiration, which again alters regional and even global climate systems.

Another common climatic indicator is the July isotherm, which defines the Arctic as starting when average temperatures fall below 10° Celsius. The zone usually coincides with the northern limit of tree growth and thus is seen in conjunction with treeline. However, the isotherm varies and extends across different portions and regions of the Arctic, depending on whether the focus is on the North American, Greenlandic, and/or Eurasian Arctic. In the case of Greenland, virtually every part of the island lies north of the 10° isotherm, but in the milder southern region of the country sheep farming is a viable and expanding activity. The treeline and 10° isotherm coincide with the northern fringes of Alaska, Fennoscandia, and Russia; with greater variance in the case of the Canadian North because of the large number of islands and marine areas.

For many, the entire Arctic is often considered synonymous with the North Pole. There are actually a number of North Poles. The most commonly understood is the geographic North Pole, sometimes known as "true north," lying in the central Arctic Ocean where lines of longitude meet. There is the magnetic North Pole, the so-called furthest point north on earth to which a compass needle points. This moves about every few years, because of magnetic changes at the earth's core. There is also the "geomagnetic North Pole" (a residual spot marking earth's variable magnetic fields), an "instantaneous North Pole" (where the rotational axis of the earth meets its surface), a North Pole "of balance" (which lies in the center of the circle the instantaneous pole makes as it moves around), and a "northern pole of inaccessibility" (a supposed spot in the Arctic Ocean that is the farthest away from any coastline). None of these North Poles coincide, and if anything, they distract from the geography of the Arctic region, which is one where the North American, European, and Asian continents converge around a semi-enclosed water mass, the Arctic Ocean.

Perhaps one of the most distinctive geographical facts about the Arctic is that a large part of it consists of that ice-covered ocean. Bordering the Arctic Ocean are numerous remote islands and archipelagos, the names of which most people would be hard-pressed to identify. In this way, the Arctic differs from the Antarctic, which is an ice-covered land mass surrounded by an ocean.

Politically, the circumpolar North has been largely defined by the eight countries self-identified as Arctic states. As we have seen, how much territory they might call "arctic" varies, but this labeling clearly matters. The United Kingdom describes itself as the closest neighbor to the Arctic and draws on a history of polar exploration and scientific activity to establish its credentials as a country with Arctic interests, while China has positioned itself as a "near-Arctic state." Swiss government officials and scientists describe Switzerland as the "vertical Arctic nation." Parts of northern Scotland (most notably the Cairngorms) have been classified as being subarctic, and some have pressed the case that Scotland might actually be an Arctic nation on account of its geographical location, historical connections to the Nordic world, and industrial and transport connections to the circumpolar North. Scottish nation-builders have also looked northwest to Greenland as inspiration for greater autonomy and independence.

We have found multiple ways to mark the boundaries of the Arctic and near-Arctic. What is clear is that for all those endeavors, there is no one definition of the "true north." The Arctic is in the eye of the beholder.

Who lives in the Arctic?

A mosaic of indigenous and non-indigenous communities characterizes the Arctic today. Indigenous peoples in the Arctic include Sámi in the northern regions of Fennoscandia and Russia's Kola Peninsula; Nenets and Chuckchi in Russia; Aleut, Yup'iit, and Iñupiat in Alaska; and Inuit in Canada and Greenland. Iceland is the only one of the eight Arctic states without a recognized indigenous people. Some indigenous communities are closely tied to specific activities, such as reindeer herding, fishing, and subsistence hunting, whereas others live in cities such as Whitehorse, Yellowknife, Anchorage, Nuuk, Murmansk, and Yakutsk.

Indigenous and non-indigenous peoples living in the Arctic are politically under the sovereign authority of the eight Arctic states; what varies is the strength of their civil and political rights. Inuit living in Canada and Greenland alongside indigenous peoples in Alaska and Fennoscandia enjoy far greater autonomy or political representation than Russian indigenous peoples. Non-indigenous people in Iceland (where the main period of Norse settlement took place between 870 and 930), northern Norway, Sweden, Finland, and Russia have long made Arctic regions their home, while more recent settlers in Alaska, Canada, and Greenland have also added to the social and cultural diversity of the contemporary circumpolar North.

The majority of the population of the Arctic live in Russia (around 2 million), and the balance between indigenous and non-indigenous people varies across the circumpolar North. Only 10% of the total population living in the Arctic is estimated to be indigenous. There is cultural diversity within indigenous societies. In North America, for example, Athabaskan peoples dwell in a substantive territory of some 3 million square kilometers covering several ecological zones, both above and below the Arctic Circle, from tundra to boreal forest and subarctic mountains and plateaus, stretching across Alaska and into Canada—in Yukon Territory and the Northwest Territories, and down into northern British Columbia, Alberta, Saskatchewan, and Manitoba. The Apache and Navajo are Athabaskan-speaking peoples who live far to the south of the northern forests, in California and Arizona. Many northern Athabaskans call themselves Dene or Dena, which means "human beings," and speak languages that belong to the Athabaskan branch of the Na-Dene family of languages. In Canada's Northwest Territories, Dene Nation has become the preferred self-designation to refer to Athabaskan peoples collectively.

The total Inuit population numbers about 160,000, and they are spread across a vast area, stretching from east and west Greenland across the north of Canada to the coasts of Alaska and Chukotka. And only in Alaska would the term "Eskimo" be recognized (although not always so) as a non-offensive description of an indigenous Arctic person (elsewhere in the North American Arctic, in Canada and Greenland, Eskimo—often thought to have an origin in an Algonquian word meaning "eater of raw flesh"—is considered derogatory by those who self-identify as Inuit, which means "people"). The acceptance of "Eskimo" in Alaska is usually attributed to the fact that "inuit" is not a word in the Yupik languages of Alaska and Siberia. Inuit culture represents one of the most extraordinary environmental adaptations found on earth. Traditionally, Inuit livelihoods have been based on hunting marine and terrestrial mammals and on fishing. Today, hunting and fishing remain vital activities for the economies of many communities, but commercial fishing, sheep farming (in Greenland), and oil-related business or financial enterprise, among other things, are increasingly important. The word Inuit (sing. "inuk"; person) is applied generally across the Arctic. However, it obscures the diversity of Inuit groups: Kalaallit in west Greenland, Inughuit in northwest Greenland, and Iit, or Iivit, in east Greeenland; Inuit and Inuvialuit in Canada; Iñupiat, Yup'iit, and Alutiiq (or Sugpiat) in Alaska; and Yuit in Siberia. However, Inuit as a more general and political term of reference was adopted by the Inuit Circumpolar Council (ICC) upon its formation in 1977 (ICC was then known as the Inuit Circumpolar Conference) in preference to the term "Eskimo."

Indigenous peoples living in the Arctic often do not have a rigid view of where it begins and ends, nor, contrary to some popular misconceptions of them, do they live on ice packs close to the North Pole. In Alaska, Canada, and Greenland, many Inuit live south of the Arctic Circle (and many have settled further south in urban centers such as Anchorage, Edmonton, Montreal, Toronto, Ottawa, and Copenhagen). The most northerly Inuit community (indeed the world's most northerly indigenous community) is the village of Siorapaluk (which has a population of under sixty) at 77°N in northwest Greenland, while Rigolet (with a population of around 300), located at 54°N, at the entrance of Hamilton Inlet in Nunatsiavut on Labrador's east coast, is the most southerly. The ICC focuses less on the geographical boundaries between Arctic and non-Arctic states, and more on an Inuit circumpolar homeland— *Inuit Nunangat*, meaning "the places in which Inuit live," and is a term for surroundings that include not just land but also ice and water—where Inuit are to be found across Alaska, Canada, Greenland, and Chukotka.

Sápmi is used by the Sámi to refer to the transnational region of northern Fennoscandia and the Kola Peninsula (Lapland is not a name favored by Sámi to describe their homeland). The area in question is around 400,000 square kilometers and cuts across the national borders of Norway, Sweden, Finland, and Russia. Unlike the territorial nation-state, the idea of homeland is more capacious and not easily enclosed within a modern political imagination shaped by exclusive claims to sovereignty and defined international boundaries. Sámi remain embroiled in struggles over land and over the recognition of specific rights. Victoria Tauli-Corpuz, the UN special rapporteur on the rights of indigenous peoples, examined the human rights situation of Sámi in Norway, Sweden, and Finland in 2016. In her report, based on a visit to the Sápmi region, including a conference organized by the Sámi Parliamentary Council in Bierke/Hemavan, Sweden, Tauli-Corpuz emphasized that all three countries fall short of their stated objectives of ensuring Sámi human rights. Russia is even more hostile to any sort of recognition for Sámi and their claims to a distinct Sápmi.

While there are no accurate or reliable census figures (the last census of Sámi in Sweden was in 1945), around 100,000 people identify themselves as Sámi (approximately 50,000 in Norway, 40,000 in Sweden, 9,000 in Finland, and 2,000 in northwest Russia). Traditionally, Sámi reindeer herders ranged far and wide in northern Fennoscandia and the Kola Peninsula, crossing national borders as they followed their animals between winter and summer pastures in nomadic spaces composed of tundra, forest, fell, and coast. Government action and border controls have restricted migration routes over the last one hundred years or so, as have government attitudes toward Sámi culture and language, while economic development, such as mining, forestry, railways, roads, hydroelectric power, and tourism have all had a significant impact on Sámi livelihoods, encroaching on grazing lands and hindering migration routes.

Archeology, ethnographic research, oral history, traditional knowledge, and contemporary indigenous narratives have shed considerable light on how Arctic hunters, herders, and fishers have adapted to, as well as anticipated, shifts and changes in the size, distribution, range, and availability of animal populations. They have dealt with extreme seasonal variability, flux, and change in northern environments by developing techniques for seeking out animals and maintaining livelihoods with significant flexibility. Being flexible made sense when living in a world that was and is highly capricious. Yet the ecological and social relations among indigenous peoples; animals; and land, water, and ice; and to seasonal movements within nomadic spaces are affected not just by environmental shifts or climate-induced disruption, but by the historical development and the contemporary influences of trade relationships and regional and global markets. They are also determined to a considerable extent by government policies and wildlife management.

Today, in the face of a changing climate, shifting animal migration routes, and wildlife management, seasonal patterns of movement by indigenous people are curtailed. Strict and inflexible regulatory practices and conservation and management systems have been put in place by Arctic states and by federal and provincial agencies, often adhering to international conventions that increasingly regulate hunting, herding, and fishing activities.

Arctic peoples, whether Sámi or Evenki reindeer herders or Inuit seal hunters, cannot always adapt to the changes they are confronted with, as they may have been able to do in the past. Changes to settlement and residential patterns have also resulted from government intervention. In northern parts of Russia and Siberia, for example, in the mid-twentieth century, Soviet authorities "industrialized" reindeer herding as a way of settling indigenous people, facilitating the large-scale development of the Soviet North and expanding the extraction of resources. In some regions of Siberia, the new settlements that grew rapidly and heavy industries that developed came to depend on reindeer herders and reindeer farms to supply them with meat. Today, in post-Soviet Russia, privatization and the transition to a market economy, as well as oil and gas development and its associated infrastructure such as pipelines, and its movement of people needed for construction and operations, bring new challenges.

The contemporary history of the increasing presence of non-indigenous peoples in the Arctic and their relations with indigenous peoples has its origins in the sixteenth century, even earlier in the case of the fur trade in northern Russia and Siberia. The nineteenth and early twentieth centuries saw regular and extended contact between indigenous peoples and outsiders who ventured into northern indigenous homelands. Explorers, whalers, traders, and missionaries brought economic, cultural, ideological, and new religious influences when they traveled to the Arctic. They also often brought infectious diseases with them, such as smallpox and influenza, to which indigenous peoples had little or no resistance or immunity, and many communities were devastated by epidemics. For example, in Canada's Mackenzie Delta and Beaufort Sea coast region, Inuvialuit communities were affected dramatically by disease, epidemics, and famine after Euro-American commercial whalers arrived in the second half of the nineteenth century. When the whalers first went north, around 2,500 Inuvialuit lived in the region. By 1905 there were only some 250 left.

Over the past century, indigenous societies and cultures have been transformed by social, economic, and political changes and have borne a heavy burden in terms of colonial appropriation, forced resettlement, residential schools, and cultural and geographical displacement. In the 1950s and 1960s, the Canadian government settled Inuit, who lived predominantly in camps and outposts, to permanent communities scattered around the country's Arctic coasts. This exacerbated the erosion of the subsistence hunting culture (which had long been influenced by the trade activities of the Hudson's Bay Company), and Inuit were drawn into a position of greater dependency on the Canadian government and its institutions. The prevailing Canadian government attitude at the time was one of incorporating Inuit into the mainstream economic, social, and cultural life of Canada. Through education and training, the indigenous inhabitants of the Arctic were to become modern Canadians, able to improve their lifestyle options and take their place in the new period of economic development on the Canadian Arctic resource frontier.

Similarly, in Greenland, Inuit society was transformed in the 1950s, 1960s, and 1970s by Danish government policies aimed at modernization, which involved the resettlement of people from small communities to towns, rapid urbanization, and a transition from a way of life based primarily on small-scale subsistence hunting and fishing to a modern, export-oriented economy based on commercial fisheries. A large number of Greenlandic villages were closed, and their inhabitants moved to newly built apartment blocks in places such as Nuuk, Sisimiut, Maniitsoq, and Ilulissat on the west coast, which have since developed into the country's largest towns.

In northeast Russia, the economic life of the Siberian Yuit was collectivized during the Soviet era through the organization of whaling and walrus hunting boat crews into seasonal hunting co-operatives. Many Yuit villages were closed down; major social, economic, and infrastructural changes swept across the region; Soviet bureaucracies were introduced; and Yuit children, like their counterparts from other indigenous communities across the Russian North, were sent by authorities from camps to village schools in other regions or to boarding schools. There are compelling similarities across the circumpolar North in the experience of indigenous peoples and state policy, especially in terms of resettlement, education, social and cultural change, and language loss.

For indigenous peoples, therefore, the "Arctic" is more often than not associated with the colonial practices that brought designs for permanent settlements and forms of agricultural and industrial colonization, and a classification of their homelands and surroundings as remote Arctic spaces, empty wilderness areas, and frontiers. Attempts were made to replace indigenous languages with English, Danish, Norwegian, Swedish, Finnish, or Russian. As we discuss in chapter 3, for indigenous peoples, recovering autonomy over the management of Arctic environments, animals, and other resources, and over their own lives, is at the heart of land claims negotiations, resistance against historic settler colonialism, and social and political movements for self-government.

How alike are the Arctic and the Antarctic?

The Arctic and Antarctic are quite distinct even though they often get lumped together. While they may share some super-ficial similarities, such as cold temperatures, migratory ani-mals such as seals and whales, and widespread distribution of snow and ice, the regions are different. As should be clear, the Arctic is made up of regions that are part of nation states and are inhabited by diverse societies and cultures. The Antarctic is the world's only continent without an indigenous human population.

The Arctic is a semi-enclosed ocean surrounded by conti-nental fringes, whereas the Antarctic is a continent surrounded by a vast Southern Ocean. The geographical North Pole is located in the central Arctic Ocean, whereas the South Pole is situated in the interior of a polar continent, some 10,000 feet above sea level. While the central Arctic Ocean is covered with sea ice, the extent and thickness of that ice varies year to year, depending on prevailing weather conditions, namely surface and ocean temperatures and wind and water currents, and is being affected by climate change. Ice thickness might extend to twenty feet in parts of the central Arctic Ocean rather than thousands of feet deep in the case of the polar continent. The Arctic Ocean is clas-sified as the world's smallest ocean. The circumpolar Southern Ocean, on the other hand, is vast and extends into the southern fringes of the Atlantic, Indian, and Pacific Oceans.

Compared to the Antarctic, the Arctic is less isolated from the prevailing influences of the earth's climatological systems. One manifestation of this is the presence of the warming Gulf Stream, which ensures that there are parts of west Greenland, Iceland, and the Nordic and northwest Russian Arctic that re-main largely free of sea ice, even though cities such as Murmansk and Tromsø are located north of the Arctic Circle. There are no parts of the Antarctic that escape the grip of sea ice. The Antarctic does not receive any warmer air from the temperate and tropical parts of the earth, and there is a well-established bio-geographical borderland called the Convergence Zone, where the colder polar waters meet warmer temperate waters. Once you cross the zone (often known as the Antarctic Convergence) toward the Antarctic continent, the water and air temperatures change markedly. Icebergs become more noticeable and the occurrence of sea fog is common.

Antarctic and Arctic fauna share some similarities because there are birds and whales that migrate between the Arctic and Antarctic, depending on the respective summer seasons. One impressive example is the Arctic tern. Its commonplace name does not do justice to its extraordinary mobility. Weighing only 100 grams, this bird flies up to 80,000 kilometers a year, and, while Arctic terns breed in Iceland and Greenland, they fly south to Antarctica to take advantage of the austral summer season (October–March). Terns can live for up to thirty years, so the distances they travel during their lifetimes are mind-boggling.

Iconic polar animals such as penguins and polar bears travel great distances on foot and by swimming but are less "migratory" in terms of those vast distances covered by many bird species, and so are more accurately regarded as associated with the Antarctic and Arctic, respectively, as they do not move out of their polar surroundings. Penguins, however, are found across the southern fringes of South America, Africa, and Australasia, while polar bears live both above and below the Arctic Circle. Scientists have classified polar bears into nineteen subpopulations across the Arctic (there are estimated to be around 26,000 polar bears), thirteen of which are managed or co-managed by Canada and number a total of 16,000 animals. The polar bears spotted in and around the town of Churchill, Manitoba—which make up the western Hudson Bay subpopulation—are comparatively southerly to the polar bears living in the Canadian High Arctic and in other higher latitudes such as northern Greenland and Svalbard.

Sometimes animals associated with the Arctic have been introduced into sub-Antarctic territories, with the most notable example being the reindeer brought by Norwegian whalers to the island of South Georgia in the early twentieth century, to provide recreation hunting and a supply of fresh meat. With the end of whaling and the absence of a permanent human population, the reindeer population increased and extended its range (also made possible in part because of glacial retreat), resulting in overgrazing and severe environmental damage. In 2012–2013, the South Georgia government and South Georgia Heritage Trust started an eradication program of the resident reindeer, which was achieved in 2016.

However, the biggest contrast to the Antarctic lies in the Arctic's human dimension. Unlike the Antarctic, the Arctic is inhabited with small, remote communities, as well as large and growing urban centers, ports, airbases, extensive road networks in some areas, aluminum smelters, hydropower systems, mines, oilfields, and pipelines.

Apart from some areas of uncertainty regarding national boundaries in maritime areas, there are no major territorial disputes pertaining to the Arctic. In the case of part of the Barents Sea, for example, it was shown by Norway and Russia in 2010 that a forty-year-old dispute over a maritime border, which had originally flared up over fishing rights, could be resolved effectively by negotiation and agreement. Whereas in the Antarctic, there are major disagreements about ownership and sovereignty. Seven countries are so-called claimant states in the Antarctic, including Australia, New Zealand, Argentina, and the United Kingdom. The United States and Russia reserve the right to make a claim in the future. Under the terms of the 1959 Antarctic Treaty, the claimant states and now over forty other countries have agreed to a governance regime, which promotes international cooperation and demilitarization in return for all parties agreeing to put the knotty issue of ownership to one side for the duration of the treaty. At the moment, there is no mining in Antarctica in contrast to the Arctic that has mature mining sectors, including coal, oil, gas, and other minerals such as copper, zinc, and uranium.

The Arctic and Antarctic are thought by some to be "cold places," and venerable institutions such as the Scott Polar Research Institute at the University of Cambridge have studied them comparatively since the 1920s. But we need to be cautious about how far those comparisons are useful. The Arctic and Antarctic are, in so many ways, poles apart. And while it is not unusual for comparative study in some countries, many would blanch at the idea that an inhabited Arctic would be studied in conjunction with an uninhabited polar continent with a very different history and geography of human encounters let alone inhabitation.

How has the Arctic been represented in public culture?

As the vast majority of humanity is unlikely to visit the Arctic region, imagination and representation play a significant role in locating, placing, and defining the Arctic's landscapes, waters, ice, flora, fauna, and human communities. Media such as television and film are integral to the exposure of the Arctic to global audiences. For British audiences that might mean watching a BBC nature program hosted by Sir David Attenborough.

For the ancient Greeks and medieval European geographers, northern lands were Hyperborea and Ultima Thule, respectively: faraway places with mystical properties lying beyond existing bodies of geographical and cartographic knowledge. For classical scholars, the location of the Arctic was also subject to flux with some positing that such a northerly land was to be found north of Britain and Ireland, and later Iceland and Greenland.

Other stories were prevalent about ancient civilizations living at and around the North Pole—the Greeks populated Hyperborea with the Hyperboreans who, according to Herodotus, extended to the sea and lived north of the gold-guarding Griffins and the Arimaspi, "the men with one eye," while Bal Gandadar Tilak put forward a theory in his 1903 book *The Arctic Home in the Vedas* that some Hindu Vedic texts hinted at the Arctic being the place of origin for the Aryans.

In the later part of the sixteenth century, geographer and cartographer Gerard Mercator depicted the North Pole on his map of the Arctic as an enormous black rock, the Rupes Nigra, surrounded by a whirlpool and into which four great rivers flowed (the map appeared as an inset on his world map of 1569). These rivers themselves divided a vast landmass into four islands. At the top of the map, Mercator placed the Strait of Anian, which early cartographers and mariners believed allowed a northern passage between Europe and Asia by way of the Arctic to the Pacific. When such a strait was determined in 1728, it was named the Bering Strait. Mercator's sources for his representation of the Arctic were various speculative geographers and authors who themselves drew on the texts of early travelers, and his map referenced and modified Martin Behaim's view of the North Pole, which had appeared on the terrestrial globe he constructed between 1491–1493.

As European exploration of the north continued, the onset of further northerly drift ensued. The furthest point north kept traveling northward with ever more detail regarding its possible qualities; maps, charts, and atlases were reworked and updated. Mercator's map of the North Pole was revised, for example, following later voyages of discovery, yet scholars and writers continued to contribute to the speculation and intrigue regarding this northerly point as temperate and ice-free by some and by others filled with darkness and warring peoples.

In the European and later American worlds, the Arctic attracted an array of cultural media, ranging from the scientific and narrative records of explorers to popular outputs such as paintings, panoramas, drama, fiction, lantern shows, exhibitions, and mainstream media such as newspapers, photography, and film. In the nineteenth century, countries such as Britain and the United States were gripped by what was termed by some an "Arctic fever" as governments and sponsoring agencies, such as the Royal Geographical Society, initiated expeditions to search for the fabled Northwest Passage. In the 1810s and 1820s, men like John Ross and William Parry were at the fore of this quest. Nineteenth-century visual culture pertaining to the Arctic challenged existing aesthetic categories such as the picturesque, and instead the sublime was enrolled into the descriptions of the Arctic; a space represented as capable of being very beautiful but also terrifying, confusing, bewildering, and even overwhelming to humans and their senses.

One important corollary of this representational work was to portray the Arctic as a largely blank space where indigenous communities were rarely represented. Despite European explorers and travelers being dependent at times on indigenous knowledge and contact, as well as actually being guided to places they felt they were "discovering" (and which they often claimed for the countries that had sent them off to far northern reaches), the Arctic was predominantly imagined and depicted as empty, timeless, and unoccupied, waiting to be claimed and named. Later critics contend that this prevailing visual culture, especially in the nineteenth century, was integral to how the male European explorer was depicted as a heroic, adventurous figure battling the elemental odds to travel through and even survive the dangers of the Arctic environment. British and American depictions of the Arctic are held to be complicitous with an imperial white masculinity, which viewed the Arctic as a testing, or even proving, ground.

Among other European representations, Casper Friedrich's *The Sea of Ice* (1823–1824) was instrumental in perpetuating this view of the Arctic as pictorially sublime—beautiful but deadly. The icescape depicted is one in which a ship lies encased in a tomb of ice pointing dramatically into the sky. The ship in question was HMS *Griper* and was one of two ships involved in an ill-fated expedition to the North Pole led by the British explorer William Parry. Later, Edward Landseer's *Man Proposes, God Disposes* (1864) depicted the loss of the

Franklin expedition in 1845. While Inuit reported later that they had seen some survivors, it was only very recently that the ships that accompanied the expedition (HMS *Erebus* and HMS *Terror*) were discovered at the bottom of the waters of the Northwest Passage (*Erebus* in September 2014 and *Terror* in 2016). Landseer's painting was unstinting in his depiction of two polar bears scavenging among the wreckage, which included some human bones, the remnants of a flag, and a telescope.

While the Arctic was central to eighteenth- and nineteenth-century intellectual debates across the physical sciences, humanities, and emerging social sciences, regarding the earth's human and physical history, it remained a place riven with speculation and intrigue. The search for the Northwest Passage and the quest for the North Pole provided a powerful backdrop to this imaginative labor, as did maps and nautical charts positing the possible existence of an open polar sea at the top of the world. For much of the nineteenth century, the Arctic, and in particular the North Pole, was a blank space in conventional cartographic terms.

Yet it was a zone for something capable of hosting an array of representational schemata. John Cleves Symmes, a nineteenth-century American writer and former US Army officer, posited what was later termed "hollow earth" theory, in which the immediate areas around the North and the South Poles were imagined as hollow and open for possible entry, passage, inhabitation, and exploitation. In his novel *Symzonia* (1820), an expedition travels to the earth's core via the poles, represented as gateways or portals to another world, rather than points of interest in their own right, in search of resources and to explore the possibilities of settlement. Once the sea ice was cleared—like his contemporary Mary Shelley did in her novel *Frankenstein* (1818) and Percy Bysshe Shelley did in his poem *The Revolt of Islam* (1818)—Symmes imagined the Arctic as a warm, open polar sea, an enticing place that would unlock the mysteries of planet earth.

Scholars at the time rejected his theory on the whole, but Symmes persisted in promoting his ideas and set about raising support for an expedition to prove it. He found a keen supporter in Jeremiah N. Reynolds. Following a bout of ill health, Symmes died in 1829, but Reynolds set off for Antarctica by ship that year having secured the backing of a wealthy sponsor. Failing to find the polar void, and encountering icebergs and sea ice beyond which they could not venture, the ship turned away from the Antarctic region, and the crew mutinied and stranded Reynolds in Chile. Reynolds returned home eventually, after many adventures, and remained an enthusiastic lecturer on polar exploration and the hollow earth theory. The works of Symmes and Reynolds caught the imagination of a number of writers, who, in developing a genre that is tempting to label "hollow earth fiction," contributed further to that view of the Arctic as a portal to the inner earth. Most notably, Symmes and Reynolds influenced Edgar Allan Poe's novel of 1838 *The Narrative of Arthur Gordon Pym of Nantucket* (which, in turn, influenced H. P. Lovecraft's Antarctic-set novel *At the Mountains of Madness*, first published in 1936) and Jules Verne's *Journey to the Centre of the Earth* (1864). Verne was similarly taken by Poe's work and penned an essay, *Le Sphinx des Glace*, intended as a sequel in which he reflects upon Pym's journey and describes the discovery of his body.

It might be tempting to think of people like Symmes as an eccentric and something of an intellectual outlier. But that would be unfair. As Duane Griffin points out in a fascinating article published in the journal *Physical Geography* in 2004, the idea of a hollow earth and theories about concentric spheres and polar voids and openings were widespread long before Symmes had speculated and elaborated on his theory. And in his short story "A Descent into the Maelström" from 1841, Poe described how "Kircher and others imagine that in the centre of the channel of the Maelström is an abyss penetrating the globe, and issuing in some very remote part—the Gulf of Bothnia being somewhat decidedly named in one instance." The reference is to the sixteenth-century German Jesuit scholar Athanasius Kircher, and in particular to a theory set out in a passage in his *Mundus subterraneus* of 1665 that the maelstrom off Norway's Lofoten Islands was a sea-vortex that sucked water under Norway and discharged it in the Gulf of Bothnia.

The views and arguments of Symmes and his supporters coincided and resonated with nineteenth-century exploratory concern with finding an open polar sea in the Arctic, and with the development of new imaginaries about the interior geographies and geological structures of the earth. Pillars of the British naval and exploratory establishment, such as Sir John Barrow, head of the British Admiralty, were convinced that there was an open polar sea lying beyond the sea ice that once breached would facilitate further transpolar movement; hollow earth theory also had some bearing on how Arctic explorers such as Isaac Israel Hayes and Charles Francis Hall thought of the far north. By the first decade of the twentieth century, public attention shifted its attention to the North Pole and the news that American explorers Frederick Cook and Robert Peary were claiming they were the first to reach it in 1908 and 1909 respectively. While much controversy and argument ensued regarding the provenance of their respective claims, it did reinforce a view of the North Pole as inherently frozen and cold rather than a warm open polar sea.

Today, interest in polar interiors, subsurface environments, and ocean depths challenges the horizontal and linear view of the Arctic. There is a great deal more interest and understanding of Arctic depths and distinctly interior geographies, and how this requires us to ponder deep time and the Anthropocene, rather than simply a concern with the surfaces of the earth, horizons, geographical areas, lines of latitude and longitude, political boundaries and borderlands, exclusive economic zones, baselines, and maritime regions.

The film *The Last Winter* (2006) captured well the subterranean, even volumetric, qualities of the Arctic. In this fictional tale, a disastrous release of methane endangers a project team's attempts to build surface-level infrastructure in order to exploit the energy resources of northern Alaska. One of the survivors posits that the relentless desire for fossil fuel exploitation unleashed the wendigo, an Algonquian folklore spirit or monster native to northern North America. At its worst, the spirit was said to cause humans to turn on one another and commit acts of cannibalism. Expressions of greed triggered its appearance, which induced horror among the survivors as they began to appreciate that the land and its spirits were indifferent to their fate. As with Mary Shelley's *Frankenstein*, the film ends on a gloomy note, positing the dangers that have been unleashed from below and the consequences for the Arctic and global humanity. The Arctic emerges in all of this as a relentlessly productive resource to posit a wild, eruptive nature endlessly challenging humanity in the here and now as well as the future. Triumphant geopolitics gives way to disaster geopolitics.

What should guide how we look at the Arctic?

In our introduction and in this chapter, we have identified and begun to discuss five drivers that inform the rest of this book. The intersection of globalization, climate change, geopolitics, technology, and northern autonomy will determine the future of the Arctic.

Our working definitions of the Arctic will vary. Depending on what indicators we draw attention to, the geographical boundaries of the region will shift, as will our ideas of place, space, land, forest, tundra, water, and ice. What makes sense to us is to think about the consequences of using one or multiple definitions, and the ramifications that follow when decisions are made about who, what, and where are considered part of the Arctic and non-Arctic. The boundary between Arctic and non-Arctic has become politically sensitive even within the Arctic state community. Iceland, Sweden, and Finland have felt excluded from talks in recent years on the Arctic Ocean held by the five Arctic coastal states of Canada, Denmark/ Greenland, Norway, Russia, and the United States.

We are best off thinking of the Arctic in multiple forms, a region with a diversity of places and homelands. Our definitions of the Arctic have to be adaptable and flexible. There is no one "true north." A line is never ever just a line.

2

LAND, SEA, AND ICE

Humans and non-humans make their homes in many Arctic places. Cultures, societies, and ecologies have formed in relation to northern surroundings over millennia, over centuries, or mere decades. Environmental biologists warn of a new generation of invasive species entering northern terrestrial, freshwater, and marine environments, while meteorologists seek to understand how the transport of aerosols and air pollution in the Arctic affects cloud formation. As waters warm, air flows alter, and landforms shift, we can expect ever more migration northward and transformations in atmospheric processes. For longer-term residents, human and non-human, the implications of all this change might not be so welcome.

The intersection of land, sea, and ice, as well as air, is integral to how we make sense of the Arctic. It is a rather different way of understanding the Arctic; less focused on fixed lines and more on the entanglement of elements, territories, and forces, and the things, the movements, and the processes that make and remake the Arctic.

To give one example, in the early 1970s, it was normal to find mackerel off the western edges of Norway. Forty years later, the same species of fish are now found off the coasts of Svalbard, which lies some 80°N, around the coastal waters of Iceland, and off the east coast of Greenland. So, we could say that mackerel are "Arctic fish." Some species of Atlantic cod and haddock are also moving into Arctic waters. At the same time, species of fish that would typically be found in the Pacific Ocean are also expanding their range northward—for example, Chinook salmon are moving from the warming waters off the coasts of California and Oregon to Arctic rivers that empty into the Beaufort and Chukchi Seas.

The Arctic Council's Arctic Monitoring and Assessment Programme (AMAP) working group has incorporated a mixture of political and bio-geographical factors to arrive at its working definition of the Arctic, and it has argued that it includes all areas north of the Arctic Circle but, because of physical geographical and climatic characteristics, it should extend further south to north of 62°N in Eurasia and 60°N in North America, and marine areas north of the Aleutian chain, Hudson Bay, as well as sections of the North Atlantic Ocean such as the ice-filled Labrador Sea, areas south of Iceland, and the waters around the Faroe Islands. The Arctic Council's Conservation of Arctic Flora and Fauna (CAFF) working group has a similar definition, but its delineations extend to include almost all of Labrador and northern Québec.

The point of all this is that even when we work with lines of latitude, such as the Arctic Circle, there are changes afoot that mean things that we once found in the Atlantic and Pacific Oceans are now being discovered in Arctic waters. So, by focusing on the volumetric content rather than the lines of the Arctic, we initiate a very different understanding of the world's high latitudes.

What was the Arctic like in the distant past?

The Arctic Ocean is currently attracting a great deal of attention, and much of this is because of the scale and pace of change affecting it. We have satellite observations, dating from the late 1970s and early 1980s, that provide snapshots of reductions in sea ice cover during summer, and recent observations show that the melting of sea ice is freshening the ocean, so much so that the Pacific side of the Arctic Ocean could move away from being a sink to a source of CO_2.

If we want to know what the Arctic Ocean was like in the past, we need to turn to the work done by paleo-climatologists. The same would be true of terrestrial environments in the Arctic. Scientists use sediment cores and examine fossilized remains of organic matter to detect and reconstruct environmental and geographical histories. Using careful detective work, scientific analysis suggests that the Arctic has undergone substantial changes in sea ice thickness and extent. At various times, the geological record suggests that the Arctic Ocean was either ice-free and/or smothered with ice. The first evidence for Arctic sea ice has been dated to some 47 million years ago and coincides with a period of earth cooling. Perennial sea ice is a regular feature of the Arctic Ocean around 14–18 million years ago. The interaction between ocean and ice sheets, coupled with fluctuations in temperature and atmospheric concentrations of carbon dioxide, matter greatly for the extent and endurance of Arctic sea ice. The more recent geological record, coinciding with the onset of the Holocene (some 11,000 years ago), adds further understanding to the underlying physical dynamics of the contemporary Arctic.

Paleo-sea-ice records point to an Arctic that has undergone fluctuation, with variations in sea ice cover. For the last 10,000 years, it does not seem that the Arctic was ever ice-free. What the paleo-records suggest across the Arctic region is that the influx of warmer waters from the Atlantic and Pacific Oceans plays a pivotal role in determining the range of sea ice extent. As the paleo-archive of the last couple of thousands of years improves, with tree ring, lake sediment, and ice core records to draw upon, it shows that the Arctic sea ice extent is related to periods of noticeable climatic variability including the medieval warming period (800–1300 AD) and the Little Ice Age (1450–1850 AD).

For the last century, the climatic record is unequivocal. The Arctic Ocean has warmed because of inflowing Atlantic and Pacific waters. Sea ice melt is pronounced due to warming waters, and the albedo (a measure of the reflexivity of the earth's surface) of the Arctic disrupted by a decrease in ice and snow cover. Warmer waters are not the only driver of a warmer Arctic, however. The Arctic is also being affected by shifts in atmospheric and oceanic circulation patterns leading to further evidence of geophysical- and biological-state change. Recent observations also show, however, that current climate models do not accurately account for how some snow, sea ice, and cloud processes may accelerate the rate of melting Arctic Ocean ice, and how these processes are significant for our understanding of climate change. The challenge for Arctic natural scientists is to understand better the interplay between natural variability and anthropogenic climate change across diverse temporal and spatial reference points.

Future understanding of a warming Arctic will depend on how we make sense of the Arctic past and present. Ice-free (formally defined as having less than 1 million square kilometers) Arctic summers will be a reality in the twenty-first century. To give a sense of the scale of all this, in September 2018 the minimum Arctic sea ice extent was assessed at 4.59 million square kilometers. We are talking about the Arctic Ocean losing another 3 million square kilometers in the coming decades. Little wonder that a new international science project called the Multidisciplinary drifting Observatory for the Study of Arctic Climate (MOSAiC, 2019) will see a German icebreaker, *Polarstern*, enter the Arctic Ocean and attempt to collect new information on sea ice distribution and thickness. We don't know nearly enough about sea ice in the winter months, and 600 people from seventeen different countries are going to do their best to improve our situational awareness and scientific understanding.

What are the defining physical characteristics of contemporary Arctic environments?

While some scientists who work on research vessels, such as *Polarstern,* focus on understanding the changing nature of Arctic sea ice, others continue to try and make sense of other elements of the Arctic. The region's terrestrial, marine, and freshwater environments vary greatly. Northern Fennoscandia and the Kola Peninsula in Russia, as well as parts of west Greenland, are comparatively mild due to the warming presence of the Gulf Stream extension, which contributes to the milder climate and ice-free coastlines of those regions. Other parts of the Arctic such as northern edges of Canada and Greenland are cooler and more likely to witness multiyear sea ice.

We'll start with *land*. Biologists distinguish between a "high Arctic" and a "low Arctic" to recognize that the terrestrial Arctic varies according to the distribution of tundra and boreal forest. As we described in chapter 1, tundra is defined as a particular kind of biome (or ecological region) where tree and vegetation growth in general is hindered by low temperatures, frozen ground, and short growing seasons. The ground is perennially frozen (permafrost), and the frozen subsurface sometimes extends to well beyond 500 meters below ground level. Much of the Russian and North American "high Arctic" is characterized by permafrost. Soils in this part of the Arctic are generally poorly drained and characterized by low productivity except in the short summer season when the upper layer of the soil thaws, allowing some plant growth. In 2017, tundra greenness expanded due to Arctic warming and unseasonal temperatures played their part in ensuring that Alaska and Yukon were beset by wildfires and fire danger throughout the North American Arctic. Arctic greening is disruptive.

Boreal, or taiga (the Russian word for boreal), forests are populated by pines, spruces, and larches that are well-adapted to temperature extremes, low levels of precipitation, and nutrient-poor soils. Wildfires play an important role in aiding and abetting species reproduction, including the jack pine and the lodgepole pine that require the heat of fire to reproduce. Other species benefit from the fire ecologies when ground-level vegetation is exposed to sunlight. In Alaska, Canada, northern Fennoscandia, and Russia, boreal forests cover vast areas of their respective northern territories and represent 30% of world tree cover. Boreal forests, despite their low biodiversity, do nonetheless support an array of mammals, fish, insects, and birds, including the Siberian tiger in the Russian Far East and the great grey owl, which can be found across the Northern Hemisphere and is the world's largest owl by length.

The biggest threat to the terrestrial Arctic and to its biodiversity is posed by human activities such as logging and mining, as well as oil extraction and pipeline development. But there may be other subtle changes we should be wary of as well. Habitat warming, for example, with implications for earlier seasonal snow melt and the wind-drying of the subsurface, will have implications not only for native species but also encourage the encroachment by invasive species, including microorganisms, plants, and animals. Warmer winters have also meant that sources of disease and pestilence are not killed off by the extremes of cold, and there is concern that spruce-bark beetles and spruce worms are growing in number with dire consequences for the health of boreal forest ecology, as currently witnessed in northern British Columbia and parts of northern Alberta. The net result is to produce a vista of bare and broken trees that stretch as far as the eye can see, akin to the scene of a wildfire's aftermath.

Next, *sea*. The marine environment of the Arctic is varied and variable depending on variations in sunlight, density of sea ice, and a host of other factors, such as ocean and wind currents, salinity, seabed depth, and temperature. The circumpolar Arctic region is characterized by the central Arctic Ocean allied with adjacent seas, such as the Barents, Beaufort, Chukchi, Kara, Laptev, and large marine features such as

Hudson Bay. The Arctic Ocean is bisected by the Lomonosov submarine ridge and divided into the Eurasian and North American basins. The net effect of the underwater geology of the Arctic marine environment is to ensure that sea ice distribution and thickness varies depending on ocean circulation patterns (such as the Beaufort Gyre and Transpolar Drift), relative salinity, and sea temperature variations brought on by the intersection of warmer waters from the Atlantic and Pacific Oceans. The waters off parts of the Russian Arctic coasts tend to be less covered with sea ice packs compared with the North American and central portions of the Arctic Ocean. Arctic sea ice tends to be transported by ocean and wind currents in an east to west direction, ultimately exiting through the Fram Strait and Barents Sea.

Warming seas and oceans carry with them the specter of change. As Arctic waters warm, fish and other species migrate. We mentioned mackerel and cod earlier, and the movement of mackerel, in particular, might be a potential bonanza for fishing vessels working in the far north. But other things have made the journey north. Different types of Phytoplankton, a microalgae integral to the marine food chain, are now found spreading northward. The resident zooplankton depends on indigenous phytoplankton that in turn help sustain Arctic fish and indirectly seals, whales, and polar bears. The Atlantic phytoplankton are less nutritious than their Arctic brethren, and thus marine biologists believe that this might then have knock-on implications for the health of the entire marine food chain. But it is also a complicated picture because more open water in the Arctic also warms waters and more light encourages more algae. So, what is happening is the importation of a southern marine ecosystem into the Arctic.

Finally, *ice*. The range and thickness of sea ice is integral to the Arctic marine environment. Since the late 1970s, satellite monitoring has provided good coverage of the distribution of sea ice across the Arctic Ocean and allowed us to track sea ice maximums and minima. Sea ice thickness has been harder to measure, but underwater voyages by nuclear-powered submarines helped gather information on this very subject. What makes it a tricky subject matter is that it is a slippery subject par excellence. As we have already mentioned, variations in thickness and extent owe greatly to ocean currents, sea temperature, freezing and melting, and the balance between brine and water—and changes in Arctic winds, on timescales of decades, are driving a considerable amount of change to the Arctic Ocean's freshwater content and its variability.

Two-dimensional maps do a poor job of representing the dynamism of the substance itself. Whatever their virtues, those maps matter because the state of sea ice often provokes a series of debates about the environmental and human state of the Arctic itself. What we can say with some confidence is that the maximum extent of Arctic sea ice in September 2017 and September 2018 were some of the lowest figures recorded. In the last decade, we have witnessed successive shrinkage of sea ice coverage and thickness—and in parts of the Arctic, such as in northwest Greenland, the past decade has seen the most reductions in sea ice cover over the past 150 years. Warming seas interfere with sea ice formation, and typically prevent multiyear ice (which is thicker than first year ice) from enduring in the Arctic Ocean. Taking the longer view of some 2,000 years, contemporary Arctic air and sea surface temperatures are unprecedented.

One of the most intriguing environments is the "underside" of sea ice, where marine biologists have discovered surprising evidence of biodiversity. Far from being an inert or biologically barren space, the underside of sea ice is filled with algae that are largely indifferent to variations in sunlight. Ice algae provide food resources for other living organisms, including crustaceans and fish. Crucially, ice algae can survive in a world characterized by twilight, and the algae are assumed to be dormant in the depths of winter. When spring returns, the biological productivity of algae changes markedly and again provides a vital food source for other living organisms.

The sea ice, scarred by cracks and ridges, also provides a natural refuge for young fish, such as polar cod. As the cod mature, they leave the underside of sea ice floes and begin to swim in open waters. Underwater robotic technology has been pivotal in enhancing scientific appreciation of these oceanic worlds because of the difficulty of securing diving access; humans are not well-suited to prolonged exposure in polar water.

While there is still some debate about how dependent some species, such as polar cod, are on the Arctic sea ice, there is little doubt that it is crucial to polar bears on the surface who prey on seals and to other animals, such as crustaceans, which themselves prey on the algae on the underside of ice. They in turn provide a vital food source for Arctic fish, sea birds, whales, and seals. Ice melt in the summer alters the ecological balance of Arctic marine environments, and as sunlight penetrates the ocean and seas in the summer season, so algae growth provides nourishment for sea life closer to the bottom of the seabed. But, as we noted in the introduction, all this could be up for grabs if the "Atlantification" of the Arctic Ocean and northern seas continues.

Arctic freshwater environments are shaped by the prevailing energy balance. The melting of snow and ice releases spring meltwater, and this in turn accumulates in rivers, lakes, and ponds. Soils, depending on the extent of the permafrost, become saturated and swamp-like in the summer. Arctic wetlands are widely distributed and particularly prevalent in northern Canada, Fennoscandia, and the Russian Arctic. The latter is shaped in the summer season by river discharge, as Siberian rivers, such as the Ob and Lena, along with the Canadian Mackenzie River, flow into the Arctic Ocean.

Put simply, the Arctic environment is shaped by the presence of snow and ice, and by periods of cold and darkness. Regardless of warming, the "high Arctic" will remain shrouded in extensive darkness for at least four months of the year. Warming, however, does interfere with seasonality and environmental characteristics. A warmer summer means that sea ice formation is delayed or permafrost continues to thaw. If sea and glacial ice disappear then the albedo of the region alters; less ice means more solar heat is absorbed by the terrestrial and marine environment rather than reflected back into the atmosphere. Additional heat is generated by warming seas and landforms. A vicious heat cycle takes hold, and living creatures have to adapt, migrate, or die.

How has life adapted to the Arctic?

Although there are not nearly as many species of animals in the Arctic as in equatorial regions, large populations of marine and terrestrial animals have adapted to life in one of the world's most extreme environments. It has been estimated that perhaps as many as 20,000 species of life make the Arctic home on a year-round or seasonal basis and that includes endo-parasites and microbes. Many, such as migratory species of whales, seals, and birds, are seasonal visitors from more southern latitudes. They begin their annual arrival in late spring to spend the brief summer at the floe edge, at sea, and on lakes. The brief Arctic growing season restricts opportunities for animals. The land produces little vegetation during the summer that can sustain life during the long, harsh winter, so birds migrate back to southern lands, to more temperate ocean coasts, and to interior plains and forests; caribou herds leave the rich summer lichen pastures for the boreal forest; humpback whales head to warm waters. Other animals, such as polar bears, Arctic foxes, wolves, narwhals, and ringed seals remain in the Arctic year-round.

Because food sources are often scarce and meager, Arctic animals have adapted to specific niches and are opportunistic. Born in snow banks on the Arctic coasts, polar bears spend most of their lives patrolling the ice pack for their dietary staple, the seal. Omnivorous creatures, they move with ease between marine and terrestrial environments. During spring in eastern Nunavut, concentrations of narwhals appear along ice edges on the east coast of Baffin Island, at the entrances of Lancaster Sound and Jones Sound, and in Smith Sound. They also move along the ice edges off west Greenland—some head to summer areas in Melville Bay when the sea ice begins to break up along the northwest coast between May and July, while others concentrate in the North Water polynya in spring before entering Kangerlussuaq (Inglefield Bredning) in the Qaanaaq area. Their summer range includes most of the waters of the Canadian Arctic archipelago and northwest Greenland. Their summer range includes most of the waters of the Canadian Arctic archipelago and northwest Greenland. When fast ice forms in autumn, narwhals move south and spend the winter in areas along the west Greenland coast and in Baffin Bay, which are covered by dense offshore pack ice.

From the fringe of the ice pack to the limit of Arctic waters, there is a wealth of marine life. The ice edge is a unique ecosystem in motion in that it moves thousands of kilometers each year, north in spring and south in autumn. Walrus, numerous species of seal, and cetaceans, such as belugas and narwhals, have a high fidelity to this environment and follow the ice edge as it moves, taking advantage of the ready access to rich sources of food. Walrus and seals haul themselves out of the water and onto sea ice to bask in the sun, or to mate and to raise pups, in late winter and spring. Seals, walrus, whales, and millions of fish thrive on the microscopic life that abounds in the chilly waters of the north.

We have learned from traditional indigenous knowledge and scientific observation that human and non-human life is not only entangled but has proven to be also highly adaptable. What counts most is whether animals, plants, and humans have been able to cope and take advantage of the intersection of ice, water, and land.

Animals such as polar bears and Arctic hares have developed place-based strategies for survival over winter, or in the case of birds and caribou they have migrated elsewhere. Those who stay throughout the winter have special features designed to endure extreme cold. Polar bears, Arctic hares, and muskok trap warm air close to their bodies, have a layer of insulating fat, and have thick, largely water-resistant fur. In the case of the Arctic hare and Arctic fox, the color of the fur changes from brown to white as winter makes its presence felt. The polar bear can move backward and forward from the frozen seas to the edge of the sea ice with complete indifference while hunting.

For Arctic plants, the art of survival lies in not only taking full advantage of a short growing season (with long hours of light during the high summer) but also keeping close to the ground to avoid the cold and moisture-sapping winds. Root structures tend to be shallow and have a capacity to survive on the surface of permafrost. Arctic lichens survive and thrive on exposed rock and provide an essential food source for caribou, reindeer, and other animals during winter.

Human survival and adaptability have also depended on finding shelter, using clothing from Arctic animal skins and fur (such as sealskin), and using local knowledge of the land, sea, and ice to seek out hunting opportunities. One of the most fascinating areas of research involves questions about whether, after thousands of years of adaptation to the Arctic and a particular high-fat diet based on whales and seals, Inuit in the Greenlandic and Canadian Arctic have developed a distinctive genetic history. In 2015, the journal *Science* published a story suggesting that a genetic mutation had enabled Inuit to counteract the potentially harmful effects of sea mammal fat and fish with high levels of omega-3 polyunsaturated fatty acids. The genetic mutations discovered were found in nearly all the Greenlandic Inuit population sample but were thought to be typical of less than 2% of Europeans.

So when sea ice in the Arctic, for example, disappears it affects the lives of all those who depend upon it—human and non-human. And when sea ice shrinks, it no longer acts as a barrier between polar seas and polar atmosphere, or constitutes a buffer zone between Arctic seas and North Atlantic or northern

Pacific waters. Water, ice, air, and coastal areas are impacted as a consequence, and ice and ocean properties are influenced.

How has land, sea, and ice been represented?

The Arctic has long been viewed as one of the few places on earth scarcely disturbed by humans. Snow, ice, cold, and darkness frustrate those seeking to explore, map, and travel through it or design and build infrastructure such as towns, cities, harbors, and airfields. Nowadays, the view of an ice-covered Arctic as untouched by human impact is unsustainable.

Modern European and North American representations of ice, more so than land or sea, have been largely indebted to what has been termed the sublime. Developed in the writings of seventeenth- and eighteenth-century literary critics and philosophers, such as Edmund Burke, John Dennis, and Immanuel Kant, the sublime signified a particular engagement with nature and wilderness where the viewer experiences a sense of awe, amazement, or even terror at the immensity of spaces seemingly free of human interference and human presence. In 1757, Burke distinguished the sublime as a distinct aesthetic category to beauty, and he argued that it helped explain why wildness could both captivate and terrorize. It also contributed to an aesthetic response from those venturing into the Arctic that focused more on mountainous icebergs, expansive tundra, and extensive mountainous peaks. What was often missing from those depictions of Arctic sea ice were people.

Inspired by the voyage of Edward Parry and his search for the Northwest Passage (1819–1820), Casper Friedrich's representation of Arctic ice was based on his sketches of river ice on the Elbe River, which would freeze over in winter. In *Sea of Ice*, Arctic ice is piled high in a manner more reminiscent of a Swiss alpine peak like the Matterhorn. A barely visible ship has been crushed by immense slabs of ice and thus acting as a rather sinister impromptu cemetery for those trapped inside. It is not clear from the picture whether oceanic and wind currents could ever free those man-made objects. Friedrich never visited the Arctic, so his picture offers a fateful, if imagined, warning to those who would dare to venture into this ice-filled realm.

Norwegian explorers, such as Fridtjof Nansen and Roald Amundsen, became celebrated for being adept at using skis and dog-sleds, as well as airships, ships, and planes—all the more so because things could go terribly wrong. In the summer of July 1897, the balloon of the Swedish explorer S. A. Andrée and two other colleagues plummeted to the ground. Although the men survived the crash, they were overwhelmed by ice and cold. Photographs taken by the crew members record the stricken balloon on the ice and the men's belated attempts to survive the punishing conditions north of Svalbard were discovered in 1930. In June 1928, Amundsen and five colleagues disappeared while searching for members of the crew of Umberto Nobile's airship *Italia*, which had crashed on its return from the North Pole. Amundsen's aircraft is believed to have crashed into the Barents Sea—no bodies were ever found.

With the onset of the Cold War (1945–1991), the land, sea, and ice of the Arctic were substances of considerable interest to the rival American and Soviet militaries. Billions of dollars were invested in infrastructure for the explicit purpose of "opening up" the Arctic to further economic development and national defense planning. Images of Cold War era radar stations, submarines emerging through the Arctic sea ice, and planes flying over vast tundra landscapes detailed the indomitable power of the Soviet and American armed forces. And vast sums of money were spent on scientific research into the marine environment of the Arctic. Defense planners wanted to know as much as they could about sea ice, northern waters, extreme weather, and continental shelves. At its bleakest, the Arctic was the most important Cold War frontline.

While militaries invested huge sums in cold weather defense planning, the Arctic was also a place for environmental politics where the ice, sea, and land were represented as vulnerable and in need of rescue. Since the late 1970s, non-governmental organizations, such as Greenpeace, had proven adept image-makers and storytellers of the Arctic, using film, images, and narratives to represent the Arctic and its wildlife as endangered. Initially the focus was on the fate of seals, whales, and polar bears but, more recently, the fragility of sea and glacial ice has been highlighted.

The idea of the Arctic being a vast and empty icy wasteland is rooted stubbornly in popular culture. In 1534, Jacques Cartier sailed along the southern Labrador coast and into the Gulf of St. Lawrence. He wrote, "there is nothing but moss and short, stunted shrub. I am rather inclined to believe that this is the land God gave to Cain." Cartier described how he met "wild and savage folk" along the coast, dressed in the furs of animals. Dionyse Settle, who provided a narrative of Martin Frobisher's third and last voyage to the Arctic in 1577, wrote of encounters with "monstrous islands of ice" and expressed abhorrence at how Inuit ate meat and fish raw, calling it "a loathsome spectacle, either to the beholders or hearers." Many accounts of exploration and whaling voyages to Greenland and the Canadian Arctic in the nineteenth century are colored by the experiences of the hardships endured in high latitudes; the difficulty of sailing and navigating through the ice, especially in waters such as Greenland's Melville Bay, where many whaling ships were trapped and crushed in the ice; the harshness of Arctic winters; catastrophe; scurvy; tension and violence; and the deaths of crew members. At times, however, there are poetic descriptions of wonder and delight in the literature of Arctic exploration and discovery. In *Narrative of a Voyage to the Polar Sea during 1875–76*, George Nares wrote how the "surface snow on the floes sparkles and glitters with the most beautiful iridescent colours, the ground on which we walk appearing as if strewn with bright and lustrous gems."

Such images of the Arctic derived from early paintings, narratives, and other visual materials are difficult to dispel, and they permeate and resonate in culture and literature. Toward the end of Mary Shelley's *Frankenstein*, Arctic explorer

Robert Walton writes to his sister from his ship: "We are still surrounded by mountains of ice, still in imminent danger of being crushed in their conflict. The cold is excessive, and many of my unfortunate comrades have already found a grave amidst this scene of desolation." The Arctic tends to have an irresistible appeal partly because of these enduring images of awe, grandeur, harshness, and even terror, and the modern tourist heads north in search of witnessing the Arctic sublime before it disappears under conditions of climate change.

The Arctic sustains a rich imaginative ecology that can and does support mysteries about ancient ice and in deep fjords, police detectives chasing murderers in the snow through dark forests, dramatic mountains, and across frozen lakes, and thrilling narratives situated amongst the tundra, under the permafrost, and in the forbidding waters of the Arctic Ocean. They are recurrent and compelling themes, cropping up in a vast literature over the past few decades, of which Alistair MacLean's *Bear Island*, Kerstin Ekman's *Under the Snow*, Peter Høeg's *Miss Smilla's Feeling for Snow*, Lalline Paul's *The Ice*, and Juris Jurjevics's *The Trudeau Vector* are just some examples. Nordic noir is probably the best known with popular television shows such as *Borgen* (mainly set in Denmark, but with some occasional references to Greenland) and the Icelandic police thriller *Trapped*.

For fans of the climate fiction or cli-fi genre, the Arctic also acts as a powerful accomplice to images of a world being radically altered by global warming. J. G. Ballard in *A Drowned World* warned his readers back in 1962 of an Earth overwhelmed by biblical-scale flooding after the ice caps were melted by solar radiation. Set in 2145, the shift in global surface temperatures is attributed to extraterrestrial forces. More recent examples pin the blame on the avarice of human beings and their addiction to fossil fuels. Ian McEwan's novel *Solar* (2010) posits a jaded nuclear physicist working on alternative energy sources while contemplating in Svalbard the implications of continued global warming for ice loss. Finally, Michelle Paver's *Dark*

Matter (2010) is a spine-chilling account of an ill-fated expedition to northeast Svalbard in the 1930s.

We might have imagined, represented, and thought of the Arctic as cold, dark, and characterized by an abundance of ice and snow, but is that no longer fit for purpose?

Do our representations of Arctic land, sea, and ice still fit?

Our images and representations of the Arctic are often contradictory. Fading snow cover, starving polar bears, and vanishing indigenous cultures coexist with monstrous ice, hostile weather, and ferocious polar bears. Philip Pullman's *Northern Lights* (1995) shows that the fantasy genre can still posit an ice-filled Arctic graced by the presence of armed polar bears and witch clans, while the silence, mysteries, myths, and folktales of far northern frozen lands remain inspirational themes to explore in children's books—Kiran Millwood Hargrave's *The Way Past Winter* (2018) being a recent example.

For those with a professional interest in the Arctic, this range of representations in popular culture has an impact. The communication of Arctic science in part depends on finding visual hooks designed to capture the attention of public audiences. The Arctic Council's Arctic Climate Impact Assessment (ACIA), for instance, in both its key findings document and full scientific report, published in 2004 and 2005 respectively, drew attention to snow and ice as perhaps the "most striking features" of the Arctic. The drastic nature of the effects of climate change on these features, exemplified by sea ice loss in the Arctic Ocean, the melting of the Greenland inland ice, the worsening of coastal erosion, and the loss of animal habitat does provoke wider public (and political) interest. Satellite imagery, time-lapse photography, and documentary films have been used by scientists and others to aid and abet their work on Arctic change. The award-winning documentary *Chasing Ice*, for instance—which followed the work of photographer James Balog and his team on glacial retreat in several northern places—includes footage from Greenland's Sermeq Kujalleq of the largest ice-calving event captured on film.

New productions such as *Profiles from the Arctic*, which came out of a 2012 International Polar Year conference, pull together images, stories, and interviews with scientists working in a number of circumpolar places. Much of this work deals implicitly with an environmental warning about disruption to the Arctic's land, sea, and ice and hopes to explain to the public why scientific research is so necessary and even vital.

The message from a great deal of contemporary science is that the Arctic is changing and what we thought we knew about the Arctic, intuitively and professionally, is proving far from robust. In the summer of 2018, the European Arctic experienced temperatures over 30° C and many parts were affected by heat waves and forest fires. Below the water's surface, meanwhile, the Atlantification and Pacification of the Arctic continues apace. We might have grown up with images of the Arctic as cold, ice covered, and inhospitable, but those elemental qualities are being turned upside down by warming. Winter sea ice is in retreat, and summer sea ice is disappearing. We might well need to develop new mental maps of the Arctic, which more directly address excess heat, melting ice, and biological newcomers to the northern latitudes.

As Karl Marx once noted, all that is solid melts into air (or in this case water). For a warming Arctic it is no joking matter. Warmth is not good news for animals and indigenous communities who have adapted to prevailing cold for millennia. Warming brings with it opportunities for other species and human actors to migrate, settle, and flourish, and make their impact felt on resident communities and ecologies.

3

ARCTIC HOMELANDS

The Arctic, if defined by land and sea (and ice) lying north of the Arctic Circle, is home to 4 million people. The majority of residents are found in the Russian North, and overwhelmingly non-indigenous. Development policy and population movement in the 1930s onward in the former Soviet Union led to the creation of distinct mining/resource cities such as Tiksi, which is around 2,500 miles east of Moscow. With only 4,500 people, the town served as a port designed to help the Soviet Union secure the Northern Sea Route. It fell into disrepair in the aftermath of the Cold War. Beyond Tiksi, around 2 million people live throughout the northern territories of Russia, and most of these settlements were part of Soviet collectivization. Non-indigenous citizens were moved to the North and outnumbered indigenous Nenets, Dolgans, Evenks, Nentsy, and Chukchi. Indigenous numbers in the Russian Arctic are small, representing around 5–10% of the total population of 2 million.

Elsewhere in the Arctic, population distribution and type vary greatly. The highest proportions of indigenous communities in the Arctic are found in Greenland (around 85–90%), Canada (around 50%), and Alaska (20%). The figures drop markedly in places like Norway, where Sámi are well-integrated into mainstream society. Most Arctic residents are urban based and non-indigenous. The largest Arctic city is

Murmansk in northwest Russia with over 300,000 people. But again, there are variations to the overall urban picture, as population numbers are declining in the Russian Arctic with some growth in Alaska, Iceland (where some 10% of the total population of 350,000 are foreign born), and Canada.

When we speak of Arctic homelands, we draw attention again to the fact that the social and cultural landscapes of the North are varied. Northern residents travel around the North, and many move back and forth from the Arctic.

What factors are shaping Arctic communities?

Arctic homelands are dynamic. The population of 4 million, as we have noted, is geographically distributed and uneven in terms of the percentage of indigenous and non-indigenous residents. Population dynamics are highly variable across the eight Arctic states. There are five factors to highlight— variability and distribution, fertility rates and migration, gender dynamics, legacies, and transnationalism.

First, Arctic residents live in cities, towns, villages, and hamlets. In Alaska, cosmopolitan cities such as Anchorage (over 298,000 people) are found alongside small villages in the north of the state such as Wainwright, home to 500 people. Migrant labor can and does transform the look and feel of local communities. Red Dog Mine, in northwest Alaska, has a population of 300, which is composed of miners and support staff who stay in accommodation provided by the mining company. The population is seasonal—and the mine is the world's largest source of zinc and has a considerable deposit of lead. There is no one typical Arctic settlement.

Second, fertility and migration rates in the Arctic matter as much as they do in any other part of the world. For example, fertility rates are high in Nunavut where young people represent a significant presence. The 2016 national census revealed that Nunavut's population increase was 12% between 2011 and 2016. The current population is 36,000 and the fertility rate (defined as number of live births in women in a calendar year) is 2.9, which is considerably higher than the national figure of 1.6. For the record, fertility rate is defined as the total number of children born or likely to be born to a woman in her life time. Population increase brings with it accompanying challenges such as provision of adequate housing and schooling for a burgeoning young population as well as employment opportunities. In other areas of the Arctic, young people have left smaller settlements for education, employment, and other opportunities in larger Arctic and subarctic towns and cities.

Third, the politics and culture of Arctic homelands are shaped by the notable presence and prominence of women in leadership positions within communities and beyond. Access to formal education in areas of high indigenous representation has favored girls and young women, as men and boys might spend more time learning to hunt, fish, and herd. One notable example is the Greenlandic politician Sara Olsvig who has been a Danish parliamentarian and leader of Greenland's Inuit Ataqatigiit Party, as well as a member of Inatsisartut, Greenland's parliament. She was also a former chairwoman of the Conference of Parliamentarians of the Arctic Region among other political positions previously held. In 2018, Olsvig announced she was leaving Greenlandic politics and blamed an enduring "poor political climate" that "hampers and obstructs the political process" for her decision to quit.

Fourth, and as we pointed out, the histories and experiences of Arctic homelands have been profoundly influenced by federal and national state policies toward northern residents. In Russia, for example, indigenous rights were rarely protected in the face of demands for national economic development and military security. From the 1930s onward, Soviet elites moved people northward and eastward, invested in infrastructure, and militarized the Russian North. While there is a greater recognition accorded to indigenous cultures and native rights today, the net result has been to suppress the cultures of northern homelands, with consequences for population numbers and communal vitality.

Finally, it is important to acknowledge the role of transnational and circumpolar interaction and familial networks. Language, culture, and politics work to create distinct national and transnational senses of homeland for Sámi, Inuit, and other northern residents. Sámi in northern Fennoscandia, as we mentioned, actively promote a cross-border homeland of Sápmi (and the Saami Council, since its creation in 1956, encourages that dialogue), but their experiences as indigenous peoples are shaped to a considerable extent by their relationships with national governments in Norway, Sweden, Finland, and Russia. Federal and national authorities in all the eight Arctic states have demonstrated a renewed interest in entrenching their authority and presence in northern territories. So we have an intriguing mixture of political and cultural devolution, uneven population growth and migration, national centralization, and new infrastructure projects, which can bring with them hotspots of social and economic activity.

Are there tensions between indigenous and so-called settler populations in the Arctic?

The Arctic is also home to northern communities that trace their origins to more recent settlers—they may either owe their existence to specific mining/resource development projects and/or to employment opportunities in a variety of sectors, including working for local and regional governments; national park management; health and education; the armed forces; tourism and the service sector economy, including travel and hospitality. The vast majority of Arctic residents would be identified as non-indigenous and, as noted, live in towns and cities across the circumpolar North. In Russia, for example, northern economic development dating from the 1930s and 1940s onward precipitated the movement of people into cities that were designed for resource-exploitation purposes. During the Cold War, these were closed cities and access to them was sharply restricted. Even today highly sensitive cities and regions associated with strategic industries and the armed forces are still closed to foreign visitors, and in some cases domestic citizens require permits to travel there.

In other parts of the Arctic, northern cities and towns are often little different to their southern counterparts. The northern city of Tromsø, home of the University of Tromsø—the Arctic University of Norway—is similar to the southern cities of Oslo or Bergen in terms of high levels of infrastructure and governance. Residents are well integrated into the Norwegian state, and the Sámi Parliament is found in the northern town of Karasjok. What makes the northern territories of Norway arguably distinct is their geographical proximity to Russia and the Norwegian-Russian border zone. Residents on both sides have an ability to cross over comparatively straightforwardly compared to other Norwegian and Russian citizens living elsewhere. There is a special visa and customs regime in place. While the border remains strategically sensitive, and was a frontline for the location of NATO and Soviet Union military forces during the Cold War, both sides are committed to the promotion of trade and cultural cooperation. This has been a bit more strained in recent years following Russia's annexation of Crimea and controversies over refugees, mainly from Syria, entering northern Norway from Russia, prompting the Norwegians to build an eleven-foot-high steel fence.

With 4 million people living north of the Arctic Circle, and over 13 million people living north of 60° latitude, then, there is a great deal of diversity in terms of everyday lives. Apart from costs, other areas of concern for remoter communities are food security and health and well-being. Local sources of food such as whales, seals, fish, reindeer, and muskox are integral to Inuit livelihoods and culture. In Greenland, it is not uncommon to witness hunters and fishermen informally selling "country food" to people living in towns.

Indigenous peoples living in the North continue to be disproportionately vulnerable to poor health and often live in inadequate housing without access to safe water, which clearly has a profound impact on life-chances. In Canada and Greenland, a great deal of concern has been expressed about the living conditions of indigenous communities, and stories emerge regularly of young people committing suicide (or attempting to) as a consequence of frustration over their everyday lives. But there is a longer, more brutal history of indigenous peoples being uprooted from local communities, sent to residential schools, forced to learn non-indigenous languages, and act in ways dictated by others, while their lands were expropriated by national authorities eager to cement their sovereignty claims and appropriate resources. The Danish historical drama film *The Experiment* (2010; called *Eksperimentet* in Danish), addressed for Danish, Greenlandic, and international audiences, revealed the psychological trauma of twenty-two children, aged between six and eight, who were taken from their families in 1951 and sent to school in Denmark, as part of the Danish state's commitment to "modernize" and "civilize" Greenlanders and turn them into Danes.

In Canada, the Trudeau government committed in 2016 to a "nation to nation" dialogue where the relationship with indigenous peoples is respectful of their rights and wishes. The issue remains how resourcing will be directed toward communities where housing, educational and health provision and infrastructure, including broadband connectivity, is still precarious and of a standard that non-indigenous Canadians living in the south of the country would find unacceptable. The historical drama film *We Were Children* (2012) provides a chilling reminder of how many indigenous children and young people were abused in residential schools and how that legacy of abuse and neglect continues to make itself felt on individuals and communities—including a failure by federal and provincial/territorial governments to provide adequate housing, safe water supplies, and appropriate support for indigenous communities.

Overall, Arctic residents are highly diverse in terms of their everyday lives, movements, occupations, and relationships to the land and sea. Some will leave the place of their birth and become part of an Arctic diaspora, heading southward to other parts of Arctic states, to live, work, and study. Some will return and some will not. In that sense, the Arctic as an inhabited region is no different to other comparatively isolated (and again there is a spectrum here from the more isolated parts of the Canadian North and Greenland to the highly urbanized Russian and Nordic Arctic) parts of the world in terms of those human trajectories. And we also need to remember that there are plenty of people traveling northward who have been attracted to the region's economic, cultural, environmental, and aesthetic qualities.

How have the Arctic's indigenous peoples been represented, and how do they represent themselves?

There has been a long history of images and stories of Arctic peoples as either exotic or alien. In the former, indigenous peoples were often depicted as "noble savages" who were to be admired for their ingenuity and resilience. The silent documentary film *Nanook of the North* (1922) is often cited as emblematic in this regard. Filmed and directed in 1920–1921 in Port Harrison (now called Inukjuak) in northern Québec by Robert J. Flaherty, it follows the life history of an Inuk man (Nanook, portrayed by Allakariallak) and his family in the Canadian Arctic. The film continues to attract much controversy. Flaherty was accused of faking elements of the documentary and of being deceitful by claiming to offer a realistic introduction to the lives of Inuit. It also later came to be seen and critiqued as an example of salvage ethnography, or the recording of cultures before they disappeared. As a filmmaker he had no qualms of manipulating social and physical environments in order to generate the story he wished to tell. Flaherty at the time was also asked by his sponsors to evaluate the fur-trapping potential of the region and its prospects for further resource exploitation. *Nanook of the North* was widely distributed and became a global phenomenon, and it influenced later generations of filmmakers and directors. Within two years of the making of the film, however, Allakariallak died—stories that suggested he died of starvation added to the Arctic's mystique as empty and deprived, although his death was probably from tuberculosis.

Indigenous peoples have reacted to films like *Nanook of the North* in part by making what is termed Fourth World cinema, such as *Atanarjuat: The Fast Runner* (2001) and *The Journals of Knud Rasmussen* (2006), by Isuma Productions, which is based in the Nunavut community of Igloolik, and *Angry Inuk* (2016), which was directed by Alethea Arnaquq-Baril in defense of Inuit rights to hunt seals. The three films received critical acclaim for their sensitive interrogations of Arctic histories, landscapes, and indigenous life, and their interactions with settler populations and European explorers.

Indigenous filmmaking does not produce and distribute films only about traditional indigenous lifestyles. In an environmental documentary film called *Silent Snow* (2011), for example, a Greenlandic woman, Pipaluk Knudsen-Ostermann, collaborated with a Dutch filmmaker, Jan van der Berg, to depict her journey around the world meeting people affected by pollutants and environmental degradation. In *On the Ice* (2011), Alaskan Iñupiat filmmaker Andrew Okpeaha MacLean turns to the film noir genre to explore the consequences of a suspicious death on the Alaskan sea ice, and the ramifications for two teenage boys and the community of Utqiaġvik (previously Barrow).

Although very different, each film points to a noticeable trend in indigenous and northern self-representation. Cultural events such as the Greenland Eyes International Film Festival, Tromsø International Film Festival, and the Russian-based International Arctic Film Festival have provided venues for the screening and circulating of indigenous film. Scandinavian films, such as Amanda Kernell's first feature-length film *Sami Blood* (2016), have not shied away from addressing how indigenous peoples were forced to assimilate and acculturate in mainstream Swedish, Danish, Norwegian, and Finnish societies. *Sami Blood* considers how young Swedish Sámi were sent to boarding schools and instructed not to speak their native language and adopt Swedish instead. More than that, the film suggests that there was a heavy price to pay in terms of family disruption and revealed an education system that reinforced ideas about the Sámi (renamed by mainstream society as Lapps) as uncivilized. This experience was not unique to Sámi, as tens of thousands of indigenous people across the Arctic were sent to residential schools from the late nineteenth century to as late as the 1980s and 1990s.

The introduction and diffusion of the Internet and social media in Arctic communities from Alaska to Russia has given new opportunities for self-expression and cultural production, though in many Arctic communities Internet access and connectivity is still very expensive and patchy.

Indigenous self-representation is ongoing. Inuk artist and renowned throat singer Tanya Tagaq is a case in point. In 2012, Tagaq, who was born in Cambridge Bay (Iqaluktuutiaq) in Nunavut, wrote a soundscape for a retrospective on First Peoples Cinema organized by the Toronto International Film Festival. Her intervention was shown alongside a re-screening of *Nanook of the North* and designed to be an act of cultural reclamation. She said at the time that she wanted to hit back against the stereotypes imposed on northern peoples as uncivilized, deprived, antediluvian, and incapable of understanding and engaging with Western technology.

Do the interests of indigenous and non-indigenous northern populations converge or diverge?

Indigenous peoples have asserted the right to self-determination and self-government based on historical and cultural rights to the ownership, occupancy, and use of lands and resources. Campaigns for land claims settlements have been carried out against the backdrop of major resource-development projects such as oil and gas exploration, mines, and pipeline construction. We will return to this in our discussion of the resourceful Arctic in chapter 6 because land claims agreements also encapsulate ice and water. In recent decades, the United States, Canada, and Denmark have recognized, to varying degrees, the claims of indigenous peoples for land rights and for self-government. In Canada, for example, the approach has been to negotiate comprehensive land claims, which are, in a sense modern treaties; they address Aboriginal land and resource rights, but they also extinguished some existing rights enshrined in early treaties in exchange for rights to land, resources, and limited self-governing powers.

Land claims and self-government agreements have been negotiated and implemented since the early 1970s. Notable are the Alaska Native Claims Settlement Act (ANCSA) of 1971; Greenland Home Rule in 1979, followed by Self Rule in 2009; and in Canada the James Bay and Northern Québec Agreement (1975), the Inuvialuit Agreement (1984), comprehensive land claims agreements with the Gwich'in and Sahtu Dene in the early 1990s, a number of land claims with Yukon First Nations, and the creation of the new territory of Nunavut in 1999. Nunatsiavut, the Inuit region of northern Labrador, achieved self-government in 2005, but self-governance and regional autonomy are still works in progress in the Inuit homeland of Nunavik in northern Québec. These political changes not only accord specific rights to indigenous people, including subsurface rights to hydrocarbons and minerals, they often include changes in the ways that living and non-living resources are managed. A greater degree of local involvement in resource use management decisions and wildlife conservation has been made possible, including in some cases the actual transfer of decision-making authority to the local or regional level, which allows for indigenous governance initiatives that incorporate traditional knowledge and local monitoring.

There are notable differences in the claims settlements and self-government arrangements that have been negotiated. Nunavut and Greenland share some similarities. Greenlanders became the first population of Inuit origin to achieve a degree of self-government when Home Rule was introduced by Denmark in 1979, while the Inuit of Canada's eastern Arctic assumed control over their lives and lands when Nunavut was carved out of the Northwest Territories in 1999. Nunavut and Greenlandic Home Rule and Self Rule are seen as models for indigenous land claims and self-determination elsewhere in the circumpolar North, but also in many other places in the world.

Nunavut and Greenland are related to one another, in that Inuit have achieved self-determination and self-government. They are also similar in their colonial legacies binding them to trade economies based on the resources of these Arctic regions, and the ways in which Inuit lives were implicated, and changed, in these economies. They are comparable in the Inuit cultural sense. They are akin to one another in that they both face the challenges arising from unprecedented and possibly irreversible climate change. Yet the working out and defining of governance has been markedly different, and the direction they should take in the future could vary. Nunavut and Greenland may well be Inuit homelands, but the creation of Nunavut occurred within the Canadian national territory, while Greenland achieved a significant degree of autonomy within the Danish realm and remains a constituent part of the Kingdom of Denmark.

The Nunavut legislature and the Greenlandic parliament are instruments of public government, but one fundamental difference between Nunavut and Greenland lies in the ethnic dimension. The inauguration of Nunavut was preceded by an Inuit land claims process—the Nunavut Land Claims

Agreement (NLCA) was signed in May 1993 and gave Inuit title to some 350,000 square kilometers of the total area of Nunavut (which is 1.9 million sq. km)—whereas there was no land claim in Greenland, and Home Rule was worked out, defined, and implemented as a non-indigenous settlement. The Greenlandic political system is similar to the Danish style of parliamentary democracy. It comprises a thirty-one-seat parliament (*Inatsisartut*) and the government (*Naalakkersuisut*), which is headed by the premier.

For all their apparent similarities, Inuit in northern Canada and Greenland have their own political stories to tell. The Nunavut land claims process was a long one. Beginning in the 1970s, it involved the careful and extensive mapping of Inuit land use and occupancy, resolving different claims between Inuit organizations and the Canadian federal government. It involved the issue of indigenous rights, and Nunavut was the desire of an indigenous people to achieve control over their lands. By contrast, the beginnings of the Home Rule movement in Greenland had its roots in social and economic change, disruption, and rapid urbanization in the 1950s and 1960s (although anti-Danish colonial sentiment can perhaps be traced back to the first nurturing of a sense of Greenlandic national identity in the nineteenth century), but indigenous land issues did not figure in debates about self-government in the same way they did in the land claims process in what is now Nunavut.

In Fennoscandia, the political experiences of indigenous peoples are varied yet again. Sámi parliaments have been established in Norway, Sweden, and Finland. These are not forms of self-government, but they are institutions that promote political initiatives and manage the directives and laws delegated to them by national authorities. To take Finland as an example, Sámi were recognized as an indigenous people in the Finnish constitution in 1995, and they have a right to maintain and develop their language and culture as well as their traditional livelihoods, which are based mainly on reindeer herding. Since 1996, the Sámi have had constitutional self-government concerning their language and culture in their homelands in northern Finland and are entitled to service in their own language in official matters. Of the roughly 9,000 Sámi living in Finland, more than 60% live outside their northern homeland, though, and a significant number live in Helsinki and regional centers such as Oulu. Finnish Sámi continue to struggle to secure land rights because 90% of the land they claim as traditional lands by virtue of occupancy and use belongs to the government. In reality, Sámi in Finland often tend to be regarded and treated more as a linguistic minority rather than an indigenous people.

The most complex and unresolved issues relating to the autonomy and self-determination of the Arctic's indigenous peoples are found in Russia. Indigenous minorities of the Russian North were given certain rights and privileges under the Soviets, and today they are protected by Article 69 of the Russian constitution and three federal framework laws that establish a range of cultural, territorial, and political rights, even if they are often precarious. A problem often arises when indigenous rights conflict with other interests and stakeholders in the Russian North, such as tourism and the mining industry. In 2017, Russia declared that it was the official Year of Ecology and Protected Areas, but that might not deliver positive outcomes for Russian indigenous peoples.

Growth in protected areas like the Russian Arctic National Park and other conservation zones can quickly lead to disruption for those who live and work in the region as hunting, herding, and fishing rights are restricted. In 2000, the Russian federal government introduced a framework entitled Traditional Nature Use of Indigenous Minority Peoples of the North, which was supposed to guide future policy on environmental protection and indigenous rights.

It has not been implemented, and many indigenous groups complain that their interests are quickly sacrificed in favor of national economic development and security planning. The actual implementation of regulations contained in these laws, however, has been challenged by changes to legislation concerning natural resources in recent years, as well as government policies on extractive industry projects in the North. Indigenous rights have not always been recognized—indeed, there has been a gradual erosion of these rights—and many indigenous groups are calling for self-government and regional autonomy.

The definition of who is indigenous complicates matters, however. There are some forty distinct peoples in Russia recognized legally as "indigenous, small-numbered peoples of the North, Siberia, and the Far East." Together, they number around 260,000 people, or some 0.2% of the population of the Russian Federation (ethnic Russians account for around 78% of the entire population of the country). This status has a numerical and geographical qualification and is tied to specific and precise conditions. People recognized as indigenous must have no more than 50,000 members, practice and maintain a traditional way of life, live in certain remote regions of Russia considered traditional territories, and identify itself as a distinct ethnic community.

So, Evenks, Nenets, Chukchi, Yup'ik, and Sámi are recognized as indigenous under these criteria, whereas other peoples of northern Russia, such as Sakha (Yakuts), Buryat, Komi, and Khakass, who may identify themselves as indigenous, do not hold this formal, official, and legal status because of their larger populations. A definition of "indigenous" without the numerical qualification does not exist in Russian legislation. Regional and national associations representing indigenous peoples, such as the Russian Association of Indigenous Peoples of the North (RAIPON), have become subject to increasing interference, surveillance, and control by the state over the last decade or so. Conflicts have also arisen in the Russian Far East as traditional indigenous lands have been distributed to settlers from other parts of Russia.

How is the nature of indigenous peoples' relationships with their Arctic homelands expressed?

Indigenous peoples have a rich and extensive repertoire of stories, mythologies, and beliefs pertaining to the Arctic and beyond—about humans, animals, land, water, ice, air, wind, the sky, and the atmosphere. These stories matter because they give shape to those communities and help guide current and future relationships with northern settlers and national governments.

This repertoire details how an indigenous view of the environment includes the human and the more than human. Inuit, for example, know the land as *nuna*. But it is not completely accurate to translate *nuna* simply as "land"—it is the place which is underneath, above, and all around, in which people live and relate to animals and other non-human entities. It refers to more than terra firma and encompasses water, ice, soil, rock, sky and wind, what Tim Ingold calls the "weather-world," surroundings that include the air, atmosphere, subsoil, and earth processes, what is above and below, as well as what appears to be on the surface.

While many indigenous peoples may have adopted Christianity due to waves of European and American colonial encounters, Inuit and other indigenous cultures continued to be shaped by beliefs that inanimate objects, animals, and plant life possess spiritual properties. Indeed, indigenous worldviews reveal that there is no distinction between animate and inanimate entities, and there is no rigid distinction between the spiritual and physical worlds. The Arctic is an aware world, made up of humans, animals, and spiritual entities. Inuit belief systems were literally rooted in the unpredictability and environmental extremes encountered in the Arctic and often operated as a warning system to community members about how to live cautiously and respectfully in their surroundings. Within Inuit communities, elders, and shamans in particular were critical in ensuring that social rituals including taboos were enacted and observed, and warned of the perilous consequences if the spirits of animals and other elements of their surroundings were disrespected, disturbed, or agitated.

For all Inuit groups across the Arctic, the *angakkoq*, the shaman, once played a central role before the introduction of Christianity in organizing and maintaining the relations and exchanges between humans and animals, and between humans and spirits. The *angakkoq* acted as an intermediary in transactions between humans, animal souls, and the guardians of animals. Setting out to become a shaman was to embark on a difficult journey into darkness, isolation, and loneliness, and onward to the world of spirits. Inuit stories relate how the *angakkoq* first had to undergo a long, solitary, and arduous initiation, in the mountains, on the tundra, or in a deep, dark cave, away from friends and family, and far from the lives of other people, wrestling with spirits to acquire his or her powers, pulled apart limb by limb and being reassembled as a new person before returning home. The essence of shamanic practice was the trance, and it represented the journey of the shaman's soul to the spirit world to bargain with the animals' guardian so the animals would be sent to the human world to be hunted and so give themselves up to be consumed by humans who would be regenerated through the sacrifice of the animal as a non-human person. The shaman could also go into trance and search for the souls of human beings that had been captured by malevolent spirits that sought to do harm to people through sickness and death. Shamans depended on a variety of helping spirits to assist in these journeys to the spirit world. Most commonly, the helping spirit was an animal, such as a polar bear, which carried the shaman on its back, flying silently through the air or swimming effortlessly to the bottom of the sea to visit Sedna.

Sedna (the Woman of the Sea—Nuliayuk in parts of Canada, Sassuma Arnaa, or Arnaqquassaaq, in Greenland) guards over marine mammals, making gifts of them to humans and punishing the disrespectful with hunting failure. For a culture dependent on hunting whales, fish, and seals, appeasing Sedna was considered vital to the long-term survival of local communities. There are several variants of the Sedna story, but all share common elements. Sedna married a hunter, who turned out to be a petrel who could assume the appearance of a human. Sedna's father and brothers attempted to rescue her in their boat, but the petrel caused a great storm at sea. In an attempt to save their own lives, the men threw Sedna overboard. As she clung to the side of the boat, Sedna's father cut off her fingers. As they fell into the sea, the severed fingers were transformed into seals, whales, walrus, and narwhals. Sedna herself slipped beneath the waves to descend to the world at the bottom of the sea, where she became guardian of the sea mammals which had formed from her fingers.

Sedna is usually generous to the Inuit, ensuring the sea mammals can swim in the waters so they can be caught by people for food. Yet, there are times when she refuses to let the animals go, especially if hunters have caused pain to an animal's spirit or have failed to give a newly killed seal a drink of fresh water. She can bring bad weather and has the ability to whip up the sea into a frenzy and cause violent storms. Sedna's hair can also become clogged with dirt if people violate a taboo or a rule, or neglect to observe a ritual, and then the animals become entangled in it. When seals, whales, and other sea mammals are scarce and people have no luck with hunting, a shaman must plead with Sedna to release them. By combing her dirty and tangled hair, the shaman can calm Sedna and free the animals.

The Sedna story reflects a fundamental belief in the unity of all human and animal life, and it reveals much about how the world is populated by human and more than human entities, but it also symbolizes the tensions between humans and animals that can exist. It serves to inculcate a strong moral code, which would have been so vital in small and highly isolated communities even if they were part of a larger collective scattered over vast areas of the Arctic. Inuit activists often point to how it can also be interpreted as a cautionary tale, or even an explanatory account, in the contemporary context of discussion about unprecedented climate change. Human activity, it is widely accepted, has contributed to the dramatic changes now being experienced in the Arctic climate and around the globe. If animals no longer come to people, or are no longer present, then the explanation must be found in human action.

Many stories describe how, in the distant past, humans and animals were not as clearly distinguished from each other as they are today. Animals can become humans at will, and vice versa. Some humans have the power and ability to change their form. Similarly, not only can the guardian spirit of an animal assume the shape of the animal it protects, it can also take the form of another animal or a person. Hunters face a dilemma: when they encounter an animal—be it seal, whale, polar bear, caribou, or petrel—they can never be entirely sure of its real character or nature. The world and everything in it can take one by surprise, and so being ready for such surprise and anticipating danger and uncertainty, as well as opportunity, is essential to daily life.

Why do indigenous oral histories and stories matter about Arctic homelands?

Storytelling in the Arctic not only built group identity but also acted as a reservoir of legends and myths to help make sense of living in a highly dynamic and variable environment.

Take the stories of Athabaskan peoples, whose traditional homelands are the forests, rivers, and lakes of the vast subarctic boreal regions of Alaska and northern Canada. The social organization of Athabaskan communities still often revolves around annual seasonal activities of hunting, fishing, and gathering in a wide ecological niche.

Moose and caribou provide a source of meat for the entire year, as well as hides and fur. Smaller animals, birds, and fish are also a key part of people's diets. In the Alaskan interior, especially for communities on the banks of the Yukon, Tanana, and other rivers, hunting large animals is a vital part of local economies, but fishing provides stability to daily life and settlement patterns throughout the year. The Gwich'in of northeast Alaska and northern Yukon rely on the migratory Porcupine caribou herd, while the Denaina of Cook Inlet and the Kenai Peninsula in southern Alaska engage in sea mammal hunting.

Historic settlement patterns corresponded to—and were reflected in—the annual hunting and fishing cycle, and winter dwellings were sometimes temporary or semi-permanent; people were always ready and prepared to be on the move around the nomadic landscape. While contemporary Athabaskan hunters and fishers travel great distances in search of game—along rivers and traplines, or out to sea—and often spend the summer at campsites that have been used by the same families for generations, they live in permanent communities and their daily lives are circumscribed by the institutions of North American society.

Archaeologists generally say that Athabaskan-speaking peoples probably crossed the Bering Strait from Siberia to Alaska between 10,000 and 15,000 years ago, moving further into North America and exploring opportunities for hunting and places to settle as the great glaciers and ice sheets of the Pleistocene period receded. However, there are considerable gaps in the archaeological knowledge of Athabaskan prehistory. Most Athabaskan artifacts from known dwelling sites can be dated to only about 2,000 years ago.

Much of what is understood by non-indigenous people about Athabaskan origins comes from both archaeology and linguistic research, yet that research is often at odds with Athabaskan oral traditions and religious beliefs, and with indigenous relations with subarctic environments. This is especially germane given the latest research concerning the peopling of the Americas. Recent dating of an archaeological site in California to 130,000 years ago has caused some controversy amongst scientists and thrown conventional theories into disarray, especially as this was a time when *Homo sapiens* had not yet left Africa. If the artifacts and materials found at the site means that the history of early humans in North America needs to be rewritten, then it is likely that an ancestor of *Homo sapiens* moved into the Americas during the last interglacial warm period rather than the current one.

An Athabaskan view of their emergence is that it happened in Distant Time. Although the Distant Time is a remote, ancient time, oral histories and stories nonetheless recount its events in incredible detail, reflecting an immensely rich spiritual and cultural heritage about the environment and how Athabaskan people think about and relate to it. The stories of the Distant Time provide accounts of Athabaskan origins, movement, and migration; people and significant events; and the place of people in relation to the world around them. Distant Time stories provide indigenous accounts of the origins of the world, the elements, and animals. For example, Raven (or Raven Man) is a central figure in Athabaskan origin stories: before the beginning of time—in fact even before the beginning of Distant Time—there existed only darkness until Raven created the world by revealing the daylight. Having revealed the daylight, Raven then created the first people. These stories also reveal how, as for other northern peoples, everything in the world (humans, animals, rivers, lakes, trees, thunderstorms, etc.) has consciousness. Many features of the landscape were originally human or other beings whose spirits are now embodied in aspects of the natural world.

How has indigenous storytelling guided our sense of Arctic homelands?

The Arctic has its own time and seasons that defy the imposition of boundaries and classification. Visitors from temperate regions who are accustomed to dividing the calendar year into four seasons must abandon their preconceptions of how the world moves, shifts, and transforms, and adjust their orientation to this high latitude world to include at least six seasons— there could be even seven or eight, depending on which part of the Arctic they visit. In Baffin Island communities, for instance, there are at least six Inuktitut words that describe seasonal change and variation. The period from November to March it known as *ukiuq*, winter; from March to April *ukiuq* gives way to early spring, *upirngatsaaq*, before changing to *upirngaaq*, late spring, between April and June; *aujaq* is the short season of summer, lasting from the end of June to early September; then, from mid-September to October *ukiatsaaq* describes the period of early autumn, followed by *ukiaq*, when darkening days and falling snow hint at the winter to come.

The boundaries between the seasons overlap, and an outsider to Baffin Island would have to learn many more Inuktitut words to understand the world they saw merging, changing, and coming into being around them. A grasp of Inuktitut vocabulary, or the indigenous language of any other part of the Arctic one happens to be in, not only enriches one's perception and understanding of the Arctic, it can also help people survive. A common misunderstanding, for example, is that Inuit have dozens of words for snow. Essentially, there are two: *qanik*, falling snow, and *aput*, snow on the ground. An extensive vocabulary does exist, however, that comprises words and terms that describe the formation, consistency, and type of snow, such as *masak aput*, wet snow, or snow that is good for making water, *aniutaq*.

Knowing this vocabulary is vital for recognizing the types of snow you may encounter, and which either make travel easy or difficult, or can frustrate, delay, or place one in danger. For example, in Inuktitut, recent deep snow that is difficult to walk on without sinking is *apijuq*, while hard snow that is good for making snow houses and can be cut into blocks relatively easily is *sitilluqaq*. Sometimes snow falls merely as light flurries, *qanniliqtaqtuq*, but a wind can also blow around snow that has already fallen, making it *natiruviktuq*—to seem as if it is snowing. Bad weather can bring strong winds, heavy falling snow, and make it *natiruviktuq* all at once. In Inuktitut, this is called *tammajarnaqtuq*, something that in English would be described as a blizzard.

Indigenous worldviews express how every feature of the Arctic environment has its own essence—for example, Inuit refer to this sense of what animates things in the world as *inua*, which also means "owner" or "dweller." In Greenlandic *qaqqap inua*, means "the essence of mountains," or *sermersuap inua*, "the essence of the great ice," referring to Greenland's inland ice. Weather, or climate, is known as *sila*—but its meaning is far deeper than a description of the conditions of the atmosphere, and people understand *sila* as the breath of life, the reason things emerge, become, take shape, move, and change. *Sila* can also mean "outside" or "the elements," as well as "intelligence/consciousness," or "mind." It is seen as a fundamental principle underlying and animating the world and the things that comprise it, a life-giving spirit, a universal consciousness that is found in each person.

In the early 1920s, at the end of his Fifth Thule Expedition across Arctic North America, the Danish-Greenlandic explorer and ethnographer Knud Rasmussen met Najagneq, an *angakkoq* in Nome, Alaska, who described *sila* as a power that could not be explained in simple words, "a great spirit, supporting the world and the weather and all life on earth." Stories told everywhere from western Alaska to eastern Greenland describe how *sila* would react angrily if people failed to observe a ritual or commit a taboo. "No one has seen Sila," Najagneq told Rasmussen, "his place of being is a mystery in that he is at once among us and unspeakably far away."

The experience of growing up and living in the Arctic has taught Inuit hunters and fishers that, in addition to good equipment and skill, knowledge of the movement, behavior, and habits of animals is vital for their successful capture, as is an understanding of how *sila* moves and affects the world and a person's moods. Knowledge of good places to hunt and the names and stories associated with the landscape, seascape, and icescape also enhance a hunter's chances of navigating and moving around successfully. Place names provide essential information about a community's past, significant events, and the astonishing things that may have happened, as well as things that may seem insignificant to an outsider. They also say much about community activities, animals, animal-migration routes, dream-trails (places in the landscape where animal spirits reveal themselves to humans in dreams), environmental changes, climate change, and significant weather-related events. Stories and discussions about the weather and climate are interwoven with stories and experiences of particular tasks such as hunting, fishing, berry-picking, or traveling. Much of this is entangled with memories of events, local family histories, and a strong sense of attachment to place and locality. *Sila*, the weather, connects people to the environment and animals, but also to their ancestral, familial, and local histories and relationships.

Anthropologist Julie Cruikshank, who has worked extensively with Yukon First Nations over several decades, has written about how subarctic peoples were constantly on the move in search of places to bring within their seasonal cycle of economic and social activities. Mobility within nomadic spaces meant being able to carry what was necessary and to carry it efficiently; anything burdensome would slow people down. Other anthropologists working in northern indigenous societies have pointed to the importance of things being portable and for people to be flexible and adaptable in their movements in their surroundings. Technology is something that is carried around by people in the form of ideas and knowledge, and in memories and stories, not just in the form of material objects. The knowledge and skills necessary for constructing a sled or shelter and for making hunting implements are vital for survival in northern environments. These are passed from one generation to the next through oral tradition and traditional knowledge and can move with people from place to place.

The sense of potential in Arctic surroundings informs local worldviews, including attitudes toward ice and snow. For many indigenous communities, bodies of ice, such as glacier and mountain peaks, are invested with not only sacred character but also indicative of other earthly forces that are responsible for avalanches, ice retreat, and inclement weather. The movement and behavior of ice and snow strongly informs the customs and rituals of everyday life. Glacial movement becomes indicative of transgression. In a pioneering study of the St. Elias Mountains in Alaska and northern Canada, Cruikshank explored how the experiences and understandings of glaciers contrasted with colonial explorers and administrators and their respective epistemologies and cosmologies. Glacial retreat provoked very different understandings from the respective communities in and around the St. Elias Mountains as indigenous and Western/scientific modes of understanding were brought to bear.

Why do indigenous peoples matter in Arctic geopolitics?

Over the last two or three decades, indigenous governments and organizations have played a pivotal and increasingly influential role in agenda-setting and political debate on the Arctic environment, the use and conservation of wildlife, resource development, and sustainability. In Norway, after decades of Sámi experiencing discrimination and marginalization, a decision was taken by the government to adopt ILO Convention Number 169, with attendant guarantees for the protection of land and resource rights. But the adoption in 1990 still proved controversial as Norwegian Sámi continued to campaign for greater recognition of their right to increased autonomy over their lives and lands. After years of activism and protest, the more wide-ranging Finnmark Act of 2005 gave Sámi and the residents of the northern area of Finnmark further legal rights to 46,000 square kilometers of land and water.

In Scandinavia and Finland, Sámi have demanded and been granted their own parliaments and formal recognition within national constitutions. In 1995, for example, Finland recognized the Sámi as an indigenous people (although the attitude that they are seen more as a linguistic minority prevails) and thus able to access resources and cultural rights protection. But all of this has involved long-term campaigning, activism, protesting, and civil disobedience. In other words, it has not been achieved in a straightforward way, even in liberal and progressive Nordic Arctic countries.

In the Arctic Council (more about which we will discuss in the next chapter), indigenous peoples' organizations have made a place for themselves in the vanguard of Arctic environmental protection and sustainable development for indigenous communities. They have become major players on the stage of international diplomacy and policymaking concerning the future of the Arctic. They are permanent participants in the Arctic Council and pivotal to the mission of this intergovernmental forum.

In Greenland, Canada, and Alaska, regional and national Inuit organizations have outlined and put into practice their own environmental strategies and conservation policies. They aim to safeguard the future of Inuit resource use; to ensure a workable, participatory approach between indigenous peoples, scientists, and policymakers to achieve sustainable resource management and development; and to support efforts focused on the co-production of knowledge. From an Inuit perspective, threats to wildlife and the environment do not come from hunting, but from airborne and seaborne pollutants entering the Arctic from industrial areas far to the south, as well as from global climate change, international conventions for conservation, and environmentalist action that does not take indigenous perspectives into account. Extraction of nonrenewable resources, such as oil and gas and minerals, poses other challenges, even if they can also bring benefits. In recent years Inuit have sought ways to counteract such threats and devise strategies for environmental protection and sustainable development. This approach has been made more effective through the support of the Inuit Circumpolar Council (ICC), which has released a number of declarations on the Arctic and works for the implementation of initiatives that consider local knowledge and Inuit cultural values.

ICC is a pan-Arctic indigenous peoples' organization representing the rights of Inuit in Greenland, Canada, Alaska, and Siberia. Its foundation as the Inuit Circumpolar Conference in Barrow (now Utqiaġvik), Alaska, in 1977, was partly a response to increased oil and gas exploration and development in the Arctic. The ICC has had non-governmental organization (NGO) status at the United Nations since 1983. Since then, it has sought to establish its own Arctic policies, combining indigenous environmental knowledge and Inuit concerns about future development with ethical and practical guidelines for human activity in the Arctic. In September 2008 in Kuujjuaq, Nunavik, the ICC organized the Inuit Leaders' Summit, which resulted in a "Circumpolar Inuit Declaration on Sovereignty in the Arctic." It reaffirmed Inuit perspectives on the Arctic as a homeland and emphasized that governments and others with interests in the Arctic should recognize and acknowledge the specific rights of indigenous peoples. It stressed that, as the world looks increasingly to the Arctic and its resources, and as climate change makes access to circumpolar lands easier, the inclusion of Inuit as active partners is central to national and international deliberations on Arctic sovereignty, development, and protection.

Notable success stories include the ICC's central role in the negotiation of the global Stockholm Convention on the Elimination of Persistent Organic Pollutants, and its lobbying of states to ratify it in their national legislatures. The Convention entered into force in May 2003, and the ICC continues to work to ensure that the Convention's obligations are implemented. In the United Nations, the Permanent Forum on Indigenous Peoples is a body of sixteen representatives, half of them nominated by indigenous organizations and half by UN member states, that meets annually to examine indigenous issues. It makes recommendations to the UN Economic and Social Council. Arctic indigenous representatives—particularly Inuit—have played a significant role in the Permanent Forum, demonstrating how global indigenous movements can find ways of negotiating at international levels.

We should expect more examples of indigenous participation in circumpolar and global geopolitics. At the July 2018 meeting of the ICC in Utqiaġvik, Alaska, over sixty Inuit leaders gathered to speak about their political priorities. The theme of the meeting was "Inuit—The Arctic we want." One area of common agreement was support for a mandatory ban on the use of heavy fuel oils in Arctic waters, with entry into effect in the early 2020s. The International Maritime Organization is developing a formal proposal for just such as prohibition. In October 2018, Inuit and other indigenous leaders were represented at the Second Arctic Science Ministerial meeting in Berlin, and the communique signed by all the participants recognized indigenous groups as indispensable to Arctic science and international cooperation.

What does indigenous legal and political activism reveal about the state of Arctic homelands?

The determination to push for the Arctic that Inuit want is the product of long-term legal and political activism.

In 2005 Sheila Watt-Cloutier, then international chair of ICC, submitted a *Petition to the Inter-American Commission on Human Rights Seeking Relief from the Violations Resulting from Global Warming Caused by Acts and Omissions of the United States.* While she was their lead representative, the petition was on behalf of Inuit living in Alaska and Canada. It aimed to draw attention to the behavior of the United States in terms of fossil

fuel consumption and the impact caused by the largest industrial economy in the world to the world's biosphere, and in
particular the change wrought on Arctic sea ice, tundra, and
boreal forest, which in turn impacted Inuit, including their capacity to move and to hunt.

The petition not only pointed the finger at the United States
as mass polluter, but it also demonstrated that Inuit were
willing and able to campaign on global issues and not just
on regional and national matters such as devolution and autonomy. The choice of submission for the petition was a deliberate one. The Inter-American Commission on Human Rights
is described as an autonomous organ within the Organization
of the American States (OAS) with the mission "to promote
and protect human rights in the American hemisphere." In
session since the late 1970s, although established in 1959, the
Commission investigates the human rights conditions of the
members of the OAS and hears from parties via petition.

The Commission's work was, up to that point, mainly concerned with addressing human rights violations in Central
and South America. The United States and Canada are mar-
ginal to the work of the Commission, despite its headquarters
being in Washington, DC, but this does not mean that the two
countries do not have international legal obligations when it
comes to human rights and climate change. The petition was
designed to explore the intersection between the two, and in
April 2013 Earth Justice and Eco Justice Canada filed a petition to the Inter-American Commission on behalf of the Arctic
Athabaskan Council (AAC). As an indigenous people's organization and permanent participant to the Arctic Council,
the AAC enjoyed a mandate to press the case that a warming
Arctic was being exacerbated by continued emissions of
black carbon due to southern Canadian industrial activity.
The Canadian government was held to be at fault because of
a failure to regulate those emissions. The petition asked the
Inter-American Commission to address Canada's failure to
live up to its obligations under the terms and conditions set

out in the American Declaration of the Rights and Duties of Man (1948).

The 2005 and 2013 petitions were designed to not only grab world media attention but also make a clear causal link between human rights and climate change. For a people, Inuit, who depend on the Arctic being fundamentally colder and ice dependent, warming and melting trends undermine a long-standing way of life. The 2005 petition enabled Inuit to present oral testimony to the Commission in November 2006 and introduce into the public record stories and experiences of what climate change meant to those dependent on the ice and snow to make their lives bearable. While the Commission later rejected the petition on the grounds that it was not able to make a clear-cut causal connection between US specified emissions and pollutants and climate change in the Arctic, it did resurrect and empower the debate about how the Arctic was being affected by other parts of the world. In the 1980s, for example, Nordic countries protested to the United Kingdom that they believed so-called acid rain originating further south was being transported by air currents and posing a devastating effect on their forests and ecosystems. In Canada, traces of pollutants and poisons were found in the breast milk of nursing indigenous women living thousands of miles from those pollutant sources.

The 2005 petition represented a milestone in Inuit self-representation, and in 2008 the UN Human Rights Council passed Resolution 7/23, which acknowledged that "climate change poses an immediate and far-reaching threat to people and communities around the world, and has implications for the full enjoyment of human rights." The Resolution makes clear that climate change as a process continues to affect the international legal obligations states have to communities around the world; through geo-physical and bio-chemical transformation, there is a danger that those obligations are not being met. So, the Resolution cited the Universal

Declaration of Human Rights because it is legally relevant when discussing the deleterious consequences of climate change. Rather than citing war and/or genocide, environmental change was named as a present and future danger to human rights protections. If unchecked, then warming in the Arctic posed grave dangers to future livelihoods, the ability to secure safe drinking water, and the right to access secure housing and sanitation. For Arctic indigenous activists, including Sheila Watt-Cloutier, climate change is a human rights issue, and they strive to have their voices heard in international policymaking fora, arguing that Inuit cultural survival is dependent on the continued presence of ice and snow. However, as we will see later in this book, this argument is not universally accepted across the Inuit world, and other Inuit politicians and leaders stress that climate change is bringing opportunities for development and greater autonomy, as well as challenges.

As the Arctic Climate Impact Assessment (released in 2004–2005 under the auspices of the Arctic Council and involving up to 300 scientists) noted, however, those threats to northern communities were already manifest and likely to hit indigenous peoples hardest given the precariousness of some smaller communities who were dependent on their relationship to local and regional ecosystems for livelihoods. A warming Arctic might bring new opportunities for some actors, but it also profoundly alters ecosystems and communities that have existed for millennia and are largely dependent on traditional indigenous knowledge of patterns and currents of ice, snow, air, water, and wind. Melting of sea ice and thawing permafrost destabilizes communities and their infrastructures, as well as provoking change within ecosystems, as flora and fauna are disrupted and thawing permafrost contributes to methane release. So, the Arctic inadvertently ends up contributing to further greenhouse gas emissions through the breakdown of ground that was previously frozen even in the short summer months.

In recent years, a warming Arctic has been held responsible for changing marine and terrestrial environments so profoundly that local communities living in coastal sites, such as central and western Alaska, have been imperiled by worsening winter storms that batter coastlines, which are no longer protected by sea ice. So the viability of communities is called into question, and if sea ice is less predictable, then the role of traditional indigenous knowledge becomes less assured as community elders can no longer transmit reliable knowledge and understanding of local and regional environments to younger generations. When Inuit campaigned about the impact of a warming Arctic on their communities, they drew attention to a wider world community about the damage done to the most intimate part of their everyday lives and the economic, cultural, and spiritual significance of ice and snow to their cultures and well-being.

The 2013 petition picked up on the groundwork done by the 2005 petition by returning to the theme of damage done by a warming Arctic to indigenous peoples. Higher temperatures, thawing permafrost, sea ice thinning, increases in forest fires, and seasonal shifts in aridity were held to be disruptive and even devastating to the traditional use of the land and sea. In both cases, the Inter-American Commission was asked to investigate whether Canada and the United States were failing to live up to their human rights obligations regarding the inhabited Arctic. A year later the Commission dismissed the petition and again cited the absence of direct causation. But yet again the petition served to remind North Americans and the wider international community that indigenous communities are bearing the climate change–related brunt of global energy production and consumption. Paradoxically, the Arctic was in danger of becoming more like the kind of place that some nineteenth-century explorers and writers imagined it to be: altogether warmer and intimately connected to the fate of planet earth.

Are there human-animal conflicts in Arctic homelands?

Inuit are not just fighting against the warming of the Arctic. They are fighting for recognition of their ways of life and respect for traditional indigenous knowledge.

The ICC's ninth general assembly, which was held in Kuujjuaq in northern Québec in August 2002, resulted in a declaration that, among other things, called upon various levels of governments to recognize the inherent rights of Inuit to hunt sustainably and to continue subsistence-based activities. It also drew attention to understanding and addressing global forces that erode Inuit rights. This reference to global forces was significant and helps one understand some of the context for those climate change petitions a few years later. Inuit were responding to what they felt were the extraterritorial actors playing a destructive role to their ways of life.

As we have discussed, the long-standing dependence of indigenous societies on Arctic marine and terrestrial animals continues for several critically important reasons. One is their obvious economic and dietary importance. Animals are the principal supply of food for many northern indigenous communities. Fish and meat from marine mammals or caribou and birds are nutritionally superior to the foodstuffs presently imported to the Arctic (and which are often expensive to buy). Another reason is the cultural and social significance of hunting, herding, and fishing that goes beyond the economic. Through hunting, humans interact and engage with the natural world, and cultural identity is founded upon and derives deep meaning from this interaction and from the relationships it reinforces between persons, animals, and the environment. In the contemporary Arctic, though, animals are often at the heart of discussions about nature conservation and environmental policies designed to halt the loss of biodiversity and/or address the ongoing warming of the Arctic. For example, seal hunting is an integral part of Inuit culture. The seal is not only a food and heating source but also has valuable materials. The thick, water-resistant skin was repurposed for clothing and kayaks, and other parts of the seal were and are still used for tools and ornaments. This proved controversial because a global anti-sealing campaign did not understand these indigenous uses.

In the last forty years, global anti-sealing hunting campaign has been mired in controversies about whether it is a barbaric and inhumane activity, with public figures, such as Brigitte Bardot and Paul McCartney being particularly active in the 1970s onward, shaping public opinion on animal welfare grounds. This campaigning, which was focused initially on commercial sealing off the coasts of Newfoundland and Labrador, was aided and abetted by environmental and animal rights groups such as Greenpeace, the International Fund for Animal Welfare, the Humane Society, and Friends of the Earth, was soon extended further north and provoked bitter resentment from indigenous communities in Canada and Greenland in particular. International opposition led to the European Economic Community (EEC, and renamed the European Community in 1993) imposing a ban on the importation of seal products into the markets of its members in 1983.

What is often forgotten is how central the harvesting of seals was to the colonization of the Arctic by European powers and their corporate agents. From the 1770s to the first decade of the twentieth century, the Royal Greenland Trade Company was in effect the sovereign agent of Denmark and divided Greenland into different zones for the purposes of resource exploitation and trading networks. Seals were harvested for their skins and blubber for 200 years. The company enjoyed a monopoly on the seal industry in Greenland, and the wealth created by sealing was essential to the exercise of Danish control over the island.

In the last decade, Inuit in Greenland have re-appropriated seal hunting as a symbol of their self-determination and cultural autonomy as part of the Kingdom of Denmark. Coinciding with Greenlandic Self-Rule in 2009, Inuit Sila was established as a counter-movement to the anti-sealing campaigning and mobilized the slogan that "the Inuit seal hunt is 100% sustainable." By using the term "100% sustainable," Inuit campaigners challenged claims that the hunt was somehow inimical to the durability of human, economic, and ecological systems. They also highlighted the damage done to Inuit communities by the seal-products ban. In the European Union (EU, established in 1993), for example, the seal-products ban was initiated in 2009, which, in effect, meant bolstering the original EEC restrictions. While some exemptions were allowed for indigenous and Inuit communities, the ban led to a huge decrease in Greenlandic seal-skin sales. The World Trade Organization, paradoxically, recommended removing the exemptions because the seal-skin industry was too commercial. The European Parliament recommended in September 2015 that the European Commission (EC, which manages the business of the EU including treaties and the implementation of EU-level decisions) maintain the exemptions and educate and inform European citizens about the importance of seal hunting to Greenlandic and Inuit cultures.

The seal-products ban was not merely imposed by the EU, however. But it has been most keenly felt in Europe and perhaps particularly in regard to Greenland's relationship to the EEC (which it left in 1985) and later the EU. Anger over the seal-products ban has also influenced the EU's relationship with the Arctic Council; Canada in particular was adamant that the EU was not going to be approved as a permanent observer to the Council until the seal-products ban was addressed. The government of Greenland, in the midst of the seal-products ban controversy, reaffirmed its commitment to support the seal hunt industry and subsidized it to the tune of 26 million Danish krone in 2015 (about US $4 million). Although a loss-leading enterprise, the argument made was that it was an essential element to Inuit identity and culture.

While international opposition to whaling and seal hunting has had long-lasting impacts on indigenous communities, other parts of the Arctic are also sites where conflicts between humans and animals, particularly when those animals are considered predators that threaten human activities and livelihoods, have been apparent and remain deeply contested. Animals such as polar bears, whales, wolves, and reindeer are seen as characteristic of places defined as wild, and their healthy population status is seen as an indicator of healthy ecosystems. In many places, however, this has led to conflicts between people and animals, as well as between people and conservation management. Such conflicts are especially acute in areas of higher human population density, urban growth, tourism activity, and agriculture. Local, regional, and national discourses often play on classificatory systems that emphasize the opposition between human society and wildlife, and they reinforce culturally and historically constructed boundaries between humans and animals. Attitudes toward wolves in Alaska, Canada, northern Fennoscandia, and northern Russia exemplify this. In parts of northern Europe and North America, the role of the state in managing wolf populations has changed dramatically in recent years, from policies supporting hunting bounties, which saw the eradication of wolves as a management objective, to state-regulated conservation policies during the latter part of the nineteenth century and into the early twenty-first century.

Also, in the last few decades, international institutions and agencies have acquired a major role in how they influence a country's conservation policies. An example of this is the debate between Finland and the EU on grey wolf (*Canis lupus*) hunting applications in the early 2000s. Wolves were once abundant throughout Finland until around 1880 when their numbers began to decline because of persecution. Historically, attitudes toward wolves in Finland have generally been negative. The wolf is still seen essentially as a problem animal, especially by farmers and reindeer herders (both Sámi and Finnish herders alike), and they are believed to cause serious disruption to domesticated animals and people's livelihoods as they prey on cattle, sheep, and reindeer. Over the last few years, the grey wolf population has increased and spread to many parts of Finland, although it is largely concentrated in the eastern part of the country. Before Finland joined the EU in 1995, it defined the content of its policy toward wolves, wolf hunting, and conservation. The wolf was defined as a game species and the population was controlled by regulated hunting. Following EU membership, Finland had to tighten its legislation concerning the conservation status of the wolf, which was now defined as an endangered species. In 2005, the EU began legal proceedings in the European Court of Justice against Finland after the European Commission accused Finland of breaching EU legislation and allowing widespread poaching.

The case illustrates a debate on the place of the wolf in a modern nation, and how Finland struggled to combine hunting and animal husbandry traditions with EU conservation regulations and directives. It also challenged ideas about nature and the environment. The EU relented in 2008 when it stated that Finland had not threatened the sustainable level of its grey wolf population. Nonetheless, no wolf culls were authorized in Finland between 2007 and 2015, despite farmers and reindeer herders arguing that wolves were killing more of their animals and their dogs. In 2015, Finland resumed an authorized trial hunt, and in 2016 authorized a culling program. Environmentalists and conservationists stress the uniqueness of the grey wolf and worry that the cull will destroy its genetic diversity, while landowners, reindeer herders, and other rural residents express concern for the safety of their livestock and dogs, as well as pointing to the dangers wolves pose to people—despite there being no reports of wolf attacks on people in modern times.

Today, it is particularly evident in the circumpolar North that human-animal relations occupy increasingly contested spaces complicated by societal, cultural, and political decision-making processes due to, but not limited by, ideas and images about animals and habitats; environmentalism; the expanding industrial use of natural resources; ecological transformations brought on by climate change; changing rural and urban ways of life and the associated conceptual changes; and emerging needs for recreation, tourism, and conservation.

What do iconic species such as polar bears reveal about the state of Arctic homelands?

For most of us, the polar bear might make its appearance either as a cuddly toy or as a taxidermied version if you travel through airports such as Anchorage, Longyearbyen, and Oslo. But polar bears are not just curiosities. For Inuit, they are a renewable resource. They aren't called Lars.

Inuit continue to speak out against the animal rights activists still opposing seal hunting, and they remain active in the annual meetings of the International Whaling Commission (IWC), working to defend aboriginal subsistence whaling and ensuring Inuit rights are taken into account when the IWC decides on quotas. When environmental organizations such as WWF and Greenpeace and multinational corporations such as Coca-Cola enroll iconic animals in their campaigns to save the Arctic, this can heighten the potential for conflict. Controversies over the future survival of polar bears and what conservation and management measures need to be put in place illustrate that the Arctic is a region of international cooperation and conflict, where the cultural interests of Inuit and other indigenous peoples can clash with those of scientists, nation-states, and environmental organizations. Polar bears are migratory—their range crosses the national borders of several Arctic nations, making them subject to discussion about international management and conservation regimes. They are threatened by contaminants, pollution, and climate change and have become symbols of Arctic ecosystems at risk. Toxic chemicals, such as PCBs and pesticides, affect their hormonal development and immune systems, and they are frequent casualties of oil contamination. They are curious animals, which leads them to explore offshore drilling sites and oil canisters and rubbish dumps in Arctic villages. Some 500–900 polar bears are hunted each year, mainly by Inuit subsistence hunters, with a few caught by sport hunters mainly in Canada, who are guided by local Inuit. For conservation groups, they have become the supreme image of the plight of all the world's animal species endangered by human activities.

The predictions for the future of polar bear populations— and the health of the Arctic generally—are alarming to some scientists and conservationists, who argue that some polar bear subpopulations are unlikely to survive if there is an almost complete loss of summer sea ice cover, the ecosystems they occupy. Heart-rending stories in the media represent the polar bear, once a majestic predator at the top of its food chain, as a helpless, starving animal seeking seals on thinning ice. For environmentalists and conservation organizations, the threat of their extinction makes polar bear management and conservation a pressing issue of global concern. Polar bears have been transformed in the public imagination from symbols of cold, unbounded polar wildernesses, to symbols of an ecosystem in crisis and a planet in peril.

At the same time, polar bears are one of the most carefully monitored, studied, and managed marine mammal species in the circumpolar world. In the 1960s, the five nations with polar bear populations (Denmark/Greenland, the United States, Canada, Norway, and Russia) grew concerned that the animals were declining in number due to overharvesting, mainly from commercial hunts. In 1967, the International Union for the Conservation of Nature (IUCN) formed a specialist group to coordinate research, conservation, and management of polar bears at an international level. Norway and Russia eventually banned commercial hunting, and the United States, Canada, and Denmark (for Greenland) limited polar bear hunting for subsistence purposes by Inuit hunters, with Canada implementing an annual quota system. These five nations signed the Agreement on the Conservation of Polar Bears in 1973.

The Agreement was one of the first international regimes to include ecological principles, and it calls for the protection of the ecosystems upon which polar bears depend and, specifically, to protect special habitat components. It allows for the hunting, killing, and capturing of polar bears for scientific and conservation reasons; to protect other resources; for harvest by local people using traditional methods; or where people had a tradition of hunting polar bears. Many polar bear scientists claim that the Agreement has been effective because resource users, and those involved in research and management, were committed to finding a solution to improve polar bear conservation and respected the cultural differences of signatories. In addition to the Agreement, polar bears are also protected under the US Marine Mammal Protection Act of 1972.

The Agreement was worked out, negotiated, and implemented at a time when climate change was not a global concern. In 2008 the United States listed the polar bear as threatened throughout its range under the Endangered Species Act. To support the listing decision by the US Fish and Wildlife Service, the secretary of the interior asked the US Geological Survey (USGS) to carry out research that would generate new scientific data and models on polar bears and their sea ice habitats. The research concluded that projected changes in sea ice conditions would result in the loss of approximately two-thirds of the world's current polar bear population by the mid-twenty-first century. Inuit leaders argued that this listing, and any conservation measures implemented that would affect hunting quotas, especially without Inuit involvement and consultation, would restrict the hunting and use of polar bears and would impinge on the rights and interests of Inuit in Canada, Alaska, and Greenland directly and substantively. Their claim is that Inuit have conserved polar bear populations at healthy levels through proper and responsible wildlife management, research and monitoring, and sustainable harvesting practices.

In Canada, for example, the Agreement on the Conservation of Polar Bears, and polar bear management more generally, is implemented in a combined effort by community and regional hunting and trapping organizations, wildlife management boards, provincial and territorial governments, and the federal government. In Nunavut the co-management of polar bears (and co-management of all wildlife) is legislated through the Nunavut Wildlife Management Board (NWMB), a public institution under the Nunavut Land Claims Agreement. It cooperates closely with Inuit hunters' and trappers' organizations, and the incorporation of Inuit traditional knowledge into its research operations and management principles is particularly strong.

For Inuit, discussions of polar bears as endangered species and the right to protect wildlife from hunting bring back emotive memories of the 1970s and 1980s, when successful anti-trapping and anti-seal-hunting campaigns by animal rights groups seriously undermined the economies and livelihoods of many Arctic economies. These activities, by southern groups who did not understand northern cultures, were perceived by indigenous peoples, such as Inuit in Greenland and Canada, as inattentive to Inuit culture. Canada, as home to Inuit peoples, has in the past chosen not to designate polar bears as either threatened or endangered as a result of sea ice loss and concomitant projections of declining numbers.

Notwithstanding their support for cross-border cooperation, the United States and Canada do not agree on polar bear conservation. This revealed itself in 2014 via the Commission for Environmental Cooperation (CEC), which was established as part of the North America Free Trade Agreement (NAFTA) as a way of monitoring pressure placed by open markets on North American environmental legislation. The CEC's role is to implement the North American Agreement on Environmental Cooperation (NAAEC) and the United States wanted the polar bear re-classified as endangered. Canada disagreed with this proposal. In November 2014, the parties to the Convention on

Migratory Species (CMS; also known as the Bonn Convention, which includes Canada and the United States) urged all parties in the Arctic to work harder to coordinate their conservation plans. They placed the polar bear in appendix II (which covers species "that have an unfavourable conservation status" and require international agreements for their conversation and management) rather than the more controversial appendix I of the Convention (which lists species as endangered and at risk of extinction in part or in all of their range). As a consequence of this listing, Canada avoided having to implement tighter prohibitions and restrictions such as a ban on killing. This provides a strong indication of the reluctance on the part of Ottawa to marginalize northern indigenous knowledge and practices, including harvesting polar bears.

International concern over the survival of polar bears has been increasing in recent years, with particular focus on the impacts of climate change and hunting on polar bear populations. It also reminds us of the role of the non-human (or perhaps the more than human) shaping Arctic discourses and practices, including region building and the positioning of the Arctic as a local/regional space but also connected to the global. Polar bears, whales, and seals have had and continue to have an extraordinary power to bring to the fore how the Arctic is understood and engaged with.

The search to find the Northwest Passage preoccupied European and, later, North American explorers. Three crew members from John Franklin's 1845 expedition to the Canadian Arctic died and were buried on Beechey Island, a peninsula of Devon Island. A fourth gravestone marks the burial place of a member of one of the many expeditions that went in search of Franklin's ships. Photo: Mark Nuttall.

The Canadian Coast Guard vessel CCGS *Terry Fox*, sailing through Canada's Bellot Strait between Boothia Peninsula and Somerset Island. The Northwest Passage has become key to some discussions about sovereignty and security in the Arctic marine environment. Photo: Mark Nuttall.

The Greenland inland ice and glaciers, northwest Greenland. Climate change is having dramatic effects on the Arctic environment and is evident, for example, in rapid changes being observed in ice sheets, glaciers and sea ice. Photo: Mark Nuttall.

Hunting and fishing camp on the sea ice during March in Melville Bay, northwest Greenland. Indigenous peoples throughout the Arctic continue to depend on traditional resource use activities. Photo: Mark Nuttall.

Qikiqtarjuaq, Nunavut, Canada. Between the 1950s and 1970s, indigenous peoples in many parts of the Arctic experienced relocation and resettlement by the state as part of policies of modernization. Photo: Mark Nuttall.

Polar bears are iconic, charismatic animals. They have become central to international campaigns to save the Arctic, but they are also subject to stringent international management. Climate change and other environmental issues, such as pollution, threaten polar bears and throw up challenges to governance. Photo: Mark Nuttall.

Finnish reindeer herders working with their animals during autumn round-up. Reindeer herding is central to the cultures and economies of many indigenous communities in northern Eurasia, from the Sámi homelands of northern Fennoscandia to those of the Chukchi of eastern Siberia and Evenki of Sakhalin Island. In northern Finland, however, both Sámi and Finns are allowed to keep reindeer. Photo: Mark Nuttall.

The Santa Claus Village near Rovaniemi in Finnish Lapland is located at the Arctic Circle. A popular destination that promotes northern winter themes and images, in recent years many visitors have arrived during the Christmas season to find little or no snow. Photo: Mark Nuttall.

DEW Line radar station, Tuktoyaktuk, Northwest Territories, Canada. The Distant Early Warning (DEW) Line was a system of radar stations constructed along the northern coasts of Alaska and Canada in the 1950s. Additional stations were built in the Aleutian Islands, Greenland, Iceland, and the Faroe Islands. It was designed to detect Soviet bombers and missiles approaching North America via the Arctic. By the 1980s, advances in military technology soon rendered the system obsolete and many stations were decommissioned and abandoned. Some stations were upgraded as part of the new joint US-Canada North Warning System in 1985. Photo: Mark Nuttall.

The annual Iditarod Sled Dog Race starts in downtown Anchorage in early March, and teams compete to be the first to reach Nome on the Bering Sea coast. In recent years, a lack of snow has marred the start of the race, and it has had to be moved to alternative starting venues. Photo: Mark Nuttall.

Two representatives from the Saami Council attending the 2017 Arctic Council Senior Arctic Officials Meeting in Fairbanks, Alaska. Photo: Arctic Council Secretariat/Linnea Nordström.

British journalist Stephen Sackur hosting a high-level discussion at the annual Arctic Frontiers conference in Tromsø, Norway. Photo: Klaus Dodds.

4

FROM COLONIZATION
TO COOPERATION

The Arctic has undergone profound human and natural change over millennia. When we record that the Arctic is home to some 4 million people, it is a mere fraction of a world population currently approaching 8 billion people. Apart from the Antarctic, the Arctic remains a lowly populated region that is characterized by vast open areas of forests, tundra, mountains, lakes, and seas. Population in many areas of the North American Arctic and Russia Arctic is sparse and intermittent.

In this chapter, we consider the human colonization of the Arctic and take the reader on a journey of some 15,000 years, starting from the earliest migrations to the North American Arctic and ending with the post–Cold War impulse for regional cooperation, environmental protection, and sustainable development. It is a complicated story, and as ever there are important regional and national differences involving settlement patterns, resource exploitation, and the lasting legacies of settler colonialism and the Cold War.

This will help us navigate toward the present and contextualize how Arctic homelands have been settled and then shaped by regional and global forces.

Who came across the Bering Land Bridge?

The first humans crossed from Siberia to Alaska across a land bridge that once connected Asia to America, some 15,000 years ago. First proposed in the sixteenth century, the existence of what was termed the Bering Land Bridge was widely accepted by scientists in the 1930s after archeological and genetic-based research confirmed that human migration from Asia to North America did occur. What paleo-ecologists and archeologists believe happened next is that as the ice age ended, ice melted and sea levels rose accordingly. Low-lying regions such as the Bering Land Bridge were inundated and became what we would now know to be the water-filled Bering Strait.

The North American portion of the Arctic was one of the last regions of the world settled by human populations. Archeological evidence has given us insights into how these early human communities survived in a world shaped by the intersection of glaciation and climate change. The means by which people moved in and across the Arctic is better understood by focusing on their stone and wooden tools, their dependence on flora and fauna, and their capacity to secure shelter. DNA evidence from bone, hair, and even teeth is yielding fundamental evidence of how ancient peoples migrated, settled, and endured.

The peopling of Arctic North America was not a large-scale migration from Asia, but a gradual process of movement across the land taking place over several thousand years. It began with the exploration of new hunting grounds, rather than a search for new land to settle. During the Pleistocene (a period of geological time encompassing approximately 2.6 million to 11,700 years ago), a series of ice ages affected the high latitude regions of the world we now know as the Arctic. However, great sheets of glacial ice did not bury the lowlands of Beringia, and the region became a unique refuge for plants and animals that were superbly adapted to these cold lands. Gradually, the animals people depended on for food migrated eastward from northeastern Asia as a result of major climatic changes during the last ice age and the immediate postglacial period. Paleo-Arctic peoples did the same and began to range far and wide in search of game along the coasts, river valleys, and interior lands of what is now Alaska, eventually moving into what is now Canada and eastward across the tundra and northern shores of the North American Arctic to Greenland. So, while we can point to large-scale environmental change as significant, it is not possible to say that there was only one mass movement of people. Instead we have a picture emerging of multiple waves, with a Paleo-Inuit population hailing from eastern Siberia occupying parts of the North American Arctic before being replaced by the Thule peoples who were whale hunters in modern-day northern Canada and Greenland. The Paleo-Inuit and Thule peoples appear to have been largely separate from one another, but they share the same origins in eastern Siberia. From what we know, through genetic records, it appears that there was no genetic contact between Paleo-Inuit and the historic ancestors of contemporary Inuit, the Thule people, who arrived and settled in Greenland around 1300–1400 CE.

Overall, there were three migratory waves into the North American Arctic. The first dates from 15,000 years following the flooding of the Bering Land Bridge. The second and third waves of migration, which helped produce the Eskimo-Aleut peoples and the Na-Dene-speaking Chipewyan peoples, respectively, followed several centuries later. This contradicts earlier research, which adumbrated the view that there was one single migratory event at the onset of the interglacial period. Earlier research also posted that the First Americans were so-called Clovis People, who were big-game hunters because of lithic evidence pointing to their use of spear points. The Clovis were thought to be the direct ancestors of all Native Americans.

Over millennia, these three migratory flows contributed to the colonization and settlement of the wider Americas by coastal and inland migratory routes. As evidence has accumulated, it appears more than ever to be the case that the last glacial maximum is the signature event for explaining how humans were prompted to cross over from Asia to the Americas. Prior to the increased European encounter from the fifteenth century onward, and the transportation of African peoples to the Americas, these ancient peoples intermingled with one another, and as a consequence scientists have found traces of what has been described as First American DNA in other indigenous groups living in Central and South America.

By the time European explorers and traders made their way along the rivers, shorelines, and bays of North America, northern and eastern Canada was home to established Algonquian and Iroquoian communities. Further north and west, the Na-Dene peoples were living in modern-day Alberta and Yukon, and Athabaskan-speaking communities inhabited what is now southern Alaska and northern British Columbia. Inuit in the High North had largely replaced the Dorset peoples by around the time of the arrival of the Norse in Greenland during the second half of the ninth century and certainly by the time of later explorers such as John Cabot at the end of the fifteenth century.

Who were the first Europeans to colonize and settle the Arctic?

Some of the earliest were Norse. Hailing originally from Norway, settling in parts of northern Scotland, Orkney, and Shetland, and then traveling to Iceland, during the second half of the ninth century, the Norse peoples were recorded in sagas as having reached the fringes of Greenland where small settlements endured for around 500 years. Norse explorers, such as Erik the Red, were instrumental in surveying the potential for settlement in the fjords of the southwest coast of Greenland. His naming choice of "Greenland" was a deliberate one; intended to encourage others to leave Iceland and settle and populate the area. For the following three centuries, the colonization process was spearheaded by two settlements—the Eastern and Western outposts. Archeologists believe that around 2,000–3,000 people settled in southern Greenland and that perhaps as many as 400 farms were established.

Apart from farming, the Norse communities established trading networks, and walrus ivory, furs, wool, whale, and seal products were traded within and beyond the Norse world. At its zenith the Norse universe extended as far as northern Africa and the Middle East. During the settlement of Greenland, however, the Norse also explored further westward and came into contact with indigenous peoples in the North American Arctic, including the Thule, whom they called *skraelings* (a Norse name for a native of Greenland or Vinland). The Thule and the Norse traded with one another, and archeologists have found evidence of objects, such as ivory figurines in ancient Inuit settlements on the east coast of Ellesmere Island in the Canadian High Arctic.

Why did the Norse settlement not endure?

Despite the trading networks and exploratory activities in the North American Arctic, by the fourteenth century, the decline of the Norse was apparent. The Western settlement was abandoned in 1350, and it is believed that that Eastern settlement followed a similar fate by the close of the fifteenth century, although it is possible that the denouement of the community was as early as the 1450s. The most plausible explanation advanced for the decline of the Norse in Greenland revolves around the onset of the Little Ice Age, a period between the thirteenth century and the end of the eighteenth century, when European weather noticeably cooled. In the case of Greenland and the North Atlantic, pack ice thickened and travel between Greenland and Scandinavia became more challenging. This would have made trade also more problematic, and scholars suggest that the previously profitable walrus ivory trade was adversely affected by ivory from elsewhere including Africa.

While both the Norwegian and Danish Crowns considered Greenland an important element in their territorial and resource portfolio, the Little Ice Age contributed to both population decline and marginalization in the face of inclement weather and extraordinary ice conditions, affecting islands such as Iceland and Greenland. Sea ice extending for miles off the coastline of these northern territories made access all but impossible for years. The Norse settlements declined, in part, because of climate change, and the areas of Greenland where they had thrived were profoundly depopulated.

What was the next wave of European settlement in Greenland?

In 1721 a Danish-Norwegian expedition led by the Lutheran missionary Hans Egede was sent to Greenland. The expedition marked the reassertion of Danish interest in Greenland and the onset of renewed trading, resource exploitation, and settlement planning. It also marked the re-population of Greenland by Nordic peoples. For the Danish progenitors, the colonization of Greenland was underwritten by a religious and trading mission and was seen as culturally and administratively distinct from other European powers because of the island's connections to the Danish-Norwegian Crown dating from the Norse era in the thirteenth century onward. At that stage, the Norse Greenland settlements were paying taxes to the Norwegian Crown as were communities living in Iceland. When Egede arrived in Greenland, Denmark and Norway were still one kingdom, and in Greenland the trade and mission stations were considered to be part of an inheritance, while other areas of the Danish Empire in places like the West Indies were colonies in the sense that they were occupied with the explicit purpose of economic exploitation and strategic advantage in the form of protecting trading networks.

Another view is that the Danish authorities, whatever their choice in nomenclature, were engaged in a colonial enterprise that was not so different from other imperial powers who believed that they had inherited territory and resources. What perhaps made the Danish colonization of Greenland rather different was that active indigenous resistance and large-scale conflict, even massacre, did not characterize it. The Danes were not looking to eradicate the hunting economies of indigenous peoples; rather, they sought to profit from them.

The Danish trading stations were designed to cement Copenhagen's authority and act as a deterrent to competition from others. Dutch whalers and traders were active and had been operating in Greenlandic and North Atlantic waters for at least a hundred years before the Egede mission. In Svalbard, for example, the Dutch had established a settlement on Smeerenburg and the Northern Company was active in whaling from 1611 onward. British whalers were also active in those northern waters. The Danes were eager to regain competitive advantage and stop other European traders from interfering with whaling and sealing in Greenland. The Royal Greenland Trade Company from 1774 onward enjoyed a monopoly of trade in the island that did not end until the early 1950s. Whaling, sealing, and mining for cryolite (used in aluminum production as well as to make caustic soda) from the 1850s contributed further to the extractive sector of Greenland and profitability for the Danish authorities.

In the 1970s, Denmark's relationship with Greenland was challenged after 250 years of paternalistic management and the development of a political-trading relationship that ensured that Greenlanders were treated as people who were not deserving of consultation when it came to resource extraction and political representation beyond limited local and regional councils. While Inuit Greenlanders regarded land, including subsurface resources such as minerals, as a communal resource, the Danish state regarded Greenland as part of the Kingdom of Denmark and in 1953 a new constitution established exactly that. Twenty years later, however, pressure for Home Rule and demands for more autonomy changed that relationship forever.

How was the North American Arctic colonized and settled?

The modern colonial history of the North American Arctic in part resides in the action of the Russian state and its investment in exploration and trade from the imperial capital of St. Petersburg. As we note below, the Russian Empire at one stage encapsulated modern-day Alaska and Russian-American Company trading posts and sea otter hunting extended as far south as California.

But there is a distinctly British element to this story, which envelops much of North America in the form of charter, proprietary, and royal colonies. In the north of modern-day Canada, the Hudson's Bay Company (HBC) was the agent of British imperial power, trading furs with indigenous peoples and facing off competition from others including the French and Métis. Established in London in 1670, the HBC earned a reputation as one of the largest landowners in the world, including vast areas of Hudson Bay, which were stitched together by sea and land routes and trading posts. Supported by royal patronage, the HBC bought furs and then transported them to London and European markets. In return for selling furs, the HBC employees traded blankets, cutlery, and knives with the trappers. The Hudson's Bay point blanket was the most notable and profitable trading item. The 'point' refers to the short black lines woven into the blanket for the purpose of determining overall size.

Trading was not always straightforward, however. Conflict with French interests became increasingly violent in the 1670s in and around Hudson Bay and ultimately led to the 1713 Treaty of Utrecht, which endowed greater territorial and resource advantage to the British and the HBC. Anglo-French conflict in Europe determined the fate of both parties in Canada, and although France was the superior power in Canada, it ended up losing to British interests at the end of the Seven Years' War in 1763.

France, up to that point, was an active agent in the North American Arctic and coastal territories on Canada's east such as Newfoundland. As with British explorers and sponsors,

French parties armed with royal patronage from Francis I in the 1520s onward were also looking for a passageway to the Pacific Ocean. French fishing and early settlement began along the St. Lawrence River on what was to become Québec. The fur trade encouraged further contact with indigenous peoples and mapping of territories toward the northeast of the modern United States in the seventeenth century. French exploration extended further south toward Annapolis in Maryland, and during this period the removal of English and Scottish settlers from Nova Scotia occurred.

As with their rival British competitors, the French contact with First Nations peoples varied in scope and tone. When the French colonized the area that became Québec in the seventeenth century, conflict erupted between them and the Iroquois, which was eventually resolved by a peace treaty in 1701 signed in the city of Montreal. A year later, Britain and France were at war again. This time it proved decisive for the history of North America. After fighting, the so-called Conquest of Arcadia in 1710 led to the diminution of the French presence in Canada. Nova Scotia became a British possession, and after another fifty years of sporadic conflicts French/Arcadian control of Québec City and Montreal was ceded in 1760. All remaining territories in North America were ceded to Britain in the north and Spain in the south under the Treaty of Fontainebleau (1762). The Treaty of Paris (1763), a peace treaty ending the Seven Years' War between Britain and France and their respective allies, signified the conclusion of the French colonial project in North America.

This largely shaped the emergence of modern-day Anglophone Canada, as the HBC and short-lived rival companies, such as the North West Company, were able to expand their trading interests northward and westward. By the 1820s, the two companies were merged by the British government, and, after a period of rationalization and reorganization, the area of commercial interest stretched to the Arctic Ocean encompassing 3 million square miles and about 1,500 employees spread out over trading posts, controlled by what were termed chief traders. While agricultural settlement proved commercially unattractive, some of the prime real estate under the control of the HBC known as Rupert's Land (and sometimes as Prince Rupert's Land) was eventually sold back to Britain and later under the Deed of Surrender given to the Dominion of Canada (formally established in July 1867) in the form of the North West Territories in 1869. It remains the largest land transfer in Canadian history, but one that had come in the aftermath of a century of conflict involving French, American, and indigenous and First Nations peoples, including the 1812 War involving British and American forces fighting one another over the borderlands between modern-day Canada and the United States.

The territorial implications for the North American Arctic were still being felt in the 1890s when Canada and the United States argued over the southern boundaries of Alaska. The Yukon gold rush made the issue far from trivial, as both parties were eager to ensure access to coastal ports so that the gold could be transported further south to relevant markets. The boundary was settled in 1903 after arbitration and the port of Skagway was awarded to the United States. Although disappointed over the outcome, Canada's authority over its northern possessions was strengthened by the establishment of the North-West Mounted Police (NWMP) intended to manage relations with First Nations and indigenous peoples, American miners, and illegal trade in liquor. In 1903 the first NWMP post in the Arctic was established at Cape Fullerton, close to an area used by American and British whaling fleets. The NWMP were responsible for administering whaling licensing and collecting custom taxes.

How and why did Russia expand northward?

Russia is the largest Arctic state. It is difficult to underestimate quite how important the Arctic and a cold climate are to Russian cultural history, literary culture, and national identity. The

French philosopher, Montesquieu, in *Esprit de lois* (1748) was one of the first to describe Russia as simply a "cold country." Ice, snow, and frost have made themselves felt in a myriad of ways through poetry, novels, paintings, and folklore.

Russia's Arctic territories are vast even if you simply start at the Arctic Circle and track northward. From 60° north, its northern territories encompass nine time zones stretching from Fennoscandia to the Bering Strait and the northern fringes of the Pacific Ocean. To the north, Russian islands are to be found in the Kara, Lapev, and East Siberian Seas, which connect to the Arctic Ocean. The history of Russia's colonization of the north is rooted in its expansion as an imperial power from the sixteenth century onward.

The establishment of the Arctic port of Arkhangelsk in 1584 was catalytic, and Russian Arctic ambition involved dealing with British and Dutch rivals eager to establish their own footholds on the northern edges of the Atlantic Ocean. By 1703, with its new capital in St. Petersburg, Peter the Great was already presiding over a country that had an administrative-military presence on the shores of the Pacific Ocean. While not systematic, the end result was driven by trade in furs, strategic opportunism, weakened local and regional political and military opponents, and the absence of other imperial actors such as the Turks/Ottomans and Persians. By the mid-nineteenth century, Russian traders and settlers in Siberia were thought to number nearly 3 million and on the island of Sakhalin a penal colony was established.

Russian explorers and scientists were also active in the exploration and study of the northern latitudes. Scientific curiosity in the north has a lengthy pedigree stretching from the Great Northern Expedition (GNE), or Second Kamchatka Expedition as it is also known, to participation in the first multinational International Polar Year of 1881–1884. The GNE was a spectacular enterprise, precipitating the large-scale mapping and exploration of the northern fringes of Siberia and the North American coastline including Alaska. Its genesis rested with Peter the Great, and was then funded and promoted by later Russian leaders, Anna and Elizabeth. Peter's vision was of a Russia dominant in the north and in control of what was termed the Northern Sea Route (NSR), linking the Atlantic to the Pacific Ocean. Vitus Bering was the leader of the main expedition, stretching from 1733 until 1743. Involving thousands of people, the GNE consumed about a fifth of the total income of the then Russian state. While the expedition discovered and mapped Alaska and the Aleutian Islands in the northwest of the North American continent, the northeastern sector of Asia proved harder to map and explore, however, due to inclement weather and sea ice.

Russian expansion in the north and west was also facilitated by comparative Chinese weakness. Russia benefited from treaties such as Aigun (1858) that witnessed territorial gains (over 600,000 square kilometers) around the Amur River region at the expense of the ruling Manchu dynasty. Later the Treaty of Beijing (1860) facilitated further Russian expansion south from the Amur River and led to further colonization, including establishing a presence at the port of Vladivostok in the same year. In 1867, remarkably as it turns out in the Arctic context, Russia sold its territories in Alaska and adjacent islands to the United States. In so doing, it ensured that the United States in territorial terms became an Arctic nation. Territorial and trading consolidation also ensured that the Russian presence in California, through its trading post at Fort Ross, ended in 1841. One can only speculate how world history, including the Cold War, might have been different had Russia not sold Alaska to the United States. In 1875, Russia also left the Kurile Islands and acknowledged Japanese sovereignty in return for control over the whole of Sakhalin Island.

In Soviet Russia, the Arctic became a place for industrial development, mining extraction, labor camps, and militarization, with large areas of the Arctic and the Soviet Far East closed off to visitors, including Russian citizens. Using prison labor, single-resource cities were established with the sole purpose of providing the mineral resources needed for the industrialization of the Soviet Union.

The exploitation and development of the Soviet Arctic began in earnest in the 1920s and accelerated in the 1930s. The Soviet Union was determined to "conquer the North" and was prepared to be ruthless in the pursuit of that goal, including using slave labor to construct infrastructure to "open up" the vast region of Siberia. It is worth bearing in mind that Russia/the Soviet Union had acquired a formidable body of experience and knowledge regarding northern environments. During the 1881–1884 International Polar Year, Russian scientist Heinrich Wild was the chair of the International Polar Commission and institutions such as the Russian Geographical Society and St. Petersburg Academy of Sciences acted as repositories of polar scholarship, including mapping and charting lands and seas. Russian research on weather and sea ice was also well established and clearly directed toward a strategic aim of better understanding how to manage and move in those northern domains.

Determined to secure access to the NSR and exploit the resources of the North, the "race for the Arctic" became integral to Russian popular culture. Individuals such as Otto Schmidt, born in Belarus with German ancestry, became a household name as the cult of the Arctic hero literally sailed and took off. He was originally an academic, but by 1930 Schmidt's fame grew as head of the Soviet Arctic Institute and later in 1932 as head of an administrative body responsible for managing the NSR. He also led expeditions on the steam-powered icebreaker *Georgy Sedov*, which established a scientific station on Franz Josef Island and traveled through the Kara Sea while discovering new islands close to Severnaya Zemlya. In 1932, Schmidt, on another icebreaker, made a nonstop voyage along the NSR and did not over-winter anywhere on route. It was a stunning achievement. Over the next seven years, he pioneered further exploration and cruising along the NSR.

The "Red Arctic" was a winter wonderland, showcasing a pioneering revolutionary state, the Soviet Union.

While Schmidt was rewriting the record books for nautical voyaging in the Arctic, he was also encouraging air voyaging. Earlier pioneers were Russian pilots, such as Yan Nagursky, who were flying in the Arctic just before the onset of the First World War. Twenty years later, a Stalinist Soviet Union was eager to recover that legacy of achievement. In 1937, he helped to establish a drift ice station called "North Pole 1" and facilitated an airborne expedition to support that venture in the far north. Soviet Arctic pilots such as Ivan Cherevichnyy, Vitaly Maslennikov, Ilya Kotov, and Nikolai Kamanin were in terms of fame and familiarity similar to the American aviator and explorer Charles Lindbergh. They appeared in books, films, and on postage stamps. The pilot embodied the ideal of the Soviet Union: brave, selfless, and visionary. Polar flying, while dangerous, was integral to northern ambitions, offering the seductive possibility of further discovery, exploitation, and colonization of the Soviet Arctic. These ambitions demanded a collective sacrifice on an extraordinary scale, and it was carried out with ruthless zeal.

The indigenous peoples of the Soviet North were marginalized and dispossessed—and treated as politically suspect because of their belief systems involving spirits and shamans. Could they be trusted to embrace Marxist-Leninism? Dependent on migratory routes for reindeer hunting and reliant on subsistence lifestyles involving hunting and fishing, they were no match for Soviet administrative and military structures designed to bring the Russian North to heel. So, while Soviet pilots and Arctic administrators acquired Hero of the Soviet Union and Order of Lenin medals, political dissidents and slave laborers were put to work in northern gulags.

The Soviet conquest of the Arctic, championed by Joseph Stalin, was not straightforward. Soviet administrative inefficiency, inclement weather, terror-related purges, and funding difficulties all contributed to an imperfect project. In their drive to industrialize and collectivize human activity, the Arctic environment bore a heavy toll. Stalin announced in 1932, "The Arctic and our northern regions contain colossal wealth. We must create a Soviet organization which can, in the shortest period possible, include this wealth in the general resources of our socialist economic structure." He ordered the establishment of the Glavsevmorput (the so-called Commissariat of Ice) and called for more strategic focus on coordinating farming, mining, transportation, timber production, and infrastructure provision. Under Schmidt's leadership, the Commissariat was intended to bring order to administrative and geographical dispersion and, while there was extraordinary success in some areas, notably the NSR, the balance sheet was uneven as institutional and personal rivalries in the Soviet Far East blocked the sort of progress that Stalin hoped for in 1932. Economic ambition often exceeded scientific understanding of working in a region characterized by temperature extremes, ice and snow, light and darkness, isolation and disconnection, and infrastructure lacking insight from cold weather engineering. Soviet ideology was willing, but the know-how lagged behind the ambition, and in private, it was not unknown for Soviet citizens to mock Stalin and his vision of the USSR as a giant "ice breaker." But the ice was "Red Ice."

What impact did World War II have on the Arctic?

By the time war erupted in Europe in 1939, the Arctic was not remote for those Arctic states that exercised sovereignty over those territories. While infrastructural provision remained less dense and population numbers lower compared to southern constituencies, anxieties about the role that hostile powers such as Germany and Japan might play in the Arctic accelerated colonialism in the North. In northern Finland, Finnish troops faced an opportunistic attack by the Soviet Union in November 1939. Stalin was determined to establish a larger buffer zone between it and Germany and improve the Soviet defense of Leningrad.

The Winter War (November 1939–March 1940) demonstrated that a determined smaller force (Finland) could frustrate a large military force (the Soviet Union) by stealth, determination, and adapting well to the frigid fighting conditions. Much of the fighting occurred in near total darkness in Finnish Lapland and freezing conditions throughout the war-affected areas. Although Finland was forced to cede over 10% of its national territory—parts of Karelia, Salla, and Petsamo, and four Gulf of Finland islands—it was not subsumed by the Soviet Union and maintained an uneasy coexistence with its larger neighbor. The Winter War became a crucial element in postwar Finnish identity politics and contributed greatly to its international reputation. In 1952, a still independent Finland was able to host the summer Olympics after the ones planned for 1940 in Helsinki were cancelled due to wartime conflict.

With the onset of war with Japan in 1941, the United States committed itself to further infrastructural investment and the movement of armed forces personnel. After the attack on Pearl Harbor in December 1941, Japanese forces attacked and occupied two islands in the Aleutian chain, Attu and Kiska. US and Canadian military forces were involved in repulsing the Japanese by 1943, and, after the expulsion of Japanese forces from Alaska, the US initiated a program of road building (the Alaska Highway), pipeline development, airfield construction, and harbor improvement. The Aleutian Islands were also transit spaces for the movement of planes sent by the Americans to the Soviets under the terms of the Lend-Lease Agreement. While indigenous peoples were employed in support roles, Alaska was militarized, and in the face of a global conflict, there was limited concern for indigenous land rights and environmental management.

In the North Atlantic, Arctic convoys were an integral part of the Allied war strategy linking the Soviet port of Murmansk. Vital supplies were transported between the UK and its wartime ally the Soviet Union in the face of terrible threats posed by a German fleet of submarines and surface vessels. Merchant vessels were sunk, along with British Royal Naval vessels, with the coastline of Norway and the Orkney and Shetland Islands becoming vital elements in this nautical struggle for supremacy. Svalbard was also drawn into this struggle as Allied forces were stationed there in 1941 in order to deny Germany access to coal supplies and harbor facilities.

Greenland's strategic importance during World War II lay not just in the possibilities it provided for access to its resources (including the Ivittuut cryolite mine in south Greenland, which was essential for the manufacture of aluminum), but as a North Atlantic stepping-stone route for American bombers. Allied military planners also needed weather information to facilitate transatlantic flying. Several American installations were built including three airbases at Narsarsuaq (known as Bluie West One) in south Greenland, Søndre Strømfjord (which was originally known as Bluie West-8 and is now the main transatlantic airport of Kangerlussuaq) on the west coast, and Ikateq (known as Bluie East Two) near Ammassalik on the east coast. These military installations contributed to the postwar consolidation of the United States' military presence, in both the south and the far north of the island.

Research on Arctic sea ice and weather assumed considerable importance, and polar scientists were asked to share their expertise in aid of Allied shipping and flying operations. A string of weather stations was established around Canada, Greenland, Iceland, Ireland, and Norway; they provided meteorological information vital for polar war planning. In 1941, British forces destroyed a weather station on the remote Bear Island in the Barents Sea in order to deny it to German naval forces. Despite an Allied presence on Svalbard, German forces were able to maintain several weather stations there until September 1945.

War accelerated the occupation and development of the Arctic. Every Arctic state, some in collaboration with others, such as the United States in the case of the Danish colony of Greenland, invested more in these northern territories. Infrastructure development accompanied a general trend in favor of a form of militarization, which spawned more restricted areas, closed spaces, and zones of exceptional sovereignty where the rights of indigenous peoples were circumscribed. It also ushered in more investment in a whole manner of things ranging from the development of cold weather training and engineering to areas of science and technology addressing cold weather challenges and problems.

How did the Arctic become a frontline in the Cold War?

The "ice curtain" descended on and around the Arctic in the late 1940s. As relations between the Soviet Union and the United States worsened following the end of World War II, the northern edges of both countries were caught up in the ensuing narratives and reports about possible American-Russian confrontation. Separated by a few nautical miles from one another, in the case of the Diomede Islands (known in Russia as the Gvozdev Islands) in the Bering Strait, the United States and the USSR began restricting the movement of indigenous peoples and prevented local peoples from crisscrossing between the islands. The indigenous Iñupiat of Big Diomede, within Russian territory, were relocated to the mainland and replaced with a military base, while Little Diomede in Alaska, just two and a half miles from Big Diomede, remains home to a small Iñupiat community of just over one hundred.

Geographical proximity was the major factor in shaping how the Cold War took hold of the northern circumpolar regions. For military planners, it was strikingly obvious that the Arctic would be the frontline in any potential conflict, and if this had not been recognized before it probably reflected the inadequacies of existing maps and their projections, which had the effect of underplaying the fact that the Arctic Ocean and Bering Strait (just like the Finnish-Russian and Norwegian-Russian borders) were areas that demanded close surveillance and military enhancement. In the case of Alaska, a wartime legacy of investment had bequeathed the Americans with a territory (not a state until 1959) filled with highways and airfields that not only needed protecting but also provided scope for force projection.

Working with Canadian counterparts, under the newly created North Atlantic Treaty Organization (NATO) in 1949, the most dramatic intervention across the North American Arctic was the construction of the Distant Early Warning (DEW) Line. The DEW Line owed its origin to a conviction that the most likely form of attack on the United States by the Soviet Union was via long-range bombers flying over the Arctic Ocean or crossing the Bering Strait. Construction started in 1955 and nearly three years later a total of sixty-three manned radar stations were built stretching from Alaska in the west to Greenland in the east along the 69th parallel. The majority of the stations were based in Canada and this led in turn to concerns that Canadian sovereignty was being compromised in favor of the dictates of US military planners. Within ten years, however, many of the sites were being decommissioned as US military planners recognized that the Soviets were more likely, from the 1960s onward, to pose a threat through their submarine fleet and intercontinental ballistic missile capability. Looking to the skies for signs of Soviet bombers appeared rather anachronistic.

The imagination of the Arctic as the new frontline also found expression in popular culture. Early Cold War films such as *The Thing* (1951) warned audiences that alien craft might be found buried in the Arctic ice and that their discovery could pose dangers to US armed forces personnel and scientists based in the Alaskan Arctic. Films such as *Ice Station Zebra*, based on a novel by Alistair Maclean, and books such as *Night Without End* (also written by Maclean) entertained audiences while warning that American and Soviet submarines, planes, and tanks were circulating the Arctic region. Early warning surveillance appeared to make sense, at least in the era of the long-range bomber, and enhanced understanding of cold environments was again shown to be at a premium. Ice and snow could play havoc on military preparedness, and sea ice could and did confuse those trying to track the movements of enemy submarines.

In the United States, the US Army Corps of Engineers established the Snow, Ice and Permafrost Research Establishment (SIPRE) in 1949, which was based in the state of Illinois from 1951 onward. Teams of engineers and scientists were funded to learn more about the properties of sea and land ice, and to appreciate better how permafrost could disrupt infrastructure. All of this was highly relevant as the US launched Operation Blue Jay in 1951 in order to construct a new airbase at Thule in northwest Greenland, as part of a new round of investment in Arctic defense. The work at SIPRE was supported by the Arctic Construction and Frost Effects Laboratory and then reorganized in 1961 into a Cold Regions Research and Engineering Laboratory (CRREL) based in Hanover, New Hampshire.

Ice and snow were no longer the stuff of romantic musings and expeditionary endurance; they were elemental to Cold War/cold weather planning.

What was Project Iceworm?

When it comes to Arctic geopolitics, some outlandish projects have been devised for Arctic environments. Their very existence tells us something about what Cold War military planners thought the Arctic was good for. As thinly populated spaces, located far away from the main centers of population, they were ideal for plotting and planning and testing equipment and military skills. After all, who would notice and who would care?

Scientists and engineers working at SIPRE and later CRREL were involved in one of the most audacious Cold War Arctic projects, called Project Iceworm, which operated on the premise that it might be possible to hide a mobile network of nuclear missiles under the Greenland ice sheet.

Initiated in 1960, the Danish government was never informed about the real purpose of Project Iceworm. Instead a cover story was launched called Camp Century, and US and Danish publics were told that American engineers were simply experimenting with cold weather engineering techniques. Camp Century was built on and under the inland ice at over 6,000 feet above sea level and was occupied under the auspices of the Army Polar Research and Development Center. It was actually a feasibility study into whether it might be possible to put into practice an extraordinary plan involving 2,500 miles of trenches and tunnels and 600 nuclear missiles designed to carry out a covert strike on the Soviet Union. A nuclear power plant was going to help support the construction activity.

Arctic science also played its part in the cover story. Polar scientists had long been interested in better understanding the Greenland ice sheet. In the postwar period, European and American scientists were working collaboratively, and ice-core research was beginning to gain traction as a hugely insightful technique for learning more about planetary history and the composition of ice history. During the project, tunnels were established, and about two miles were secured so that a small community of 200 could live under the ice. Ice-core research, however, revealed that the ice in question might not be stable and that there was a real danger that the tunnels and everything inside them, including a mobile nuclear reactor, accommodations, and a hospital, were vulnerable to being crushed. By 1966, Camp Century was closed, and Project Iceworm was abandoned by its sponsors, the US Army. Its submerged presence is a reminder of what the Arctic was during the Cold War—a space for military experimentation and grand designs, whose infrastructure is being revealed by melting ice, and worries over any remaining chemical and radioactive waste reminding us of the toxic legacies of the period.

What was the Thule disaster of 1968, and why does it matter?

No further attempt was made to hide nuclear weapons under Greenland's ice. If anything, such plans were thrown into further sharp relief by a plane crash involving a B-52 bomber close to Thule Air Base in January 1968. What followed became the stuff of legend; danger, intrigue, and lies on an industrial scale. The crash rocked Danish politics and society.

On January 21, a bomber was flying close to Thule when a fire developed on board the aircraft. Six of the crew members ejected safely and one did not. The plane crashed on the ice-covered North Star Bay and disintegrated on impact, unleashing a fuel-filled explosion. The explosives in the B28 nuclear bombs detonated and plutonium and uranium were released. The ice melted and bomb fragments were later recovered at the bottom of the bay. Operating in freezing conditions and near total darkness, Project Crested Ice was the recovery operation involving US armed forces personnel and local Danish workers based at Thule. The project team were working under extraordinary pressure to complete the mission before the spring melt made recovery even more precarious. Recovered waste was supposed to be shipped back to the United States for safe disposal. Anything remaining was assumed to be made safer by dilution.

The scandal of the Thule disaster revolves around the fact that the Danish and Greenlandic publics were never told at the time about the true scale of the crash and that it involved nuclear bombs. The other disturbing aspect of Project Crested Ice was the health consequences for the rescue workers, many of whom were not wearing protective clothing. The clean-up operation was often carried out by hand, and Danish workers in particular were at the front end of recovery, including dumping waste into huge fuel tanks. Anxious about the conditions and the threat of exposure to hazardous material, Danish staff at Thule began to monitor the health of the affected men and were concerned about the onset of cancer diagnoses. While the casual connection was disputed, some twenty years later, the United States was sued by the Danish clean-up workers and their relatives, and, even though their claim for compensation failed in a US court, it revealed the US Air Force had not been monitoring the health of the American men involved in Project Crested Ice. In 1995, the Danish government paid compensation to the affected Danish men and their families, and later a 2009 report commissioned by the Danish government concluded that there was no missing nuclear bomb despite speculation that the clean-up team could not find it.

Today, Inughuit living in Qaanaaq and other communities near Thule Air Base worry about the toxic legacy of the crash, as well as other activities, such as Camp Century. The longer term implications of the Thule air disaster also revealed a particular quality to the US-Danish relationship over Greenland. With the connivance of successive Danish governments, the United States had been allowed to establish a nuclear presence in Greenland despite never informing Danish and Greenlandic publics. The bomber's presence was explained as a one-off rather than a routine occurrence. As Greenland was considered vital to the air defense of North America and Europe, and as both the United States and Denmark were NATO members, a veil of secrecy existed over Thule and its operational mandate. Moreover, the crash also raised fears that accidental explosions that trigger nuclear weapons to explode might be wrongly interpreted by the Soviet Union that a first strike was imminent. One immediate consequence of Thule was for the United States and the Soviet Union to sign what was called the 1971 Agreement on Measures to Reduce the Risk of Nuclear War, using an upgraded hotline to inform one another of accidents.

What part did Arctic science play in Cold War geopolitical tension?

Arctic science was—and still is—essential to Arctic states and their sovereignty, security, and stewardship agendas. Reliable knowledge and understanding are needed in environments that often test the limits of human capabilities. Being able to operate and move around in cold weather environments, as well as being able to mobilize and deploy armed forces and military equipment, were considered a strategic imperative and prompted investment in scientific expeditions and experimentation. Universities and specialist research institutions within and beyond the armed forces and intelligence agencies were the beneficiaries of this sense of urgency. For most scientists and scholars, however, science works best when sharing knowledge and facilitating the mobility of scientists, which was not always easy to ensure given the sensitivity of knowledge production itself and the funding sources involved, many of which were military in origin, such as the US Office of Naval Research (ONR).

The ONR and the Naval Research Laboratory in the United States were major funders of Cold War era research on the physical environments that the US Navy has worked in, including the sea, land, sky, and space. During the Cold War, cold weather research of direct relevance included the capacity of sea ice to disrupt sonar and thus hinder enemy submarine detection, the effects of cold water on submarines and ships, the potential for disruption to communication in Arctic marine conditions, and the hazards of flying in Arctic weather. The Soviet Union was no different and funded similar cold weather research under the auspices of the Arctic and Antarctic Research Institute (AARI) and the Productive Forces Research Council of the Soviet Academy of Sciences. On the other side of the Arctic Ocean, the Arctic Institute of North America (AINA) was founded in 1945 as a joint venture between Canada and the United States dedicated to advancing Arctic physical and social science. On both sides of the Ice Curtain, science was supposed to support national development, enhance strategic capabilities, and enhance national prestige.

While the Cold War unquestionably made scientific cooperation difficult in the Arctic, there was a history of collaboration both before and after 1945. It is worth remembering that both the United States and the Soviet Union contributed to the second International Polar Year of 1932–1933, and there was interest before war broke out in 1939 in establishing a circum-polar chain of weather stations where information was shared between the United States, Canada, and the Soviet Union. After 1945, it was harder to collaborate because of a climate of mutual suspicion. The 1957–1958 International Geophysical Year (IGY), the third variant on the International Polar Year, witnessed substantial acts of cooperation in the Antarctic but less obviously so in Arctic regions. The glaciological research conducted in Antarctica during the IGY was, however, in-formed by research conducted in Greenland and the Soviet Arctic. Prior to IGY, American and European scientists were working on ice cores sourced from Greenland's inland ice.

During the IGY, the US developed plans for floating ice stations in the Arctic Ocean (Project Ice Skate), which were designed to facilitate meteorological and oceanographic re-search. Previously, US naval personnel from Thule Air Base landed in March 1952 on what was termed T-3 (Base Bravo), which was seven miles long and settled for nearly two years before temporary abandonment. As part of the IGY, plans were hatched to return to T-3 and establish a new station called Base Alpha. The latter was later abandoned as ice conditions changed and a new floating station called Alpha II was estab-lished for the remainder of IGY. The US Naval Arctic Research Laboratory at Port Barrow in Alaska provided further support for the IGY Arctic program. Canada's contribution to the IGY was south of the Arctic at Fort Churchill in Manitoba, where experiments were conducted on the effects of the auroras on long-distance communication. But throughout the IGY period, Canadian scientists were contributing to research on polar environments and weather under the auspices of the Polar Continental Shelf Project.

Sometimes the science involving the Arctic was simply fan-tasy. In the 1950s, Soviet scientists conceived of plans to bomb sea ice. New dams would be constructed to modulate the flow of warmer and colder waters through the Bering Strait. The American journal *Popular Mechanics* reported in 1956 that the

Soviets were imagining a huge dam built across the Bering Strait, designed to keep icebergs from escaping and interfering with shipping routes in the northern Pacific Ocean. To be fair, the writer concluded that the Soviet proposal was a piece of propaganda designed to rival American scheming for the Arctic. There are other examples of even more outrageous examples to geo-engineer the Arctic.

Notoriously, American scientists led by the nuclear physicist Edward Teller thought that nuclear explosions could be used to re-engineer Alaska. Project Chariot was imagined by Teller and colleagues in 1958 to be a plausible way to create an artificial harbor at Cape Thompson on Alaska's Chukchi Sea coast. Using a string of nuclear explosions, the nearly created harbor would then help promote access and development to that part of the US territory. While it did have some support within Alaska, the Iñupiat village of Point Hope was a locus of opposition. Subsequently, scientists at the University of Alaska became vocal critics, and later environmental groups added to a chorus of criticism. The Atomic Energy Commission dropped the plan in 1962 but never formally cancelled it.

Huge infrastructural investment required cold weather engineers and scientists to advise on how to construct and maintain projects such as the DEW Line. When the radar stations were built, major corporations such as AT&T, Bell, and Western Electric led the way in the coordination of around 25,000 workers. While the DEW Line's efficacy was placed in doubt by the onset of nuclear missile technology emanating from submarines, the infrastructural investment in the North American Arctic helped bring the region closer in the geographical imaginations of Canadian and American citizens. The popular iconography of the radar stations (in their distinct golf ball structures) became a mainstay of North American culture as documentaries and feature films, including the James Bond caper *You Only Live Twice* (1967), depicted the radar stations in action.

Science and scientists were integral to Cold War geopolitics, and fields such as glaciology, cold weather engineering, and sea ice studies enjoyed a substantial funding and logistical dividend.

Did science and technology produce positive results in the Arctic?

Being a Cold War frontline meant that the Arctic as a region became a space for military operations, military disasters, and military experimentation. It would be easy to conclude that the record for the Cold War Arctic is bad.

But the militarization of the Arctic brought other things as well: investment and employment. Roads were built, schools established, science and research stations funded, and local people employed at American airbases. In Alaska, northern Canada, and Greenland, as well as in the Nordic world more generally, US troop, ship, and plane deployment meant local multiplier effects. Iceland's economy received a substantial boost when US/NATO forces occupied the Keflavik airbase. After a wartime deal involving the British and Americans, the Icelandic government entered into a defense agreement with the US as fellow NATO members. The airbase became a crucial transatlantic hub for US and NATO forces and air policing in and around the North Atlantic region integral to hemispheric defense. From the late 1940s until 2006, the United States provided military security for Iceland and contributed billions of dollars to the local economy. After an initial retraction in 2006, worsening concerns over Russian behavior in Ukraine and Crimea provoked a renewed interest in restoring NATO air policing.

Both the Soviet Union and the US shared a view of the Arctic as crucial to the Cold War confrontation. As with the Americans, the Soviets were also interested in developing a better understanding of how to operate in a vast region characterized by permafrost, sea ice, and extremes of cold and darkness. They also invested huge sums of money in defense and early warning systems and used the Arctic as a testing area for military equipment and nuclear devices. The Kola Peninsula was arguably the most militarized place in the Arctic, where the Russian Northern Fleet was stationed and where nuclear-powered attack submarines were harbored. The Barents Sea was a strategic battleground as NATO and Soviet vessels, including fishing vessels acting as spy ships, patrolled and monitored the waters to the north of the Soviet Union and Norway. Tom Clancy's 1984 novel *The Hunt for Red October*, made into a big budget film in 1990, conveyed a sense of how anxious US strategic planners were about the ability of Delta-class Soviet submarines to avoid NATO detection. Having excellent surveillance abilities and advanced maps of the seabed and the Arctic seas, including the Arctic Ocean, was deemed vital—and as North American NATO planners discovered in the 1990s, the Soviets possessed detailed oceanographic charts and maps of the North American seabed and coastline.

Science and technology could and did play a positive role in the Arctic, however. While travel for Soviet scientists outside the communist bloc could be challenging and subject to restrictions, it was not impossible for Western and Soviet scientists to share information about Arctic science, including hosting and participating in workshops and conferences. The most notable boost to cooperation came at a period of relative détente. Under the Nixon-Brezhnev era, restrictions were lifted and contact encouraged in areas such as outer space and in the Arctic in areas like the Bering Strait, where both the United States and the Soviet Union shared mutual interests in meteorology, oceanography, and sea ice extent and thickness. Ship cruises were organized, and US-Soviet scientific cooperation led to joint projects on marine biology and oceanography, some of which addressed the ancient history of the Bering Land Bridge. American academics, such as David Hopkins of the US Geological Survey, were leading lights in building and sustaining cross–Bering Strait collaboration, involving in this case scientists specializing in the Quaternary-era from Russia, Canada, and the United States.

Other areas of notable cooperation included the 1973 Polar Bear Agreement signed in Oslo, involving Norway, the USSR, the United States, Canada, and Denmark. Even at the height of Cold War tensions, Arctic cooperation could occur in surprising ways. In 1984, for example, Canada and the USSR signed a protocol on Arctic science and indigenous exchanges, and in 1987 Canadian and Soviet scientists undertook a skiing trip across the Arctic Ocean starting at Severnaya Zemlya (an island group, which lies north of Siberia's Taymyr Peninsula, where the Soviets had carried out nuclear tests in the 1960s) to the Canadian island of Ellesmere. Ostensibly the trip was supposed to collect information about sea ice, but few failed to see it for what it was—a confidence-building measure that helped in 1989 to renew Soviet-Canadian agreement on science exchanges.

Arctic science cooperation suffered again between 1979 and 1985, when relations between the two superpowers worsened. The Arctic, once again, became a highly militarized space where restrictions on access, including sites where Western scientists wished to carry out field research, were affected. For researchers on snow, ice, and permafrost, this was deeply frustrating as large parts of Siberia and the Soviet Far East were forbidden zones. This did not change until the 1990s when renewed improvements in the relationship between the United States and now Russia allowed Western scientists to re-establish linkages. The establishment of the International Arctic Science Committee (IASC) in 1990 was pivotal after a preliminary meeting in Sweden in 1988. IASC was charged with encouraging circumpolar Arctic science, while American and Russian Arctic scientists were able to meet at the Pacific Ocean port of Vladivostok in 1994. Supported by the Far East Branch of the Russian Academy of Sciences, the meeting was renowned for the US American Association for the Advancement of Science having to bring $60,000 in cash along with their overheard projectors and other conference equipment (because the Russians did not have any resources to run the meeting). But the result was highly significant. American scientists were given permission to work with their Russian counterparts in northern Siberia, including Arctic coastal environments around the Lena River.

Did the end of the Cold War provide a new opportunity to reshape Arctic governance?

Mikhail Gorbachev famously evoked the ending of the Cold War in the Arctic in a speech in October 1987.

> Comrades, speaking in Murmansk, the capital of the Soviet Polar Region, it is appropriate to examine the idea of cooperation between all people also from the standpoint of the situation in the northern part of this planet. In our opinion, there are several weighty reasons for this.
> The Arctic is not only the Arctic Ocean, but also the northern tips of three continents: Europe, Asia and America. It is the place where the Euro-Asian, North American and Asian Pacific regions meet, where the frontiers come close to one another and the interests of states belonging to mutually opposed military blocs and nonaligned ones cross.

Gorbachev's meta-geography is noteworthy because he repositioned the Arctic as a meeting place for three continents rather than the frontline of a superpower confrontation. The Arctic Ocean, rather than being just a place for nuclear submarines and icebreakers to circulate in mutual suspicion of their opposing numbers, might be thought of as a meeting ground for the eight Arctic states who have shared interests in its future management. It is difficult to underestimate some of the challenges that Gorbachev was hinting at—for forty years the Arctic had been treated as a military frontier with attendant environmental costs, including a legacy of nuclear weapons testing in the Soviet Arctic and degradation of nuclear and nonnuclear facilities and vessels including submarines.

Science, the legacy of militarization, and the quest to promote environmental conservation helped rebuild relationships between the Arctic states. In September 1996, Norway, Russia, and the United States signed the Declaration on Arctic Military Environmental Cooperation (AMEC), which encouraged the three parties to support and enhance Russia's ability to manage its radioactive waste and longer term degradation of the Northern Fleet, after the country introduced funding cuts to its armed forces. Norway, as the one of nearest neighbors to the former Soviet Union in the High North, was particularly anxious about pollution and radioactive waste management in the Barents Sea region. Apart from security concerns, in the aftermath of the collapse of the Soviet Union, Norway was also concerned about the long-term health of its fishing industry.

Another neighbor, Finland, initiated a new era of scientific and environmental collaboration. After a meeting in Rovaniemi in September 1989, the eight Arctic states supported the writing of a series of reports on pollution including radioactivity and metal/oil pollutants. This investment paved the way for what was to become an Arctic Environmental Protection Strategy (AEPS), leading to the establishment of an Arctic Monitoring and Assessment Programme, supported by Finland and Norway. The premise of the AEPS, which took two years to negotiate, was "preserving environmental quality and natural resources, accommodating environmental protection principles with the needs and traditions of Arctic Native peoples, monitoring environmental conditions, and reducing and eventually eliminating pollution in the Arctic Environment." Acknowledging the role of northern and indigenous communities was integral to the Finnish vision, and AEPS then supported additional projects leading to the creation of the Protection of the Arctic Marine Environment, the Conservation of Arctic Flora and Fauna, the Sustainable Development and Utilization, and the Emergency Prevention, Preparedness and Response Working Groups. The AEPS used science and conservation to build political confidence and promote a vision of a circumpolar Arctic, as Gorbachev articulated in 1987.

Five years after the AEPS was agreed upon, the eight Arctic states gathered in Ottawa in September 1996 to sign an agreement establishing an Arctic Council to "provide a means for promoting cooperation, coordination and interaction among the Arctic States, with the involvement of the Arctic indigenous communities and other Arctic inhabitants on common arctic issues*, in particular issues of sustainable development and environmental protection in the Arctic." The asterisk (*) is faithfully reproduced from the original text because it highlighted something rather significant—"The Arctic Council should not deal with matters related to military security."

Both the United States and Russia did not wish the Arctic Council to tackle issues regarding military security. For Russians, NATO member states were already well represented in the convention (Denmark, Canada, Iceland, Norway, and the United States), and thus any attempt to introduce a military dimension was judged not to be conducive to collaboration. The Arctic Council created three types of members—the Arctic states, the six Permanent Participants (indigenous peoples' representatives who were thus acknowledged in their own right to be significant in any discussions about the future Arctic—the Inuit Circumpolar Council, Saami Council, Russian Association of Indigenous People of the North, Arctic Athabaskan Council, Gwich'in Council International, and Aleut International Association), and observers who were described as "non-Arctic states," "inter-governmental and inter-parliamentary organizations, global and regional" and "non-governmental organizations." Some of the earliest observers were European states such as the UK, Germany,

France, and the Netherlands who had historically long-standing interests in the Arctic.

With a rotating chairmanship lasting two years, each Arctic state is responsible for managing the Arctic Council and shaping its priorities. Over the last twenty years, it has been recognized as the premier intergovernmental forum for Arctic affairs. It is a forum and not a treaty-based organization. Thus, it relies on consensus and goodwill rather than hard laws and formal obligations. For much of that period, through the efforts of its working groups and later task forces, it developed a well-earned reputation for producing significant reports and statements on the challenges facing the Arctic, such as the *Arctic Climate Impact Assessment*, which released its findings in 2004 and 2005; the 2009 *Arctic Marine Shipping Assessment*; and the 2016 *Arctic Resilience Assessment*. As the workload of the Arctic Council increased, the parties agreed to fund and establish a permanent secretariat in Tromsø in 2011. The secretariat is charged with helping the rotating chairmanship coordinate and manage Arctic Council affairs, including the working groups.

What are the latest developments in international cooperation in the Arctic?

The Arctic Council is a good place to start to identify the latest, and largely positive, changes influencing Arctic governance. For one thing, under the auspices of the Arctic Council, the eight Arctic states secured three binding legal agreements on search and rescue (2011), oil-spill response management (2013), and scientific cooperation (2017), which indicates a willingness on the part of the eight to strengthen their cooperation with one another. The Russian annexation of Crimea in 2014 led to profound concern about conflict spillover and renewed militarization of the Arctic, but this did not prevent the agreement on scientific cooperation being signed in May 2017. Second, in May 2013, the Arctic Council agreed to a new round of observers such as China, South Korea, Japan, India, Singapore, and Italy joining. While not unexpected given the growing interest and investment in polar science, it did signify a major change in the observer body, which hitherto was dominated by European states and international and regional bodies such as the World Meteorological Organization. Membership issues have not always been straightforward, however. The European Union has not been granted permanent observer status thus far because of Canadian and Danish/Greenlandic anger over the seal-products import ban and then later Russian discontent over EU sanctions in the post-Ukraine crisis era. At present, the EU is allowed to attend major Arctic Council meetings as an ad hoc observer. In 2017, the Arctic Council announced its approval of new observers and these included states such as Switzerland and non-governmental groups such as Oceana.

We should not be uncritical of the work of the Arctic Council. It is a consensus-based body, and thus there are areas where it has to act with caution. Maintaining a cordial relationship with Russia is clearly integral to its future fate. Canada was very censorious of Russian activity in Ukraine and Crimea but reluctant to disrupt Arctic Council business—bar refusing to participate in one Moscow-based meeting. Under the chairmanship of Canada (2013–2015), there was criticism that too much attention was given to economic development and thus attention was taken away from its traditional areas of interest, namely science and environmental conservation. Under the US chairmanship (2015–2017), science cooperation and the challenges posed by climate change took center stage with former president Barack Obama visiting Alaska in September 2015 in order to highlight the impact of climate change on the Arctic itself. But with the election of President Donald Trump in January 2017, it is likely that the emphasis on climate change will be downplayed given Trump's reported comments, which cast doubt on the scientific validity of a warming planet.

The Finnish chairmanship of the Arctic Council (2017–2019) has placed considerable emphasis on circumpolar cooperation and what is described as the pursuit of "common solutions." Finnish foreign minister Timo Soini noted:

The Arctic has a great potential. Better access to natural resources and the opening of new sea routes in the Arctic will bring benefits, but also challenges. The new opportunities oblige us all to work for sustainable development in the Arctic region. This will emphasize the leading role of the Arctic Council in producing outstanding scientific assessments and addressing the impacts of globalization and climate change.

Do the legacies of settler colonialism still shape Arctic politics today?

While indigenous peoples and northern communities are partners in the work of the Arctic Council, the pursuit of "common solutions" can be troubling. The history of colonialism and the colonization of the Arctic region is complex. With the launch of an Arctic Council in 1996 and talk of a "global Arctic," attention can and does become resolutely forward looking. While foreign and environment ministers can focus on "new opportunities," others worry that the past is glossed over.

European encounters with the Arctic were and are transformative. Drawn by the search of new trading routes to the Orient, commercial companies and expeditioners precipitated transnational economies based on the exploitation of furs, whales, seals, and later minerals and timber. Whaling in the nineteenth century was a global industry, and whale oil used for heating and machine lubrication and baleen used in corsetry were hugely profitable. Inuit and other aboriginal peoples were involved in those trading and resource-intensive activities acting as skilled labor, but their involvement was precarious. Equivalent to zero-hours contracts, Inuit involved in whaling could be dropped when not needed, and sexual unions involving Inuit women and European and American whalers produced generations of children with mixed heritage who were adopted into those communities.

During the gold rush in Canada's Yukon, indigenous peoples once again provided local expertise and services to visiting miners who were again extracting Arctic and northern resources for the benefit of southern constituencies and markets. So, the onset of a European colonial era, from the fifteenth century onward, contributed to a view of the Arctic/far north as a resource base for European, Asian, and American markets located thousands of miles from the ecosystems and communities servicing those needs.

With European encounters came not only trade and interaction but also a history of disease and dispossession. The struggles of indigenous peoples in the Arctic share similarities with other areas of the world. Conceived of a *terra nullius*, the Arctic/far north region has its own histories and geographies of conflict, land theft, and exploitation by others. Even countries that pride themselves as being socially progressive, such as Canada, have a troubling history of relationships with indigenous peoples, including conflict with Métis communities in the north west. The 1876 Indian Act witnessed the use of legislation to ensure further governance and control over Indian and indigenous lives, setting out how people were classified and treated under a growing body of Canadian law pertaining to indigenous peoples. The 1885 North West Rebellion, involving Métis pitted against Canadian forces, was eventually ended after an indigenous insurgency. The rebellion was informed and inflamed by accusations and experiences of settler Canadian racism, indigenous dispossession and economic marginalization.

The history of indigenous peoples in the Arctic is also one shaped by the experiences of residential schools and repeated attempts to assimilate children into settler colonial societies. These strategies of assimilation occurred in Canada, Russia, the Scandinavian Arctic, and the Danish territory of Greenland. Often run by churches, and funded by national governments, it is difficult to underestimate how awful the experiences were for indigenous peoples sent to these schools. In some cases, they were repeatedly abused and/or raped. Children were punished if they spoke their native languages, were forced to learn alien languages, such as Danish, English, and Russian, and expected to become "model citizens." In Canada, the residential school system began in the 1870s and finally closed in the 1970s. In 2008, forced to apologize for the abuse and displacement, the Canadian government instituted a Truth and Reconciliation Commission to investigate said abuses and crucially allowed victims to speak of their experiences. Many children died in schools—many from suicide. Indigenous peoples have spoken of a cultural genocide enacted against them with profound implications for personal and communal well-being, social cohesiveness, and societal resilience.

In Canada and Greenland, for example, the damage done by residential schools still reverberates in indigenous communities. Aboriginal children are more likely to suffer serious health issues; be in foster care; and indigenous girls and women are more likely to be victims of abuse, rape, and murder. Housing conditions are often poor and overcrowding is common in northern communities. A failure to encourage traditional activities, such as fishing and hunting, can and does contribute to a loss in personal esteem, especially in young men. High levels of unemployment and under-employment are not uncommon. Indigenous peoples in Russia are also on the receiving end of troubling statistics—more likely to be killed, to commit suicide, to endure high infant mortality rates, and to have a lower life expectancy than ethnic Russians. As with other Arctic states, the Soviet authorities also instituted a policy of forced relocation, residential schools, and greater state interference in the way indigenous peoples managed their traditional activities, such as herding and hunting. The Cold War was often cited as the imperative for these interventionist and assimilationist strategies.

The Cold War years brought far more indigenous peoples into contact with southerners as military personnel, scientists, miners, contractors, and builders journeyed north to defend, study, and build the Arctic. In some places that contact was less unusual, perhaps as in the case of Greenland, where some communities had been exposed to American soldiers and airmen during World War II. In the Soviet Union, the far north was visited by another group of people who did not want to be there, namely political prisoners and dissidents sent to the gulags in Siberia. As we have noted, Cold War investment and attention brought opportunities to local communities, but it also ushered in an era of prohibition as well, with some areas of the Arctic being declared out of bounds due to national security reasons.

Finally, we return, briefly, to land claims and autonomy. In Canada, land claims regarding specific (e.g., addressing past disputes and grievances) and/or comprehensive claims (e.g., ongoing treaty-making activities) involve aboriginal peoples, federal Canada, and the province and territory implicated. Initiated in the early 1970s, negotiations over claims remain ongoing in many parts of Canada, and the scale and substance of the negotiations are considerable, involving twenty-six comprehensive land claims and four self-government agreements embracing over 450,000 square miles of land, CAN$3 billion capital transfers, and participation in and governance of land and resource-related projects. Indigenous peoples are also supposed to enjoy guarantees regarding traditional lifestyles and political recognition. While there is plenty of evidence of progress in Canada, addressing the grievances and losses of indigenous peoples is ongoing, and there is plenty of evidence suggesting that in many parts of the Arctic they are often treated as either barriers to further southern-led economic development or obstacles that have to be managed.

As many indigenous peoples and their representatives complain, just because one acquires rights and representation, it does not mean that struggles for autonomy and recognition are resolved in the Arctic. In Scandinavia, Sámi complain that their traditional livelihoods remain vulnerable to state-level decision-making regarding resource projects and access to traditional reindeer herding and hunting territories. In February 2016, a Swedish court upheld a case involving nomadic reindeer herders seeking to protect their rights to control hunting and fishing in northern Sweden. Giving a judgment in favor of the herders, it reversed a decision by the Swedish parliament in 1993, which stripped such powers to exercise control over traditional subsistence activities from Sámi. The Swedish government could appeal the judgment, and thus the struggles involving indigenous peoples to secure autonomy, recognition, and rights remains a work in progress.

Indigenous peoples might be recognized as permanent participants by the Arctic Council member states and observers, but their participation remains sharply shaped by the national governments that dominate their homelands. The history of Arctic exploitation, settlement, and governance is one where northern communities have played second fiddle to southern powers and constituencies, located thousands of miles away from the Arctic.

5

WARMING ARCTIC

Climate change and its effects on Arctic societies, wildlife, and environments has been a recurring theme of this book. And for good reason. In many parts of the Arctic, these effects are inescapable, and, given that Arctic temperatures are rising faster than anywhere else on earth, they are often dramatic. The Arctic—and in particular the Arctic Ocean—has become one of the regions of greatest concern to the global scientific and political community because of the speed of visible and observable changes there. Both sea ice and glaciers—and dislodged ice shelves and crumbling icebergs—have become climate signals. Since 1979, satellite observations have reaffirmed this trend of loss and have provided compelling juxtaposed images of repeated record low years of sea ice distribution and thickness. These observations and images are integral to a vision of runaway environmental change and a narrative of tipping points. We can see and measure such loss and retreat of ice—and capture it through photography, film, and remote sensing—perhaps more easily than we can detect and visualize the effects of climate change in other parts of the world, such as assessing the increases in water stress and excessive heat in other environments.

Some of the ways in which we think about climate change and imagine its consequences have been articulated in recent years through an expanding scientific and environmentalist vocabulary of forewarnings of imminent danger, and of hazards, crisis, and risk. This sense of unwelcome futures has been exemplified over the last decade by the use of the term "tipping points," with scientists warning of the crossing of climate thresholds after which a system experiences irreversible ecosystem shifts.

Climate change and its impact on regions such as the Arctic is indicative of a "hyper-object," and people struggle to get a handle on what this catastrophe is, and what it will mean, precisely because of its reach and its extent. We have chosen to weave discussion of climate change throughout the various chapters of this book, as so many of the issues and topics we consider intersect with and are affected by a warming Arctic. In this chapter we return, inevitably, to a discussion of climate change processes and impacts, but our intention is more to reflect upon terms like "warming Arctic" and "tipping points" and draw attention to how they undermine the notion of a stable region with a fixed boundary line, and how they inform narratives that all our fates are tied to places like the Arctic. Indeed, the very idea of a stable and unchanging environment seems particularly inappropriate for a part of the world where sea ice is disappearing and permafrost is thawing.

A warming Arctic demands a reordering of how we think about and classify the world, but it also requires new scientific and conceptual ways of thinking across disciplinary boundaries and how we address environmental change. Assessing, understanding, and responding to climate change (and not just in the Arctic) requires the political will for a coordinated international response. We then ponder what a warming and ice-free Arctic may mean for international cooperation and climate diplomacy in the region. There is now a vast body of significant evidence of dramatic transformations in Northern Hemisphere climate patterns and a growing literature on their environmental and societal effects, but how states decide to consider and act upon this will determine the kind of diplomatic engagement needed to deal with the challenges climate change brings and the Arctic categories and boundaries it disrupts. This will certainly influence Arctic geopolitics and power dynamics.

Why does a warming Arctic matter?

In October 2017, scientific observations of Arctic sea ice extent for that month showed that it averaged 6.71 million square kilometers (2.60 million square miles), which was the fifth-lowest in the 1979 to 2017 satellite record. To put this figure in context, it was 1.64 million square kilometers (633,000 square miles) below the 1981 to 2010 average extent and 820,000 square kilometers (317,000 square miles) above the record low October extent that had been recorded in 2012. In 2016, the Arctic Council's Arctic Resilience Assessment initiative released its full scientific report, which underscored how the region, its peoples, societies, and economies will need to be increasingly resilient in the face of feedback mechanisms that will have implications for human and non-human communities and ecologies everywhere. A special report released by the Intergovernmental Panel on Climate Change (IPCC) in October 2018 warned that even to limit the global temperature increase to 1.5°C will require action that involves "unprecedented" transitions in every aspect of society.

The shape-shifting geographies of the Arctic are made manifest by diminishing glacial ice, the retreat and thinning of sea ice, fiercer storms, and coastal erosion. Scientists may have recorded very low extent figures for Arctic Ocean sea ice in September 2007 and September 2012, but it is now common to read that ice-free summers will be routine in the near future. Satellite images of surface melt on Greenland's inland ice and receding coastal outlet glaciers provoke further alarm over an Arctic meltdown and global sea level rise. With less sea ice in the winter, storms hitting Arctic coastlines mean communities are more exposed to the violent interaction of wind, water, and ice. Beaches get eroded and infrastructure is undermined. And with less sea ice in the Arctic Ocean and diminishing snow cover on land, then ocean, air, and land temperatures rise because less heat from the sun is being refracted from ice.

As the climate changes and the Arctic warms, and as terrestrial, marine, and freshwater environments are affected, Arctic societies face disruption and expensive challenges. But these challenges are global ones too. A recent major EU-funded research program called ICE-ARC (Ice, Climate and Economics—Arctic Research on Change), which concluded its work at the end of 2017, investigated the regional and global consequences of Arctic sea ice loss. It was a significant international project, with members of the research team working from icebreakers and aircraft, and using drones and remote sensing, and with north Greenlandic hunters and their dog teams. One aspect of the research was to assess the economic impact, not just for the Arctic but also for the world. Economists used data from the scientific research and from climate models to consider a changing Arctic under a range of global emissions and socioeconomic scenarios. Results suggested that the acceleration of climate change driven by thawing Arctic permafrost and melting sea ice could cause up to $130 trillion worth of economic losses globally, over the next three centuries, under a current business-as-usual trajectory. However, if global warming is limited to 1.5°C by the end of this century, the researchers argued, that additional projected additional cost will be reduced to under $10 trillion.

Indigenous peoples across the circumpolar North observe and experience climate change in immediate ways, and their abilities to harvest wildlife and food resources are already being tested. Becoming resilient to climate change, and preparing to respond, cope with, and adapt to its impacts, risks, and opportunities will require urgent and specific policies and action at local, national, and international levels. When placed in a global context and quantified in economic terms, the projected effects of climate change appear shocking, and the question of how to deal with them seems an overwhelming one that is difficult to answer.

Greenland in particular has come to represent both the image and reality of catastrophic climate change in the Arctic. Climate models suggest that average temperatures in Greenland will rise by more than 3°C this century, which would mean large-scale melting of the inland ice. Airborne, satellite, and seismic data indicate pronounced thinning of the edges of the inland ice in places where summer melt has been increasing over the last twenty years, while there is evidence of slower rates of thickening of the ice much further inland. The entire Greenland ice sheet contains enough water to raise global sea levels by seven meters. In January 2011, for example, the *New Scientist* published an article entitled "Last Chance to Hold Greenland Back from Tipping Point," which reported that new data and models showed that Greenland's inland ice was on track to hit a point of no return in 2040. Although this may have seemed alarmist at the time, just a few years later many scientists appear less cautious when expressing concern that Arctic ecosystems are approaching tipping points beyond which changes will transform the ecologies, economies, and societies of the region irreversibly. A continued warming trend of less than 2°C until the end of this century would tip the Greenland inland ice to a state where it will melt completely, some scientists warn, although this process would take a few hundred years. In June 2018, a team of Norwegian scientists published the results of their research in the journal *Nature Climate Change*, based on data going back some fifty years, and it suggested that the Barents Sea had crossed a tipping point. The loss of sea ice, they argue, has transformed the Barents Sea from a transition zone between the Atlantic and Arctic Oceans to an ecosystem that was more like an extension of the Atlantic. Some scientists suggest that a tipping point has already been passed for the entire Arctic Ocean sea ice regime, meaning that ice-free summers will be the norm from the middle of this century.

The drastic nature of this reshaping of the northern regions of the globe provokes scientific and public anxiety in some and denial in others, itself stimulating the further commissioning and production of talk shows, television documentaries, and feature films warning of disappearing ice and vulnerable animals, as well imperiled northern communities. The scenario of an ice-free Arctic Ocean in the not too distant future and the prospect of polar bears and Inuit culture disappearing from the far north are irreconcilable with popular images and conceptions of how the Arctic has always looked. The Arctic is increasingly observed and monitored by science; but having more data about sea ice loss and permafrost melt, or more data on the interplay between larger scale atmospheric, sea ice, and ocean processes, does not necessarily lead to greater comprehension. We can be simply overwhelmed by something that appears to challenge our capacity for human action and long-term planning.

What, so far, has been the impact of warming in the Arctic?

Current research on the effects and consequences of climate change for the Arctic focuses largely on impacts and adaptations. The growing social science literature is capturing local experiences of crisis and risk as a result of global warming. The significance of these studies goes far beyond the northern reaches of the globe and enriches our understanding of living on a planet undergoing constant change rather than one assumed to have a climate and biosphere that is benign and predestined for further human activity.

Ethnographic literature, archeology, historical ecology, the ethno-historical record, and traditional indigenous knowledge reveal how the peoples of the Arctic have exhibited a great degree of social and cultural creativity in the face of dramatic environmental and social change. Far from living in an environment that constrains human action, the Arctic is an environment that has often provided opportunities and possibilities for indigenous peoples, who have anticipated the possibilities of successful engagement with it as well as adapting to changes affecting it. In turn, this might encourage a view that indigenous peoples become unwitting "poster communities" for climate resilience, and paradoxically reinforce a skepticism toward the more deleterious consequences of Arctic warming— in other words, a view that assumes the people of the Arctic will cope with climate change and that we should not underestimate their ability to adapt to the challenges that warming might bring.

We are nonetheless witnessing the emergence of a "new Arctic" in an era of climate change, with the likelihood of shipping routes transecting previously inaccessible ice-covered waters and the development of extractive industries in what have until now been relatively remote and underdeveloped areas. Climate change in the Arctic becomes another business opportunity rather than a sustained moment to pause and consider the long-term consequences. Paradoxically, therefore, strange weather and warming trends add nourishment to a worldview that redemptive adjustment is possible. Environmental shifts help resurrect a sense of human mastery over natural obstacles and bring forth stories of previous episodes of adjustment and resilience.

According to the most recent IPCC assessments, the average temperature on the earth's surface increased by 0.85°C between 1880 and 2012 (IPCC 2013, 2014), reinforced by the IPCC's special report published in October 2018. Climate scientists no longer appear hesitant to say that the warming observed in the past fifty years or more is attributed to human activities, particularly activities related to burning fossil fuels. The Anthropocene, a term popularized by biologist Eugene Stoermer and atmospheric scientist Paul Crutzen in 2000, does indeed seem apt to describe the era of extensive, dramatic, and deep human influence on the planet and how we are implicated as capitalist agents of geophysical reconfiguration and climate change in our current environmental predicament.

Few areas encompassing the air, water, rock, ocean, and animals of the biosphere have been untouched by the human imprint. The Arctic is bearing the brunt of this ongoing geophysical transformation.

How has the Arctic changed in the past?

Like land forms and waters anywhere else on earth, the Arctic has undergone many dramatic changes, ruptures, and shifts throughout its geological and climatic history. Complex geological processes have moved continental and oceanic terrains, resulting in the present geographic configuration of Arctic landmasses and seas. At the beginning of the Cambrian period, for example, Greenland and the Canadian Shield were part of a continuous continent situated at the equator. Some of the earth's oldest geological features are found in the Arctic, but parts of the region are relatively young in terms of formation, such as the floor of the Arctic Ocean. Ice cores extracted from Greenland's inland ice and sediment cores from Arctic Ocean submarine ridges and plateaus provide compelling evidence of how a deep-time perspective allows us to think of the Arctic along a timeline stretching back millions, even billions, of years, and add to our understanding of how the Arctic has undergone tremendous shifts in climate, ranging from subequatorial during the Paleozoic period to arctic in the Cretaceous and the present.

The science of ice coring, which includes the analysis and interpretation of ice cores, is sophisticated, and the long-time series of paleo-climatic data it produces gives us remarkable insight into the changing climate of the entire earth, not just local information about the ice sheets and glaciers from which the cores are drilled. For example, by comparing the ice archive from drilled cores from Greenland's inland ice with glaciological studies of total mass change and temperature records from coastal meteorological stations around Greenland, we can build a picture of a range of Arctic climates that have experienced remarkably abrupt and severe changes. Like glaciers and ice sheets elsewhere in the Arctic, Greenland's inland ice is a frozen archive of the weather and climate of the past. Each accumulated frozen snow layer contains memories of what conditions were like with each annual snowfall, going back 100,000 years. Globally, this ice and temperature record reinforces our knowledge of human life on the planet, especially over the last 11,500 years, against an environmental backdrop of climatic and geological instability.

Sudden and often dramatic climatic shifts and extreme biophysical events have kept the Arctic in a state of flux rather than static balance. Fifty-five million years ago, when parts of its rim were forested, the Arctic Ocean's year-round surface temperature averaged 23°C, which may seem extremely warm compared with today's Arctic climatic conditions. Ice ages have come and gone. Prehistoric fossils have been discovered which reveal that giant redwoods, along with ferns and flowering plants, flourished in Canada's High Arctic and northern Siberia during the Eocene some 45 million years ago, while terrestrial ecologists have shown that the vast tundra plains characteristic of much of Siberia originated only in the last 10,000 years.

Based on both shallow and deep drillings, the ice core record for the Greenland inland ice is incredibly detailed, extending back through the present interglacial period, through to the last ice age (when temperatures on the ice were 20°C colder than at present), and into the preceding interglacial era, when the sea level was some five meters higher than at present. Ice cores from the Greenland inland ice reveal how, between these periods, there were dozens of periods of abrupt warming and cooling. During the glacial period, for example, there were twenty-six abrupt temperature increases of about 7–10°C. These glacial warm periods, named Dansgaard-Oeschger events, may be random, chaotic, and unpredictable.

Between the middle of the ninth century until the 1300s, during what is now known as the Medieval Warm period, or the Medieval Climate Optimum, the northern North Atlantic climate was warmer. This may have brought advantages to some, including the Norse settlers of the northern North Atlantic islands who sailed across relatively ice-free waters from Iceland to settle in Greenland and, from there, explored other parts of northern North America. Vineyards also flourished in England during this time. In the western Arctic, Inuit groups, who archeologists and historians have called the Thule Inuit, migrated eastward across Canada toward Greenland, following bowhead whales as they extended their range into increasingly larger stretches of open water. The Medieval Warm period was followed, however, by the Little Ice Age, mentioned in the previous chapter, which, interspersed with three main periods of warmer temperatures, lasted until the middle of the nineteenth century.

Following a period of 400–500 years during which mean summer temperatures were 1–2°C below current average temperatures, during the Medieval Climate Optimum summer temperatures were around 2°C higher on average than at present. One consequence of this warming was less summer sea ice in the Canadian Eastern Arctic, which also experienced longer periods of open water and ice-free summers. These changing ecological conditions opened the way for nomadic Inuit groups to venture into maritime areas with a variety of marine mammals, mainly narwhal, beluga, harp seal, and, significantly, the bowhead whale. While this climatic shift changed the ecology of the Canadian Eastern Arctic, the cultural effects of the Medieval Climate Optimum on coastal Inuit groups were far-reaching. The advantages it offered to the Thule Inuit were, however, not to the benefit of the Paleo-Inuit Dorset people the Thule eventually displaced. Major cold spells in Greenland between the sixteenth and eighteenth centuries were followed in the next 200 years by major advances by many of the inland ice outlet glaciers. Today's alarm about the melting of the Greenland inland ice, however, arises from scientific scenarios that suggest the scale and nature of climate change in the coming decades may well exceed any previous changes experienced in the earth's history. A point we have returned to several times throughout this book is that the northern circumpolar regions are experiencing some of the more profound changes we can expect in a warming world.

In examining the paleo-climate record, scientists point to the importance of understanding how the Arctic atmosphere, ocean, and cryosphere regulate global climate on a variety of temporal and spatial scales. Our knowledge of natural climate variability in the past, though, is still limited—much depends on accumulating a paleo-climate record from lake sediments, marine sediments, trees, and glacier ice cores—and this restricts the reliability of Arctic climate predictions. Writing in the journal *Science* in 2012, a team of researchers reported on a sediment core from Lake El'gygytgyn in northeastern Russia that provides a continuous, high-resolution record of Arctic environmental conditions over the past 2.8 million years. Significantly, the core revealed numerous "super inter-glacials" during the Quaternary—the extreme warm conditions were difficult to explain, the authors argued, showing just how much we still have to understand about global climate systems. Yet, much of the scientific literature examining Arctic climate change over the past 1,000 years suggests that what can be considered pre-anthropogenic causes (i.e., before 1850 or so) resulted to a considerable extent from solar irradiance and volcanism rather than greenhouse gases.

How is climate change influencing the Arctic today?

We have already described how ice is thinning, permafrost is thawing, that there are significant reductions in seasonal snow, and that glaciers are receding at a rapid rate. It would be wrong, however, to assume that these changes have only been noticed in the last decade or so. The Danish Pearyland Expedition, which explored parts of northern Greenland in the late 1940s, proved that the Chr. Erichsen Bræ glacier receded thirty-five meters annually between 1947 and 1950. The expedition referred to maps made of Independence Fjord in Greenland's far north on previous Danish expeditions in 1906–1908 and 1920–1923 and concluded that glaciers in the area had "shrunk considerably." In a preliminary account of the expedition's activities during the winter of 1948–1949, and published in the journal *Arctic*, the scientific team reported that "Today, Chr. Erichsen Bræ is practically a mass of dead ice, and the rate of movement is insignificant." In the first two decades of the twentieth century, miners on Spitsbergen were only able to load coal on ships in the summer, which accounted for a period of around ninety days. By the 1950s, the fjords were free of ice more often and navigable for an average of 191 days in the year. In Greenland, the warming of waters along the west coast during the first two decades of twentieth century saw the transformation of the economies of several towns from small-scale hunting and fishing to large-scale, capital-intensive commercial fisheries based mainly on cod. Again, as we pointed out, the difference between the changes observed between fifty to one hundred years ago and now is that the current changes are considered remarkable in their speed and extent.

One of the most dramatic examples of warming occurred in the summer of 2016 when a heat wave in Siberia caused permafrost to melt. The thawing led to the exposure of human bodies and reindeer, which had previously been buried in the permafrost. The decayed bodies released anthrax spores and bacteria, which subsequently caused the death of over 2,000 reindeer in a part of the Russian Arctic where reindeer herding is prevalent. Before this heat wave, prevailing temperatures had been sufficiently cold for corpses, human and non-human, to remain buried. This "freakish" event, however, served as a reminder that viruses have a nasty habit of being resurrected. Warming melts not only ice and snow, but it also has the capacity to reanimate things that we thought were dead and buried. The past haunts the present.

What will an ice-free Arctic Ocean mean?

A number of seas border the northern rims of the North American and Eurasian continents. Each of these stretches of water, which include the Beaufort, Barents, Kara, and Laptev Seas, has its own distinctive marine ecosystem, but they all form part of the Arctic Ocean. Sea ice in the Arctic Ocean is constantly battered by winds and shunted around by currents. Broken into floes that collide and grind together, forming walls of ice known as pressure ridges often several meters in height, it drifts slowly about in two large gyres, or circles. It is an ocean in constant movement, but the seas that surround it act as buffer zones between an ocean of Arctic ice and the Atlantic and Pacific Oceans. These zones appear to be receding and, as we noted in the case of the Barents Sea, the distinctiveness of these marine ecosystems appears to be changing as they become more Atlantic and Pacific in nature.

We have also discussed at length how the disappearance of multiyear ice in the Arctic Ocean and other northern waters is likely to be immensely disruptive. Ice-dependent microorganisms will lose a permanent habitat, and that in turn will have tremendous consequences for Arctic wildlife. As the amount of sea ice decreases, seals, walrus, polar bears, and other species will suffer drastically. Most Arctic mammals and fish depend upon the presence of sea ice and, in turn, many Inuit coastal communities depend on harvesting these species. Higher ocean temperatures and lower levels of salinity, changes in seasonal sea ice extent, rising sea levels, and many other (as yet undefined) effects are certain to significantly affect marine species, with implications for Arctic coastal communities that are dependent on hunting and fishing.

Looking further offshore, however, the implications for an ice-free Arctic Ocean are even more wide-ranging. Perhaps most relevant here might be the fate of the Central Arctic Ocean (CAO), and the possibility that ocean warming might encourage fish stocks to migrate to the cooler waters of the far north. Sea ice forms a natural barrier to commercial fishing, but it is indisputable that the CAO is in effect a zone constituting "international waters." Until recently, there has been concern that with no regulatory regime for fishing in place, the CAO might become a commercially and physically viable space for fishing. There are around 150 species of fish in Arctic waters, including some, such as the Alaskan pollock, that were subjected to devastating exploitation in the 1970s and 1980s. As we noted, mackerel have been discovered recently in Greenlandic and northern Norwegian waters having previously been thought to be largely resident in milder waters, including those off the British Isles. The northward migration of this fish serves as an indicator of what is possible in the future.

The Arctic region's history is one of consistent overexploitation, including whales, seals, finfish, and shellfish. The extraordinary collapse of the Alaskan pollock in the Bering Sea stands as testimony to commercial greed and weak governance. Fishing fleets from China, South Korea, Poland, and the Soviet Union took millions of tons of fish in the international waters beyond the American and Soviet exclusive economic zones. A moratorium on pollock fishing came in 1993, but by that time it was simply too late. The fish stocks were decimated. Even today, fish-stock levels have not come close to recovering from the heyday of the late 1970s and early 1980s when pollock biomass was estimated to be 10–15 million tons.

Mindful of past experiences of overfishing, Canada, Russia, Norway, Denmark, and the United States have met since 2013 in an attempt to work with extra-regional partners like the European Union and China on a tentative agreement for the CAO. In July 2015, the five Arctic coastal states published the "Declaration Concerning the Prevention of Unregulated High Seas Fishing in the Central Arctic Ocean" detailing their interest in developing conservation measures for the area in question. The Declaration is non-binding and was followed up with scientific and political meetings involving Iceland, Japan, China, South Korea, and the European Union in 2015 and again in 2016. After further consultation, a moratorium was agreed on in 2017 for some sixteen years and was signed by the ten parties in Ilulissat in October 2018. The agreement builds on the United Nations Convention on the Law of the Sea and the UN Fish Stocks Agreement. Important in its own right for the Arctic, it also represents an additional element in discussions leading to the development of a global framework for fisheries management.

Protecting the CAO from commercial fisheries—at least for the time being—also obligates the ten parties to each make significant commitments to fisheries research and to monitoring fish stocks. By the time the moratorium is up for review, a regional fisheries management organization (RFMO) may be established for the Arctic Ocean, in advance of any commercial fishing. Prior to the establishment of a RFMO, though, proper research needs to be undertaken as to what kind of biomass might be found in the CAO. It is unlikely that fishing will never occur. The question is more how can it be done sustainably, and thus avoid the collapse of other fisheries such as the Bering Sea Alaskan pollock. The moratorium of sixteen years was a compromise between the various negotiating parties—China wanted a four-year moratorium and Norway asked for a thirty-year stay of grace. Readers can draw their own conclusions from that disparity.

The prospect of an ice-free central Arctic Ocean will likely mean that coastal states and non-coastal states will argue over the management of international waters. What no one knows is what will happen to the marine ecosystem should sea ice continue to disappear and ocean temperatures continue to warm. The region will still be seasonably affected by limited amounts of natural light and nutrient availability. Nutrient-rich waters from the Atlantic and Pacific Oceans might well improve productivity. However, in addition to ice-melt, the Arctic Ocean is also being acidified, with mixed consequences for plankton, fish, and shellfish. Any displacement of existing species in favor of migrating species will have implications for the overall ecosystem, leading inevitably to species winners and losers.

Climate change may bring economic benefits as well as mean social and economic costs to the Arctic. Climate warming may enhance biological production in some fish species, for example, with positive results for commercial fisheries. Extractive industries have been a significant driving force for environmental and socioeconomic change in parts of the Arctic for over a century, and today, as we discuss in the next chapter, much of the circumpolar North is on the verge of major energy and mineral exploration and development. In 2016, and in the wake of the Deepwater Horizon disaster, Canada imposed a five-year moratorium on oil and gas exploration and development in the Canadian Arctic. However, operations can continue under existing licenses. A number of review processes are currently underway that feed into the Canadian government's decision whether to extend or lift the moratorium in 2021. So while the moratorium does not affect projects approved before 2016, oil and gas activities are not completely banned in the Canadian Arctic. In January 2018, Norway banned oil drilling in the waters around Lofoten for four years, but at the same time announced that new drilling operations in the Barents Sea would go ahead. That same month, the US government announced it would expand oil and gas drilling in nearly all the country's offshore areas, thereby overturning a ban imposed on activities in the Arctic, Atlantic, and Pacific under the Obama administration. Meanwhile, Russia continues to develop large oil and gas projects, and the government of Greenland is encouraging oil and gas companies to bid for exploration licenses off west and east Greenland. Exploration and development will likely continue in many parts of the Arctic as climate change contributes to reductions in sea ice; opening new sea and river routes; and reducing exploration, development, and transportation costs.

Countries such as China, India, South Korea, and European Union member states are looking to the Arctic as a crucial source of oil, gas, and minerals that could meet their energy needs in a future characterized by resource scarcity (see next chapter). Increased interest in the resource-rich continental shelf raises the prospect of disputes over Arctic sovereignty. As the world looks northward for its supplies of oil and gas, and as the ice melts, territorial challenges are provoking nations like Canada and Russia to reassert their claims over their northern hinterlands. The Northwest Passage, for example, is not recognized as Canadian waters by the United States. Instead, the United States argues the Northwest Passage is an international strait. Furthermore, there is an unresolved maritime boundary dispute between the United States and Canada, extending from the Alaska-Yukon border into the Beaufort Sea.

Russia faces similar issues over the future use of the Northern Sea Route (NSR). Once part of a major Arctic transportation system, Russian shipping in the NSR has declined, but many other countries, including the United States, China, and Japan, consider it a potentially important transportation artery. Russia is hoping to profit from international usage of the NSR through the provision of icebreaker support and transit fee income. If there were ever to be development of commercial fishing in the central Arctic Ocean, it would encourage further shipping and infrastructural investment, some of which may not be funded by the Arctic states. It would also carry with it attendant dangers for environmental pollution, search and rescue incidents, military confrontations, and fish-stock collapse if poorly regulated. The United States and Russia have a common interest in ensuring that shipping is safe and secure as it enters and leaves the Bering Strait.

Opportunities to develop new global trade links may arise as shipping routes open up across an ice-free Arctic Ocean, the oil and gas industry would benefit from lower operational costs, commercial fishing might flourish, and cruise ship tourism operators will find that access to previously remote and inaccessible places—or at least places difficult to reach because of ice conditions—will be easier. The danger, however, is that these benefits will be accrued largely by powerful trans-national corporations and foreign companies rather than by indigenous and local communities, and new shipping routes and global interest in developing extractive industries in the Arctic also raise issues of resource governance and environmental protection.

Arctic ecosystems are complex and diverse, and the nature of the seasonality and temporality of high latitude regions has enabled long-term patterns of human and non-human adaption. A warming Arctic is discombobulating for humans, plants, and animals. Having a capacity to adapt or exhibit resilience should not fool one into thinking that the Arctic's transformation is something that humans can manage let alone master.

A timely reminder of that might be the fate of the Svalbard global seed vault, which was supposed to provide a secure repository for the world's seeds in a place where permafrost was just that. In May 2017, it was reported that the permafrost underlying the seed vault had thawed, and the facility suffered flooding. The managers of the facility are now having to invest in waterproofing and further engineering works to ensure that glacial melt is drained away from the facility.

6

RESOURCEFUL ARCTIC

While awareness of the effects of climate change on the Arctic is growing and provoking anxiety over ecosystem thresholds and tipping points, circumpolar places are also increasingly presented to global audiences as dynamic, emerging, global regions that are "open for business." Depending on whom you talk to, the Arctic is no longer seen as an icy, remote space at the top of the world, but a frontier for resources, offering new markets for investment in economic initiatives and sustainable development, technological innovation, and knowledge production. This is not unprecedented given earlier rounds of resource exploitation and data collection. There is evermore interest in seeing, classifying, assessing, and extracting Arctic resources and capitalizing on the region's qualities and elemental nature, including its coldness (think about data companies locating their data servers in countries such as Iceland). At the same time, there are ventures that dream of towing icebergs to Saudi Arabia and sub-Saharan Africa. In a warming Arctic, the cold and the ice become precious resources and they encourage investment and speculation capacity in technology, communications systems, and infrastructure projects in northern regions.

Resources, whether they are animals and fish or hydrocarbons and minerals, are often tied to indigenous narratives of self-determination and aspirations for community and regional development. It is important to remember, though, that animals for indigenous peoples are not always viewed as "resources," but as non-human persons inhabiting and sharing the same surroundings. Given that land claims and self-government agreements often include ownership of subsurface resources (for example, Inuit in Nunavut have title to oil and mineral rights in about 35,000 square kilometers of the territory, and Greenland has complete ownership of its subsurface), mining and oil and gas development also seem inextricably bound up with indigenous futures.

Notwithstanding a downturn in, for example, global oil prices and the withdrawal of some oil companies from Arctic exploration since 2014 (as well as the moratorium on oil and gas activities in the Canadian Arctic), the underground worlds of the Arctic remain objects for and spaces of speculative venture. Respected assessments of resource potential carried out over the last decade or so, such as by the United States Geological Survey, suggest the Arctic could hold some of the world's largest remaining gas and oil reserves. A significant proportion of these reserves are said to lie offshore, in the shallow and biologically productive shelf seas. Such assessments make a number of circumpolar regions attractive to the oil and gas industry as the final frontier for hydrocarbon development. Most current production activity involves oil extraction onshore along the North Slope of Alaska and in western Siberia, and offshore in the Barents and Beaufort Seas. However, the Alaskan North Slope, the Mackenzie Delta of Canada, the Yamal Peninsula of Russia, and their adjacent offshore areas are known or believed to contain enormous natural gas deposits. Furthermore, exploration for oil has taken place off west Greenland in recent years.

The scientific and commercial work of marine biologists, mineral geologists, hydropower specialists, and scientists and engineers involved in geothermal and renewable energy projects will continue to be essential to the evaluation, assessment, and inventory of the Arctic's known and undiscovered

resource potential. How far and how deep this frontier of exploitation will stretch and descend will depend on the legal
and political arrangements that allow and regulate exploration
and development, the quality of the accumulated data, social
and environmental impact assessments, public participation
and community consultation in decision-making processes,
and the social and cultural attitudes about what should or
should not happen to and in the Arctic. Discussions in Canada,
for example, about the future of oil and gas activities in the
Arctic focus more on what a strong regulatory framework for
exploration and development should look like and how it will
work, rather than on expectations that there will be a permanent ban after 2021.

At the same time, though, when we talk about a resourceful
Arctic, it is important to recognize that some northern regions
of the globe are not just sites for the extraction of resources but
also for the export of expertise to other parts of the world—
whether that is Finnish know-how in energy efficiency and renewable energy moving across borders in the Nordic Arctic
region and northwest Russia, as well as water supply and sanitation projects overseen by Finnish companies in Afghanistan,
Cambodia, and Indonesia; or Greenlandic projects assessing
how glacial rock flour can revitalize depleted tropical agricultural land in Brazil or parched soils in sub-Saharan Africa.
Some indigenous businesses and companies are also major
transnational players, seeking out and investing in global
markets and enterprises.

The question of resources in the Arctic—and the nature of
those resources and the regional global networks in which
they circulate—is a complex and contested affair. Business
opportunities work both ways. In October 2018, for example,
a delegation from Greenland traveled to China to promote
Greenlandic products, including clothing, tourism, and energy
resources. This chapter explains why this is so and why we
don't all agree on what a resourceful Arctic should look and
feel like.

What is the history of resource development in the Arctic?

While climate change supposedly creates new opportunities for mining, shipping, gas, and oil extraction, as well as the development of related infrastructure in the Arctic, the reasons for such increased interest cannot be attributed to climate change alone. Regional and national economic strategies have for a long time placed emphasis on hydrocarbon development and mining projects, and this is apparent in Alaska, Canada, Greenland, and the Eurasian Arctic, or the ways other megaprojects have been part of nation-building strategies, such as hydropower in Canada and northern Fennoscandia, or nuclear power in Finland, and in Iceland with the construction of aluminum smelters.

Global connectivity is not new for the circumpolar North. As we have emphasized and illustrated throughout this book, the Arctic has long been a global region. Indigenous and local communities and the local and regional economies of the circumpolar North are not isolated from the rest of the world, even if many are relatively geographically remote. Nor have they been insulated from the effects and influences of the global marketplace or from globalizing trends. This was apparent with the financial crisis and the collapse of banks in Iceland in 2008. Tourism is now one of the biggest contributors to the contemporary Icelandic economy, and geysers, glaciers, and mountains are proving economically resourceful.

The world has ventured into, explored, exploited, influenced, and constructed ideas about the Arctic and subarctic for centuries, as well as seeing it as a resourceful space. The living and nonliving resources of the Arctic were largely bound up with the histories of European empires and national development across the circumpolar Arctic. Coal, timber, whales, seals, furs, oil and gas, and minerals such as uranium and zinc have been extracted, harvested, and processed for markets elsewhere. Fortunes were dreamed about, and some were won while others were lost in the Arctic. Mining, whaling, logging, and other activities are guides to the Arctic past, present, and future. Iron ore has proved lucrative in northern Sweden; the Russian North has been a hotspot for nickel, copper, gold, uranium, and oil and gas; Alaska's North Slope and Cook Inlet are synonymous with oil; Greenland has cryolite (which was mined for over one hundred years from the mid-nineteenth century), iron, uranium, rubies, pink sapphires, and rare earth elements; silver, diamonds, and gold, as well as iron and uranium, are found in northern Canada; and timber has been harvested in northern Finland, Sweden, Alaska, northern Canada, and Siberia. Visit places like Svalbard, and you can see for yourself how the industrial architecture of coal mining goes hand in hand with newer ventures, including tourism and a global seed vault. Commercial and indigenous fishing, sealing, and whaling activities have been pan-Arctic affairs for centuries—today, exploratory fisheries for turbot in Nunavut and in Greenland's remoter northern waters for halibut and shrimp; the development of mackerel fishing in Iceland, as well as East Greenland; and new aquaculture initiatives in Norway and Alaska illustrate how the living resources of the sea remain vital for the sustainability of many Arctic economies.

The fur trade is documented to the ninth century in the Eurasian North, and first brought northern peoples in Fennoscandia and Russia into contact with traders from regions to the south. Fur was soon sought and coveted by people living in Egypt and the Middle East, and China had become a lucrative market for furs and other products by the sixteenth century; the Chinese also extended their own trading activities and influence to Siberia.

Resources from the north, such as furs, fish, marine mammal oil, and wool were not just demanded widely as valued goods, their trade also allowed social and economic development in northern Europe, the creation of new forms of society, and the continuation of other forms of trade across the Atlantic. Parts of early Copenhagen were built from the profits of Danish trade with Iceland, while merchants from Bergen in Norway were also largely responsible for trade goods from Iceland, providing a link to the merchants of the Hanseatic League. By the 1780s the Royal Greenland Trade Company presided over a social class system in which an upper social stratum of indigenous Greenland Inuit and mixed Danish-Greenlandic families played an active role in whaling and in the trade in seal skins and blubber, as well as in the development of an emerging Greenlandic society. The Danish West Indies Company brought salted and dried fish from Nordic fishing communities to West Africa and used the fish to feed slaves traveling to the Americas. Thus, we can trace transnational connections between North Atlantic coastal communities and the growth of plantations in the Danish West Indies. Today, dried fish from Norway (or stockfish) remains central to much cuisine in West Africa and the Caribbean.

In the North Pacific, until Europeans disrupted and altered indigenous trade alliances and practices, Alaska was part of an extensive trade network with Siberia, and diverse cultures and economies were linked in a network that stretched a vast geographical distance, across Siberia and south to Korea, China, and Japan. Archeologists have found ornamental objects in Alaska that originate from Asia, including trade beads and tea, and evidence of Chinese influence on indigenous artifacts stretching back some 2,000 years. All of which serves as a reminder that the Arctic was not a peripheral space on the edge of Euro-Asian civilization but integral to wider circuits of knowledge production and exchange of peoples and trade.

Stories of vast mineral wealth, of mountains of silver and gold in Greenland and in Baffin Island and other Arctic islands, were to persist in Europe from the sixteenth century until organized mineral exploration in several regions of the Arctic in the nineteenth and twentieth centuries hinted at the realities and possibilities of actual discoveries. The extraction of cryolite began at Ivittuut in south Greenland in 1854, while a copper mine at Josva, also in south Greenland, and a coal mine at Qullissat in Disko Bay were opened during the early years of the twentieth century. In North America, the gold rush opened up Alaska and Canada's Yukon in the 1890s, bringing thousands of prospectors from all over the world hopeful of making their fortunes; while a massive industrial transformation of the Russian North and Siberia began in the 1920s with the exploitation and movement of timber, coal, and minerals to be processed in new northern industrial towns. The abundance of rivers and mountains means that power could be generated with relative ease to supply demand for the production of resources. Geography favors transportation of these materials in Russia, where they are still moved north on the great rivers of Siberia to the Arctic Ocean during the summer and convoyed by icebreaker to Murmansk, Archangelsk, and Vladivostok. Nickel, copper, and coal have been mined near Norilsk since the late 1930s, and gold, uranium, diamonds, and other minerals have been found in quantity in other parts of northern Russia and Siberia—the Mirny diamond mine in the Sakha Republic, for example, is one of the world's largest excavated holes (mining began there in 1957). Copper, nickel, and associated minerals have been mined and refined, and operations have been expanding, in Russia's Pechenga fields near the northeastern Finnish and Norwegian borders since the mid-1930s. In northern Sweden high-grade iron ore is mined at Kiruna. So vast is the operation, that the town (founded in 1900) of 18,000 people is currently being relocated some three kilometers to the east to stop it sinking into mining operations extending beneath it.

If you were to follow the resources around the Arctic, you would be taken on a fascinating journey of how objects of value get discovered, exploited, transported, consumed, and protected. You would also be made painfully aware of the difficult choices that face many Arctic communities, especially indigenous ones, eager to shape their own futures in a context in which anthropogenic climate change is being keenly felt.

*How are indigenous livelihoods affected by mining
and oil and gas exploration and development?*

The question of who has rights over access to resources and their exploitation has shaped historical and contemporary relations between indigenous peoples and Arctic states, but it also frames negotiations between northern communities, indigenous governments, and extractive companies. For many indigenous communities, the question is often not whether extractive industries should or should not be active on or near their lands, but how well they are consulted, how extraction proceeds in the best interests of people and environment, and how communities will benefit.

In Alaska, since oil first began flowing through the 800-mile long Trans-Alaska Pipeline from Prudhoe Bay on the state's Arctic North Slope in 1977, oil revenues have supplied about 85% of the Alaskan state budget. Oil has also transformed the social, cultural, and economic landscape of much of the region within the borders of the North Slope Borough, which is home to some 7,400 people, the majority of whom are Iñupiat. While there have been many benefits to indigenous communities in northern Alaska, especially through the work of regional corporations, including jobs, investment in schools, and improved medical care, oil infrastructure and development have environmental and social impacts. With production from Prudhoe Bay having peaked some years ago, and demand for energy in the United States increasing, the search continues for viable alternatives to the oil produced from these vast reserves.

Since 2001, Alaska has seen a new surge in exploration for oil and gas in underexplored areas of the state, including several parts of the interior and the Alaska Peninsula. The Arctic National Wildlife Refuge (ANWR) is also one of the last regions of the US Arctic (and ANWR's Coastal Plain is the only region of the North Slope) not open to oil and gas development. To the west and north of the Refuge, the Alaskan state government and US federal government are pursuing leasing programs in the National Petroleum Reserve-Alaska (NPRA) and in the Alaskan Beaufort Sea. A major report carried out by the Committee on Cumulative Environmental Effects of Oil and Gas Activities on Alaska's North Slope showed that more than 1,000 square kilometers of northern Alaska have been transformed into a vast industrial zone. Ongoing leasing activities and advances in oil recovery technologies on the North Slope and in the Beaufort Sea mean a substantial increase in the area of northern Alaska open for exploration and development.

Alaska's North Slope Borough is cited as a positive example of what can happen when Arctic residents have opportunities to capture some of the economic benefits from industrial development, both through employment and corporate investments. Benefits in the form of improved public infrastructure, educational services, and healthcare can be significant. Trade-offs can be decreased where communities are afforded adequate participation in, as well as authority over, development planning and operation strategies. Yet oil development—no matter how much prosperity it may bring to a region—also brings its own dilemma of how best to balance the economic benefits with major social changes and cultural impacts. For the Iñupiat of the North Slope, bowhead whales and other marine mammals are significant sources of food, and are also of cultural and spiritual importance, but they are affected by oil and gas activity. Noise from exploratory drilling and seismic exploration in the Beaufort Sea, for example, has disturbed bowhead whale migration routes. Oil spills from marine transportation or offshore oil platforms cause ecological damage, particularly in ice-covered Arctic waters.

How does oil development entail different visions of the Arctic?

Oil and gas development often leads to conflict between and within communities and different stakeholders with different visions for the Arctic. This is illustrated well by Alaska's ongoing debate about oil development on the coast of ANWR. Situated in northeast Alaska, ANWR was established in 1960, with additional lands set aside in 1980. Since the 1980s, the oil industry has lobbied for access to oil resources within ANWR, while environmentalists campaign for it to remain a protected wilderness. Supporters of opening ANWR to oil drilling include not just industry but also Republican representatives in the US government, and Iñupiat communities and businesses and labor associations. With the production levels of other American oil fields decreasing, ANWR's development remains ever-more appealing and urgent for some. Proponents suggest that the United States relies too heavily on foreign (especially Middle Eastern) oil imports, and that this dependence creates an undesirable relationship with countries that harbor terrorists. They urge that benefits should be reaped by Americans and employ the rhetoric of freedom. Such a view has the support of the American Legion, as well as other veterans' organizations. They value economic independence, hard won by US troops over the years, and see reliance on Middle Eastern oil as a threat. ANWR has thus becomes an issue of national security as well as an environmental concern.

Iñupiat communities and organizations in northern Alaska look to resource development as a source of jobs, schools, and other opportunities. The Gwich'in who live on the southern boundaries of ANWR and rely heavily on the migratory Porcupine caribou herd for their subsistence, however, are opposed to development. The herd calves in lands along the coastal plain that would be developed should ANWR be opened up to industry, and the Gwich'in (along with environmental groups) fear that significant harm may come to the herd should their traditional calving grounds be altered.

Environmental groups employ imagery and rhetoric that attempts to evoke an ideal of wilderness. Utilizing graphics of caribou, polar bears, mountains, and streams, and words such as "pristine," "untouched," and "undisturbed," helps them attract sympathy and support. They appeal to citizens to become active in protecting ANWR's wilderness from industry. Alaskan residents in support of development argue that the idea of an untouched wilderness is false (it has been inhabited and utilized by humans for thousands of years) and this mistaken notion is harmful to the people who reside there.

What are we left with then is something that often angers local communities in the north; an abiding sense that their everyday socioeconomic needs are being trumped by global appeals to protect the Arctic as wilderness, which in itself reveals a willful misunderstanding of the region's connections to global extractive and trading economies. The growing interest in Arctic resources also contributes to a redefinition or reimagining of the Arctic, such as a return to thinking about it as a frontier or extractive periphery.

For some time, it has been assumed by petro-geologists, oil and gas companies, and politicians that much of Canada's undeveloped oil and gas potential lies in its northern Arctic and subarctic areas. Extensive seismic surveys were carried out in the 1960s and 1970s on both land and of the seabed. The Northwest Territories (NWT) and Nunavut host an estimated 33% of Canada's remaining conventionally recoverable resources of natural gas and 25% of the country's remaining recoverable light crude oil. About half of these resources lie in the western Arctic, and so are strategically located north of existing infrastructure and energy hubs in the western provinces of Alberta and British Columbia. There are additional potential reserves in the Yukon Territory.

In recent years, the most ambitious, but also the most controversial, mega-project development plan in northern Canada has been the Mackenzie Gas Project (MGP), which, as originally proposed by Imperial Oil and its proponent partners, would have seen the development of three gas fields in the Mackenzie Delta and the construction of a pipeline south to northern Alberta, where it would have connected to existing pipeline infrastructure. Although Canada's federal government gave approval to the project proponents to develop it

in 2010, following six years of review, the MGP stalled somewhat because of global gas prices as well as the development
of hydraulic fracturing elsewhere in North America. The
prospects that Mackenzie Delta gas could be shipped out of
the region in the form of liquified natural gas (LNG) rather
than through a pipeline also changed the state of play over the
MGP. In December 2017, Imperial announced to the Canadian
government that the project's proponents had dissolved their
joint-venture partnership and that it would not go ahead because the costs were now too high. Much of the projected and
anticipated exploration of the potential of the western Arctic,
including elsewhere in the Mackenzie Valley, in the Beaufort
Sea, and in the western High Arctic islands, had been seen
as contingent on the commitment to build the MGP, raising
questions about future prospects.

Land claims and indigenous self-government settlements
have allowed the development of indigenous business
models, and many northern communities are now themselves   .
involved in extractive industries. For example, when the US
government settled land claims with the indigenous peoples
of Alaska in 1971, thirteen regional Alaska Native corporations
were established under the Alaska Native Claims Settlement
Act (ANCSA). Today a number of these corporations are involved in some way in the oil and gas industries. The Arctic
Slope Regional Corporation, for example, has a business portfolio that includes indigenous-owned and run oil and gas
companies, while Doyon Ltd. and Cook Inlet Region Inc. both
provide oilfield support services.

Comprehensive land claims settled in Canada in the 1980s
and 1990s have also provided business opportunities for the
participation of northern communities in resource development, and a variety of indigenous-owned companies operate
from places such as Inuvik in the Mackenzie Delta, including
those run by the Inuvialuit Development Corporation, which,
for example, has one-third ownership (with AltaGas Services
Inc. and Enbridge Inc.) in wells, processing facilities, and

pipelines further south. The MGP had promised a focus on local indigenous involvement in Canada's Northwest Territories, as was recommended in the Berger Inquiry when the project was first assessed during the 1970s.

The MGP's proponents included the Aboriginal Pipeline Group (APG), a business consortium established and led by Aboriginal groups in the Northwest Territories. The APG had the right to own one-third of the pipeline under an agreement signed with the Mackenzie Delta Producers Group. The MGP included initiatives to help identify and satisfy the training needs of northern residents to work in oil and gas, while the Northwest Territories Oil and Gas Aboriginal Skills Development Strategy aimed to provide training for Aboriginal people to find employment in the oil and gas industry. While public hearings revealed significant indigenous opposition to the project—with many people concerned about the impacts on their communities and on the environment; wildlife; and traditional hunting, trapping, and fishing practices—the APG's involvement also illustrated how a resourceful Arctic could mean economic prosperity, as well as greater autonomy and self-government for some indigenous communities based on extractive industries.

Who is investing in Arctic resources?

In Russia, energy mega-projects such as Prirazlomnoye (1989), Shtokman (1988), and Tsentralno-Olginskaya-1(2017) are found in an arc of activity stretching from the Barents Sea to the Laptev and Kara Seas. The Shtokman initiative has involved vast infrastructure investment, multiple partners, and three development phases. It suffered delays because of technical difficulties and a drop in demand in gas from European consumers. More recently, Russian energy planning is also factoring in broader geopolitical considerations, including ensuring that Arctic gas is transported across pipeline networks such as Nord Stream 2, which envisages a supply route from Russia to Germany along the Baltic Sea.

Until the imposition of sanctions by the European Union and the United States in July 2014, Russian operators needed access to western technical expertise. The sanctions include a ban on the transfer of technology for deep drilling and equipment necessary for the development of Arctic shelf resources. In September 2015, the China Oilfield Services Limited (COSL) signed an agreement with Rosneft to initiate two exploratory wells in the Sea of Okhotsk in the Russian Far East.

The Russian Arctic shelf is estimated to hold as much as $20 trillion worth of oil and gas. Russian energy strategy is predicated on the offshore Arctic providing up to 30% of the country's oil production by 2050. The effect of post-Crimea sanctions and falling oil prices, however, has created opportunities for others, such as the Export-Import Bank of China; and the China Development Bank, to provide credit support for Russian natural gas development and the Chinese sovereign fund, the Silk Road Fund, has also invested in the onshore Yamal Peninsula LNG project. The Yamal gas plant is expected to be fully operational in 2020 and should supply 85% of total gas production in the country. While European and US sanctions unquestionably did hurt the Russian oil and gas sectors, they did not hinder Russian crude oil and gas production. The ice-resistant and expanding capacity of the Prirazlomnaya offshore oil platform is world-leading and illustrates well that it would be foolish to underestimate Russia as a long-term Arctic energy player.

Global political changes, sovereignty and security issues, resource demands, and growing energy needs strongly influence the patterns and rates of resource extraction planned from the world's high latitudes. For example, much of the projected oil and gas development in northern Alaska and northern Canada was based on an assumption of strong market demand in the United States. Since the 1970s, domestic energy production in Alaska has proven popular with successive US administrations because of the potential to reduce energy dependencies with Middle Eastern suppliers. The shale gas revolution in the Lower 48 has been a game changer, and the United States' need to import energy has dropped. As American investment and interest has waned, China is now investing in both Alberta's oil sands industry and Russian Arctic energy projects. By contrast, a number of EU countries are eager to reduce their dependency on Russian energy sources and are encouraging energy diversification, including the promotion of green energy sources.

Counterintuitively, oil-rich Saudi Arabia is in ongoing discussions with Russia regarding possible investment in Arctic LNG projects. The two countries are also talking about other LNG projects around the world they might co-invest in. The rationale for Saudi Arabia lies in the fact that Russia is set to become the world's largest LNG producer, and Saudi demand for natural gas remains high. Although the country is a natural gas producer, domestic consumption continues to rise despite being the eighth-largest producer in the world. Russian gas would provide an insurance policy of sorts if Saudi gas production cannot continue to meet domestic needs in the future. The discussions are also informed by regional geopolitical dynamics as both countries have a shared interested in restraining the influence of Iran in oil and gas markets. Arctic oil and gas production and consumption reveals, as we can see, a global enterprise of networks, markets and geopolitical actors, partners, and relationships.

What are exclusive economic zones, and how do they work?

Increased interest in the resource-rich continental shelf raises the prospect of disputes over Arctic sovereignty. As the world looks northward for its supplies of oil and gas, territorial challenges have provoked nations, like Canada and Russia, to reassert their claims over their northern hinterlands.

International maritime law, specifically the United Nations Convention on the Law of the Sea (UNCLOS), should continue to provide an important framework for Arctic maritime matters including resource extraction. None of the five Arctic Ocean coastal states, including the non-signatory United States, dispute their respective sovereign rights within the exclusive economic zones (EEZs). The EEZs, under UNCLOS, extend some 200 nautical miles outwards from state coastlines. Coastal states are granted rights to do certain things in their EEZs, including explore, exploit, conserve and manage natural resources on the seabed and superjacent waters. There can be some friction as to how far sovereign rights extend beyond that 200-nautical-mile point (specifically around submarine and seabed rights to extended continental shelves), especially in maritime zones where the rights of one coastal state overlaps with another. However, the waters beyond the EEZs are international waters, and the central Arctic Ocean is a global common. Other parties such as China and the European Union are entitled to express an interest in the management of those international waters. None of which should imply that either conflict and/ or cooperation in the maritime Arctic is inevitable—there is an international legal framework (UNCLOS) in place to guide interactions and negotiations.

Fortunately, the resource potential of the Arctic Ocean seabed appears to be richest in the undisputed EEZs of the five Arctic Ocean coastal states. So, in terms of sovereignty issues, we do not expect arguments let alone conflict over resource rights. In the future, fishing and shipping in and around the central Arctic Ocean might be more troublesome because this area will require international cooperation. But as we discussed in the previous chapter, the signing of an agreement to prohibit commercial fishing in the central Arctic Ocean is a step in this direction. And, in general, if sea ice becomes less of a barrier to mobility, then Arctic states such as Canada and Russia will feel ever-more inclined to increase investment in surveillance capabilities; and if there are greater numbers of vessels operating in the Arctic Ocean, then this will in turn place more stress and strain on harboring and search and rescue facilities. It is important to emphasize that vast areas of the Arctic Ocean are still not mapped and surveyed to a standard comparable with other seas and oceans.

Arctic states, such as Russia, will continue to take their sovereign rights in the region extremely seriously. The pace and scale of resource extraction in the maritime Arctic will depend on a gamut of factors including world resource demand, pricing, and appropriate investment in cold weather technology. Historically, Russia has been a leading investor in icebreakers, and Finland a world leader in icebreaker technology. The development of the oblique icebreaker in recent years might be a game changer for Arctic development, as its design allows the ship to move ahead, astern, and diagonally through sea ice. One oblique icebreaker might be able to do the job previously undertaken by two, as transiting tankers require ice-free passages as wide as fifty meters. The new generation of ships are more fuel efficient and require smaller crews thanks to computerization and real-time usage of satellite data regarding sea ice conditions and prevailing weather. Drones are used routinely now for advanced surveillance missions in the Arctic and are considerably cheaper and safer than helicopters.

Russian investment in icebreakers provides a powerful clue as to its long-term commitment to the Arctic in resource, security, and sovereignty terms. In 2016, the Russian atomic shipping agency Rosatomflot unveiled a new nuclear-powered icebreaker called *Arktika*, purporting to be the most powerful in the world. There are also plans to develop new, immensely powerful nuclear and diesel-powered vessels for the Russian North. This is very much in keeping with Russian Arctic strategy to have the Northern Sea Route under its firm control so that resource-extraction (including the movement of extracted oil and gas) could be safely and securely carried out.

Can Arctic mega-projects be sustainable?

The term "sustainable" is used to mean different things. A national government might argue, for example, that mining is essential to ensure that remote and isolated communities are "sustainable" in an economic and social sense, whereas anti-mining protestors would contend that zinc and uranium mines proposed near small communities, such as Baker Lake in the western part of Nunavut, are rarely sustainable. Others point out that mining has been an important part of some Arctic economies and societies since the nineteenth century and remains key to the futures of some communities—without the Red Dog mine in northern Alaska, for example, the community of Kotzebue (about ninety miles from the mine) would be deprived of a vital source of employment and income. Closing the mine would bring into question the future of the community itself.

Colonial powers such as Britain, Denmark, the Netherlands, and Russia recognized that the Arctic was ripe for exploitation both in terms of its living and nonliving resources. Their resource strategies were anything but respectful of Arctic ecologies and communities. Arctic landscapes were punctuated by mines, and the Svalbard archipelago attracted a multinational coal-mining industry in the late nineteenth and early twentieth centuries. In the 1890s, the Klondike gold rush in Alaska and the Yukon encouraged the arrivals of thousands of prospectors and speculators. Many of those seeking their fortunes were Americans, including some who had experience of the California gold rush in the late 1840s. An economic recession in the United States during the 1890s proved a powerful catalyst for this northerly mobility. But it was also hugely disruptive to indigenous communities and their subsistence lifestyles, and to those engaged in the previously dominant fur trade. Mining also brought environmental problems and pollution. Canadian administrators were worried that an influx of American miners would weaken their sovereign authority in the far north. The creation of the Yukon as a distinct territory in the Canadian Federation in 1898 was a direct result of the gold rush and fears about American immigrants overwhelming local authorities in settlements like Dawson.

Subsequently, Arctic states have recognized the importance of mining to national development and security. Canada, Russia, and the United States all experienced mining booms in the late nineteenth century and revised their plans for administrating and investing in their respective northerly regions. With mining projects comes investment in infrastructure development (such as roads, airstrips, and ports) and employment and educational/training opportunities for both incomers and local communities. Mining presents challenges and opportunities for local, national, and extra-regional parties. While mining in the Arctic often attracts the ire of outside actors who decry the violation of Arctic ecosystems, some local communities might see it as essential for their long-term cultural and economic sustainability. Mining might offer the appealing prospect of further self-determination even if local communities are well aware that the exploitation of fossil fuels and strategic minerals, such as uranium, carries with it toxic legacies and consequences for global climate change.

At a national scale, Arctic states such as Canada and Russia continue to understand mining as strategically significant and indeed vital to their countries' future economic trajectories. Recent Arctic and northern strategies make this crystal-clear. In Russia's case, the 2008 Arctic strategy described the Arctic as a "resource base" for the future welfare of the country in the twenty-first century, and Canada's northern development plans assume mining will be integral. In the Canadian document, *Our North, Our Heritage, Our Future*, it is claimed, "Mining activities and major projects such as the Mackenzie Gas Project are the cornerstones of sustained economic activity in the north and the key to building prosperous Aboriginal and Northern communities." Within official public documentation, maps are playing a prominent role in highlighting where mineral deposits might be for future exploitation, but the demise of the MGP also illustrates how optimism about some projects can be short-lived.

Knowing where mineral potential might lie does not mean that mining will be economically sustainable. Low energy prices tend to deter investment, and countries, such as Russia, have vast areas to negotiate, requiring long-term investment in infrastructure, subsidies, and security. Historically, Russia has been very reluctant to open its northern territories to outside partners citing security concerns, and this in itself can make investment and development politically unsustainable as international actors might be reluctant to invest further in mining projects. There has been international engagement in relation to some hydrocarbon projects in the Russian Arctic, but these were affected by the imposition of sanctions against Russia following the annexation of Crimea in 2014 and ongoing instability in eastern Ukraine.

Mining can also be deeply controversial within Arctic communities. It can be and is divisive precisely because the changes can be unpredictable and uneven in terms of changing lives. Mining might bring more education, training, and infrastructure investment; but it also brings the prospect of migrant workers, social and environmental disruption, and worries about the long-term consequences for local ecologies and communities. National governments might also be eager to promote mining projects because of their own agendas shaped by business, commerce, security, and sovereignty rather than an appreciation of local and regional concerns and circumstances.

Mines are not only opened, they are also closed and need to undergo a process of remediation. The consequences for local communities can be devastating as a local source of employment and revenue generation simply disappears. Some plans for mining have been rejected by local communities such as a gold mine in the northern Norwegian region of Finnmark, near Kautokeino, in 2015 because of concerns about its environmental consequences. Since the introduction of the Finnmark Act of 2005, Norwegian Sámi have enjoyed far greater autonomy over land and subsurface exploitation in Arctic Norway.

The ability of local communities to comment, contest, shape, and even block mining projects varies across the Arctic. As mining is often seen as a strategic activity, it is caught up with other agendas relating to security, sovereignty, and stewardship; and sustainability might be relegated to a secondary consideration.

In Greenland, the national government, which is now in control of subsurface rights (once held by Denmark), is often caught up in messy mining politics. Greenland is often cited as a treasure house of minerals from rare earths to uranium, rubies, gold, copper, and silver. The deposits at Kuannersuit (Kvanefjeld) in southern Greenland are believed to contain up to 2 million metric tons of rare earth minerals, and thus if exploited offer a counterbalance to the global production dominance enjoyed by Chinese producers. China controls around 95% of the world's rare earth metal market and the United States imports over 90% of its domestic needs from China, principally to satisfy the smartphone market.

Mining is widely regarded as essential to political and economic strategies that drive Greenland's ambitions for possible future independence from Denmark forward. Yet, as we pointed out, local communities that would be directly affected by mining projects complain that consultation and impact assessments can be cursory and inattentive to local concerns about access to land, possible pollution, and the consequences, say, of migrant workers living close to small settlements. So, what might appear to be important for national sustainability, might end up producing pockets of local unsustainability.

One of the most controversial proposals has been an aluminum smelter proposal close to the town of Maniitsoq on the west coast, where Chinese workers were going to be invited by the company Alcoa to undertake the construction work in 2012. The involvement of "foreign workers" provoked a great deal of heated discussion not only about the impact of a large number of economic migrants but also the manner in which the municipal authorities and the government in Greenland approved the idea of the importation of cheap labor for mega-project development.

While there have been ongoing controversies about mining in Greenland, the government of Greenland approved a pre-hearing phase for the Kuannersuit uranium project being led by Australian company Greenland Minerals and Energy (GME), while Ironbark, another Australian mining enterprise, was granted a production license in December 2016 to develop a zinc and lead mine at Citronen Fjord in Peary Land in the far north of the country. Overall, there are four larger mining projects currently being considered and/or in development with many more mining sites being evaluated. One of the greatest challenges facing Greenland's government is how to regulate an expanding mining industry in a country with limited resources and staffing. At the same time, it needs to address local and, indeed, extraterritorial concerns that mining projects do not show sufficient evidence of consultation and evaluation of environmental impact.

In Iceland, the construction of hydropower dams and the power of the international aluminum industry have led to public dissatisfaction with government decisions to allow companies such as Alcoa, Rio Tinto Alcan, and Century Aluminum Corp. construct major smelters. While such projects create opportunities for local employment, civic action groups and national and international NGOs continue to campaign about the impact such development, along with geothermal energy and other forms of industrial development, has on the environment. Such opposition—expressions of which are found in Andri Snær Magnason's book (and film) *Dreamland* and the "Saving Iceland" network's website—also often accuses Icelandic authorities of "selling" Iceland and allowing multinational corporations to turn Iceland's wild places into neoliberal landscapes. Even in countries like Canada, which has a strong regulatory and environmental assessment process, some communities argue that they have not been consulted by companies about proposed projects. For example, in summer 2017, the Clyde River hunters' association won a successful case in the Supreme Court of Canada; the court's ruling agreed that the Baffin Island community had not been consulted adequately before the National Energy Board gave approval for a Norwegian consortium to carry out seismic testing for oil in waters off the east coast of Nunavut, that Inuit rights had not been considered, and that local concerns about the possible effects of seismic activities on marine mammals and local subsistence hunting practice had been ignored.

Will the Arctic become a hotspot for renewable energy?

The history of energy development in the Arctic is one characterized by surges of investment and abandonment, uncertain costs, and political determination to bring things to fruition. Public opinion across the Arctic region is divided over future energy development, and plans to exploit the North American Arctic have stalled because of high costs and demands by indigenous communities to be properly consulted over any energy projects. Large-scale projects are capital intensive, and while international demand for natural resources, including oil, gas, metals, timber, and fish, is not likely to diminish, the Arctic is one of the most demanding places in the world to operate. Further investment in infrastructure will be a prerequisite for future development.

The development of the energy sector in the Arctic will continue in Russia and Norway given their investment in infrastructure and perceived geopolitical importance of the region. The Energy Information Agency predicts that global energy demand will increase to around 720 quadrillion BTU up from 510 in 2010. Whether other areas of the Arctic become resource hotspots, such as Greenland, will depend on a host of factors, some of which will be out of the control of governments however politically supportive they may be.

Within the Arctic, we are likely to see more investment made in renewable energy sources; in particular wind energy projects will be developed in some places to replace expensive and polluting diesel generation. Alaska provides an interesting example of what is possible. Smaller communities around the state use hybrid energy systems involving wind, solar, and/or hydropower. Grants, loans, and political pressure from those affected communities proved vital to secure state and federal funding for the switch from diesel to renewable energy systems. And what has made such investment even more attractive is the capacity of harsh winters to block the supply of diesel shipments to coastal communities. In November 2011, the small Alaskan settlement of Nome was severely isolated by severe weather and sea ice. A Russian tanker eventually made it to the community in January 2012 and resupplied it with over 1 million gallons of fuel used for heating and power. The US Coast Guard created a path through the sea ice for the tanker in a well-publicized displayed of US-Russian cooperation (before sanctions and the Crimea/Ukraine crisis). As shortages mounted, there was even talk that diesel might have to be flown to the settlement, but that would have required hundreds of flights and was judged impractical.

While Alaska is a hotspot for renewable energy transition, elsewhere in the North American and European Arctic renewables are being promoted as not only more sustainable but also resilient insofar that communities are not dependent on diesel transportation from elsewhere. The Arctic in the future is going to see ever-more investment in renewable energy for cost, environmental, and logistical reasons. Nordic countries are likely to be at the vanguard given the geothermal generation in Iceland and hydropower development in Norway. The North Atlantic energy project is exploring how countries/islands such as Greenland and the Faroe Islands could further showcase renewable energy development. A more sustainable Arctic is possible.

7

THE GLOBAL ARCTIC

The term "global Arctic" has gained traction in recent years as a shorthand term for a region in transition. We have spoken at length about climate change and resource speculation and their cumulative effects are part of this accounting for change. Another aspect of all of this is a sense in which the Arctic can no longer be viewed as insulated and isolated from global economic and political networks. We use terms like globalization to convey a sense of how the world has become more integrated than ever before. It is harder and harder to be off-grid and disconnected from these integrating forces.

The discovery of microplastics frozen in sea ice is one of the most telling illustrations of how interconnected the Arctic is with the rest of the globe. Since the 1950s, plastics have reached everywhere. They are indicative of our human impact on the earth's ecosystems. Microplastics travel via rivers, oceans, and air. As they migrate through oceans and atmosphere, they pick up along the way persistent organic pollutants (POPs) and pathogens. Microplastics originating from the Northeast United States end up in the Barents Sea and infiltrate living organisms and food chains across the Arctic region.

In spring 2018, scientists from Germany's Alfred Wegener Institute gathered samples from several areas of the Transpolar Drift, which is a major Arctic Ocean current that transports sea ice from the Laptev Sea and East Siberian Sea toward the Fram

Strait. They found that sea ice in the central Arctic Ocean is not only acting as a repository of microplastics originating in Siberian waters and the Pacific Ocean "garbage patch," but it is also moving and transporting them to areas previously free of plastics, such as the Arctic seabed. A global Arctic means dealing with the pollution of others. The 1980s brought this point home through the discovery of POPs in the bodies of human communities in the Arctic. So, while not unique, it further reinforces that there are parts of the global Arctic that many who live there would not care for.

"Global Arctic" is a term of convenience. But it captures well what is at stake—a region of the world, once comparatively isolated, is no longer so.

What is the global Arctic?

The presence of microplastics in the central Arctic Ocean is a useful segue into a wider debate about how the Arctic has been and continues to be globalized. The Arctic is bearing the brunt of global warming, and these effects have the potential to trigger a series of tipping points, which, in turn, scientists worry, could irreversibly alter the balance of the earth's system, at least as it prevailed during the last 10,000 years of the Holocene. Alternatively, as we have discussed, a warming Arctic appears to be opening new, unprecedented opportunities for oil, gas, and minerals exploration and exploitation, thus offering yet another lease to life to fossil-fueled industrial civilization. Finally, the Arctic is an object of interest to "great powers" as the United States, China, Russia, and India, alongside the EU and other organizations such as NATO, invest, deploy, and co-operate with one another in energy projects, shipping, science, resource extraction, and military training respectively.

The idea of a global Arctic sits awkwardly with the national histories and geographies of northern circumpolar regions. Terms such as the "Canadian Arctic," the "American Arctic," and the "Russian Arctic" retain a powerful purchase and bring to the fore national experiences and memories of settler colonialism and national usage of land, ice, and snow by resident communities. The Arctic remains a contact zone where indigenous peoples continue to campaign over land claims, access to basic infrastructure, and demand greater autonomy, consultation, and social justice. Past mining projects, as we discussed in the previous chapter, for instance, connect to contemporary and even future struggles for a different sort of Arctic.

The Arctic Council is often described as a trailblazing model of global governance by those who champion its work. The term "global Arctic" has been used by its supporters to highlight how the Arctic becomes a net exporter—informing wider global communities and opinion formers about how they might build cooperation and crucially involve indigenous peoples as permanent participants.

How and where the term "global Arctic" gets deployed in practice is a double-edged affair. The annual Arctic Circle event—a large conference hosted in Reykjavik each October—is explicitly designed to promote, discuss, and implement a global Arctic. In October 2018, it hosted a glitzy "China night," which showcased the country's culture, while Chinese officials spoke of their desire to invest and develop the Arctic. Conversely, when indigenous peoples speak about seal product-export bans and transboundary pollution, the intermingling of the global with the Arctic is unwanted and regrettable.

The relationship between the global and the Arctic is also something that attracts policing and vigilance. Arctic states have been eager, as global interest in the region has grown, to ensure that those who are said to represent the "global," such as Britain, Germany, France, China, South Korea, and Japan, as well as NGOs and environmental groups, are respectful of their sovereignty and sovereign rights over Arctic land, sea, ice, and air. The 2008 Ilulissat Declaration was a deliberate attempt by the five Arctic Ocean coastal states to ensure a common approach to the management of their areas of interest in the Arctic Ocean. The role of observers in the Arctic Council is indicative of how the Arctic states and the permanent participants are committed to reinforcing their sovereignty and security rights and wishes. An observer manual to the Arctic Council adopted at the Kiruna Ministerial in 2013, and updated again in 2016, reminds observers that they must play a supportive (and respectful) role in the Arctic Council.

Indigenous communities in the Arctic have also appealed to the global in the form of the UN Declaration on the Rights of Indigenous Peoples (UNDRIP) to globalize the Arctic. In this case, the entanglement of the Arctic and the global is a deliberate one; designed to highlight their rights and the responsibilities of nation-states to treat their indigenous peoples with respect and dignity, and attend to outstanding land claims and natural resource arrangements. Indigenous peoples are global actors in their own right, with cultural, economic, and political portfolios. You only have to look at the interests of Native corporations in Alaska to get a strong sense of global interactions. The Bristol Bay Native Corporation, for example, has over 9,000 shareholders and includes interests from as far afield as New Zealand.

The take-away point about the term "global Arctic" is to be mindful of what Doreen Massey termed "power-geometry." The global Arctic is a beguiling sort of term. It sounds reasonable, even timely. But the terms "global" and "Arctic" mean different things to different people.

Why does a warming Arctic contribute to a global Arctic?

Former US president Barack Obama opened the Global Leadership in the Arctic: Cooperation, Innovation, Engagement and Resilience (GLACIER) conference in Alaska, in September 2015, with the following observations:

> The point is that climate change is no longer some far-off problem. It is happening here. It is happening now.

Climate change is already disrupting our agriculture and ecosystems, our water and food supplies, our energy, our infrastructure, human health, human safety— now. Today. And climate change is a trend that affects all trends, economic trends, security trends. Everything will be impacted.

Delivered approximately three months prior to the Paris meeting of the parties to the UNFCCC (United Nations Framework Convention on Climate Change), the conference reiterated a view of global climate change and its relationship to the Arctic, which was established by earlier scientific reports. What was also notable about the GLACIER conference was how the local circumstances of northern and indigenous communities in Alaska were linked to future global economic, ecological, and geopolitical world-orders. Representatives from Arctic Council observer countries, such as the UK, China, India, and Singapore, attended the conference, as did an array of officials and people attached to state, non-state, and intergovernmental organizations and corporations.

The Arctic Council has been an active player in research on climate change around the entire stretch of the circumpolar North. It has commissioned assessments on climate pollutants and has worked on making further environmental agreements possible among the Arctic states post-2009. The United States made climate change a key area of its chairmanship of the Arctic Council (2015–2017), tackling concerns such as the effects of black carbon—a major focus given its ability to disrupt the albedo (a measure of the reflectivity of the earth's surface) of Arctic sea ice and ecosystem dynamics. In short, and as we have discussed in our previous chapters, less ice means more heat from the sun is absorbed by land and water, and widespread ice loss carries with it implications for regional and global warming trends.

Under the Paris Climate Agreement, there are further opportunities for the Arctic states to show leadership and use "adaptation communications" to share good practices and ensure that indigenous knowledge is incorporated into regional, national, and circumpolar policies. Greenlandic leaders warned that the adaptation required would make it necessary for the government of Greenland to seek a "territorial opt-out" because of the importance of the oil and gas sectors and mining industry to the country's future economic development.

Much of the scientific work addressing a warming Arctic has coalesced around a number of key indicators and measurements such as maximum/minimum sea ice extent, air and sea temperatures, snow cover extent, terrestrial vegetation, and ice sheet melting trends. A good example is the Greenland ice sheet, which has attracted ever-growing concern about abnormal temperature readings taken in March 2016. Danish temperature records, dating from the 1870s, suggest that the melt season has started even earlier than the last record in May 2010. The ice melt season is defined as when there is an area of melt greater than 10% of the total ice sheet's surface. For 2016, El Niño might have been responsible for unusual warming over Greenland (the winter season of 2015–2016 was generally very mild).

One of the most reliable and insightful guides to the above is the Arctic Report Card produced and updated each year by the US National Oceanic and Atmospheric Agency (NOAA). The 2017 report concluded in bullet point form the following:

- After only modest changes from 2013–2015, minimum sea ice extent at the end of summer 2017 tied with 2007 for the second lowest in the satellite record, which started in 1979.
- Snow cover extent on land was at its lowest since 1979 and increased melting led to greater river discharge in Eurasia and North America.
- The Arctic Ocean is especially prone to ocean acidification, due to water temperatures that are colder than those farther south. The short Arctic food chain leaves Arctic

marine ecosystems vulnerable to ocean acidification events.

- Melting occurred over the Greenland ice sheet and exceptional melting was recorded in 2012 where over 50% of the ice sheet showed evidence of melting.
- Land-based vegetation and above-ground biomass has declined in productivity since 2011.

If we want a more nuanced understanding of what the Arctic in 2050 might be like, then most Arctic scientists would conclude that year-round, sustained monitoring programs are required in the region. A pan-Arctic observation network, combining traditional indigenous knowledge and polar science, is integral to realizing that strategic ambition. There are two areas of concern. First, access to the Russian Arctic is extremely patchy for historic and geopolitical reasons. Second, monitoring varies not only across time and space but also disciplinary areas (e.g., ocean monitoring compared to atmospheric observation, and summer season monitoring is far better supported than equivalent work in the long polar winter). The Arctic Observing Summit is an important milestone event, held every two years, where progress is reviewed. The Arctic Council has called on member states and observers to share information; and there are global initiatives, such as the Global Ocean Observing System, that will be significant in ensuring that information from the Arctic Ocean is sufficiently monitored, recording things like water temperature and salinity. Successful monitoring also requires capacity building in northern communities and the involvement of Arctic residents in the long-term science of the region.

All this matters to those who live and work in the diverse regions comprising the Arctic, including those involved in business and governance. Sea ice decline, especially during the summer season, will, it is widely postulated, make the Arctic more accessible to shipping, including increasing numbers of tourist vessels. In the summers of 2016 and 2017, *Crystal Serenity* traveled from Anchorage to the East Coast of the United States via the Northwest Passage. Most academic observers have, however, cautioned against the notion that Arctic shipping will automatically increase as sea ice decreases.

The melting of sea ice and thawing of permafrost, the warming of seas and oceans, and more unpredictable weather in the Arctic are just some of the factors associated with a warming Arctic. It means that the operating environment for both indigenous communities and outside interests will be challenging. Within a more resourceful context, it needs stating that achieving the ambition stipulated in the Paris Agreement, namely, to avoid more than 1.5°C of global warming, will require a substantial reduction in fossil fuel consumption. The IPCC Summary for Policy Makers stipulates that achieving such a goal would require emitting less than 1,000 gigatons of carbon from 2011 to 2050. The scale of the challenge is formidable given that it is estimated that the currently known fossil fuel reserves (excluding undiscovered potential) alone represent some 2,795 gigatons of carbon dioxide.

In June 2017, President Donald Trump announced the withdrawal of the United States from the Paris Agreement. Criticizing the accord for disadvantaging America and its strategic interests, Trump was also unhappy that the Agreement allowed countries like China to increase their greenhouse gas emissions until 2030 before asking them to make substantial cuts. Ignoring the realities of a declining coal industry in the United States and the growth of the renewable energy sector, the presidential directive was widely criticized by US cities and states such as Pittsburgh and California respectively, which have pledged to work with international partners. It remains to be seen what the United States will do more generally in the aftermath of the withdrawal, and US Arctic commentators have noted their unease with the decision given the region's exposure to global warming.

Will US-Russian relations change the global Arctic?

The election of Donald Trump in November 2016 provoked an array of commentary about how the domestic and foreign policies of the United States might change on his taking office in January 2017 onward. He is a well-known skeptic of climate change and more sympathetic to Vladimir Putin's Russia than his predecessor, Barack Obama. Members of the Trump administration have far closer personal and professional relationships with Russian industry and commerce than was the case under the Obama administration. What we don't know at this stage is whether Trump will reverse some aspects of the previous administration or simply forge a new Arctic policy based on resource extraction and closer cooperation with Russia over security matters, perhaps reversing the previous sanctions-based policies of the Obama administration.

The Obama administration, over two terms of office, achieved some recalibration of interest in the Arctic. Having inherited a presidential directive in January 2009 from the outgoing George W. Bush administration, President Obama recognized that the United States was guilty of underinvestment in northern infrastructure, including icebreaker capability. But it was not until 2013 that the administration published another statement on US Arctic policy. The National Strategy for the Arctic Region claimed, "the US is an Arctic nation" with distinct interests in Alaska and the wider Arctic region. The Strategy concluded, "We must advance U.S. national security interests, pursue responsible stewardship, and strengthen international collaboration and cooperation, as we work to meet the challenges of rapid climate-driven environment." When the United States re-assumed the chairmanship of the Arctic Council in 2015, the administration rearticulated its focus on building international cooperation and recognized that there was "One Arctic" (another way of expressing the global Arctic), which demanded that stakeholders worked closely together on areas such as climate change, environmental steward-ship, and safety in the Arctic Ocean. The chairmanship also pushed for a legally binding agreement on scientific coop-eration, which was agreed upon by the Arctic Council in May 2017.

President Trump's agenda has been very different. A new policy encouraging oil and gas development in the Arctic in-cluding Alaska and the Russian North is likely. We might also reasonably ask whether the science-based work of the Arctic Council will prevail if the experts involved in producing assessments of the state of the Arctic continue to warn about Arctic warming and advocate caution when it comes to further resource development. We expect to see a sustained push to re-verse resource extraction restrictions on ANWR and the waters off the coastline of Alaska.

The implications for defense and security in the Arctic are also uncertain. President Trump might reverse the economic sanctions against Russia and seek closer security cooperation. One project that might be revived is the joint venture between ExxonMobil and Rosneft in the Kara Sea, which was sus-pended in 2014. In a more speculative vein, the United States and Russia might find common cause and look to defend their common resource and sovereignty interests against extraterri-torial parties such as China and the European Union. Trump's support for NATO is patchy, and he might decide that his "America First" outlook is better served by working closely with Putin's Russia.

Whatever happens, Russia is not taking any chances. In the next five years, it is committed to investing in protecting the NSR and its interests in the Arctic. Investments include an Arctic drone squadron, port infrastructure, military bases, and a new generation of icebreakers and ice class pa-trol vessels, capable of handling sea ice up to three to four meters thick.

What is the Svalbard Treaty, and why is it a potential flashpoint in the Arctic?

Russia will use a combination of military and nonmilitary forces and pressures to protect its sphere of interest, it will deploy increasingly professional and well-organized special forces ("little green men") into other countries' territories, and it will defend aggressively the interests and wishes of Russian-language speakers outside the Russian Federation (or use that as pretext to act). Domestically Putin's popularity usually soars in the aftermath of such interventions—Georgia (2008), Ukraine (2014), and even recently in Syria.

It has been argued that contemporary Russian strategic thinking is predicated on the principle of "mobilization," which describes an underlying presumption that war is likely. If the international system is, as many Russian commentators believe, either unstable and/or inimical to Russian interests, then the Federation needs to prepare for crisis and instability. The Russian sphere of influence includes the "near abroad" territories of the former Soviet Union as well as the wider Euro-Asian landmass. If there is a strong likelihood of further instability, then it would make sense to ensure a state of readiness, entailing investment in military equipment, training, and infrastructure in the Arctic and elsewhere. Mobilization is not straightforward, however. The cost to the country is not insubstantial, and the Russian political and military leadership is not united on whether to commit to further investment.

The imposition of sanctions by the EU has not dented Putin's popularity, and his seizure of Crimea was regarded as justified by the Russian electorate. So, in the future, in an Arctic context, we might need to look carefully at places like Svalbard. Accessible by regular air routes from Norway and Russia, the Svalbard archipelago extends to some 60,000 square kilometers. It is about the same size as the US state of West Virginia. The largest island of Spitsbergen is permanently inhabited. Ice covers around 60% of Svalbard, and there is a total population of around 2,600 people.

Svalbard matters to Arctic geopolitics. It hosts a Russian coal-mining community of Barentsburg (the other Russian settlement of Pyramiden was abandoned in 1998 when the last coal was extracted—since then, efforts have been made to turn it into a tourist attraction). It is strategically located and acts as an entry point among the North Atlantic, Barents Sea, and Arctic Ocean. And Russia has ongoing disputes with the sovereign authority Norway over fisheries management, travel restrictions on Russian officials facing EU travel bans, and tensions regarding the interpretation of the Svalbard Treaty, including whether Norway has the right to issue oil-licensing blocks in the adjacent waters.

Ultimately Svalbard is a Norwegian territory but governed by a treaty that allows others to take an active interest in its management. The interpretation of the cornerstone of the Svalbard Treaty (originally called the Spitsbergen Treaty) could be more contentious in the future, especially if relations with Russia deteriorate. The treaty's articles set out the terms and conditions affecting the archipelago, banning "warlike purposes" but guaranteeing signatories like Russia equality of access when it comes to resource extraction.

The treaty does not make clear how Norway should exercise that sovereignty, and there have historically been disputes over how far its provisions extend over the water column and seabed. For example, Norway regards the Svalbard Treaty as covering only land and territorial sea (up to twelve nautical miles), whereas other states regard the treaty as applying to the continental shelf and fisheries zone. When Norway established a 200-nautical-mile fisheries zone in 1977, the Soviet Union saw this as a contravention of the treaty. When Norway introduced Norwegian road signs and imposed Norwegian environmental impact and health and safety standards, Russia complained that this discriminated against non-Norwegian actors present in Svalbard. Underlying Norwegian policy is a concern that unless their presence is cemented in Svalbard, then there is a danger that Russia in the future might seek to oust Norway and impose its own sovereign authority.

Contemporary Russian behaviour in Crimea and eastern Ukraine as well as the Baltic region gives some credence to these fears that a 'global Arctic' could be shaped by further geopolitical instability in the High North.

What part are Asian states playing in the global Arctic?

What makes Norway and others look on with further concern is that Russia is also developing strategic relationships with Asian states such as India and China. The impositions of sanctions against Russia following the illegal annexation of Crimea created further incentives. Cautiously, Russia has welcomed a global Arctic.

One of the most significant developments affecting the contemporary Arctic and its future is the growing role and scope of Asian states, notably China, South Korea, Japan, and Singapore. In 2009 these four states, along with India, applied for permanent observer status to the Arctic Council. The request caught the Arctic Council members by surprise, and when the Ministerial Meeting was held in Greenland in 2011, new criteria for observers was developed grounded in the expectation that observers would respect the sovereignty, sovereign rights, and jurisdiction of Arctic states and indigenous peoples. The desire to formalize further the role of observers was informed by fears that states such as China might not respect the sovereign rights of the Arctic states, and that senior Chinese officials believed that the Arctic Ocean was a global common. China's role in the South China Sea may well have strengthened the perception that it was important to ensure that new observers recognized that the maritime Arctic was not without governance and that international waters only applied to the central Arctic Ocean. At the same time, the European Union also applied for permanent observer status (which was rejected by Canada and later Russia).

The period between 2009 and 2013 was a time of institutional change for the Arctic Council, and arguably the admittance of the Asian states as permanent observers in May 2013 represented the culmination of that transformation. Arctic states and permanent participants approved their admittance. Along with the interests of Italy (and other European countries) and India, there is growing Asian involvement in Arctic regions, which has manifested in governance, science, resource development, education, and other areas such as shipping. As observers, the new members are expected to contribute to the work of the Arctic Council (even if they have little influence in Council decision-making other than contributing expertise to Arctic Council assessments); it is notable that Nordic member states were more supportive of the admission of Asian observers compared to Canada and Russia. Along with the United States, the largest Arctic Ocean coastal states were (and remain) wary of the potential role of states such as China in the midst of their ongoing negotiations regarding the limits of the outer continental shelves. This legal process is likely to be a lengthy one, and involves the United States, Canada, Russia, and Denmark/Greenland in negotiations over the delimitation of sovereign rights over the Arctic Ocean seabed.

The unease registered by Arctic states was also shared, for different reasons, by indigenous peoples/permanent participants, whose representatives expressed concern that Asian states might not be sufficiently sensitive to the rights of Arctic indigenous peoples, and that the manner in which the business of the Arctic Council might be altered by a growing interest from the global community. While the Asian observers have acknowledged the principles and values underlying the Arctic Council, their collective interest in the Arctic pivots around a series of shared concerns: the impact of climate change in the Arctic on the wider world, including near-Arctic states such as China and South Korea; the developing of transoceanic and transcontinental shipping routes and in particular the possible impact of the NSR on trade patterns; and long-term interest in securing access to Arctic energy and living resources, including fishing grounds in the Arctic Ocean. All the Asian member states are interested in polar science, and countries such as India and China conduct research in Svalbard. China established its station in 2004, and China's Polar Research Plan (2011–2015) articulated a vision for China in the Arctic, which stressed increasing scientific investment and the annual usage of their icebreaker, the *Snow Dragon,* in central Arctic Ocean scientific studies.

The long-term significance of Asian involvement in the Arctic will be felt across many sectors, including shipping, energy, and education. Some examples will convey a sense of what might be key shapers of an Arctic in 2050. China, as a major maritime nation, obtains about 50% of its GDP from international trade, and increased access to the Russian-mananged NSR (to access the NSR users must secure permission from the Russian Federation and pay for ice-breaker support) offers an alternative shipping route. China has already taken delivery of iron ore and gas condensate supplies from Norway. Chinese academics are now publishing papers examining the long-term profitability of the NSR, concluding at present that the ice-breaking tariffs imposed by Russia (as part of their regulatory authority of the NSR) coupled with overall navigation time across the Russian Arctic are the key variables. Advanced permission is needed from Russia in order to navigate through the NSR and the tariffs imposed help to fund and support the large ice-breaker fleet. By 2030, for example, it is expected that NSR trade between Norway/ Russia and East Asian markets will substantially increase in gas, dry cargo such as iron ore, and container traffic; and the Russian Integrated Development Plan for the NSR 2015–2030 assumes that the total volume of cargo trade will be equivalent to eighty million tons by 2030. Russian investment in search and rescue operations, port infrastructure, and icebreaker support is underwritten by the assumption that the NSR will be a major conduit for Russian exports to East Asia, specifically China. However, there remain substantial uncertainties regarding NSR traffic growth, including weather, transit fees, and ensuring that international operators have a simple system for liaising with relevant Russian authorities across the northern Russian coastline.

Regardless of NSR expansion, Russia is clearly invested in its further usage while China has positioned itself as an Arctic stakeholder. From defining itself as a "near-Arctic" state to encouraging collaboration with Nordic universities and research institutes, China has also worked closely with Iceland on areas of mutual interest such as shipping and energy projects. South Korea is a major shipbuilder, large natural gas importer, and investor in polar science, and it has had a scientific presence on Svalbard since 2002. Singapore's interest in the Arctic has been based on its interests in world shipping and in the development and export of technology suitable for oil and gas exploration/exploitation. Singapore and Japan are also importers of energy resources and have a keen interest in ensuring the safety and security of shipping. Japan established its science station on Svalbard in 1991 and has a long-standing interest in the Arctic and Antarctic.

There is a widespread academic consensus that the Asian states will be a growing presence in Arctic governance. The Arctic Council member states have sought to accommodate these new observers while ensuring that they in turn are respectful of Arctic states and indigenous peoples. Asian states have invested in joint initiatives involving education, training, and trade. One example is the establishment of the China-Nordic Arctic Research Centre (CNARC) at the Polar Research Institute of China in Shanghai in December 2013, some six months after the formal admittance of China and other Asian states as permanent observers to the Arctic Council. The CNARC's stated purpose is to promote academic cooperation and promote sustainable development of the Nordic Arctic region. The center has as its strategic foci: the study of Arctic climate change, Arctic resource development, and Arctic policymaking.

The accommodation of the Asian states as permanent observers within the formal architecture of the Arctic Council was considered significant for both the Asian countries and the Arctic states as well as the permanent participants. There are points of friction that may become exaggerated in the decades ahead: the Nordic states in general have benefited from Asian involvement in the Arctic, not least in terms of investment and collaborative opportunities and more so than other Arctic states and indigenous peoples in North America; the status of Arctic straits and passages might become more contentious if accessibility and patterns of usage shift; and the Asian state observers will expect to be fully involved in any discussions involving the high seas of the Central Arctic Ocean and the eventual "area" in terms of the seabed beyond the outer limits of the continental shelves of the Arctic Ocean coastal states.

One thing that should be clear is that while we use "Asia and the Arctic" as a shorthand term in conjunction with analyses titled "Asian states in the Arctic," the five Asian states themselves have distinct interests, relationships, and positions regarding Arctic states, indigenous peoples, and Arctic ecosystems and resources. There are also other Asian countries such as Thailand and the Philippines that have made their mark on some Arctic regions through investment, migration, and settlement patterns. Whether the Arctic Council membership wishes to entertain further applications from observers in the future is a moot point. Regardless of that formal decision-making process, it seems reasonable to assume that other countries will become more involved in Arctic affairs. Scientifically, countries with an established interest in the Antarctic such as Pakistan and Malaysia might wish to develop bi-polar research programs in the future.

There is also the prospect of interregional rivalries between Asian states in the Arctic arena; China, Japan, and South Korea have found cooperation challenging in many areas. China-Japan and India-China have also had difficult geopolitical relationships in maritime and mountainous border regions.

There is also variation in terms of engagement with the Arctic Council and attendance at/involvement with the working groups and task forces. In the longer term, interest in Arctic shipping will be a shared concern for the East Asian observers and that might conflict with the interests and rights of coastal states, especially Canada and Russia. Shipping and the energy sector will be the areas of greatest interest, and Asian capital and technology have potential roles to play in shaping future economic development. Notably in Greenland, the prospect of large-scale Chinese investment and labor migration did cause considerable unease and provoked public protests about size, scale, and scope of Asian investment involving Chinese companies such as China Nonferrous.

The Arctic is being renegotiated and reframed by both indigenous actors and extraregional actors, such as China, not just in symbolic or representational ways (as evidenced by terms such as "near Arctic") but also through institutional, legal, territorial, and organizational processes such as the admittance of Asian states as observers to the Arctic Council, the negotiation of trade deals, the passage of international ships through Arctic waters, and the annual meetings and symposia of a multitude of institutions and organizations designed to improve cooperation and collaboration between Asian states and Arctic states and their indigenous peoples. Terms like "Asia-Arctic" and "global Arctic" are intended to capture something of this interplay between intraregional and interregional narratives and interventions.

One thing for sure is that the global Arctic is here to stay. Russia is working with China and India over areas of mutual concern. South Korea, China, and Japan are continuing a dialogue with one another over polar matters. Iceland and other Nordic countries are eager to attract overseas business. And indigenous actors, such as the government of Greenland, are talking to Asian countries about trade and investment.

Anyone eager to understand the global Arctic would be advised to attend an Arctic Circle Assembly in Iceland.

What might the Arctic look like in 2050?

In 2014 the Norwegian Shipowners' Association, in conjunction with the Arctic Business Council, commissioned a report entitled "Arctic Business Scenarios 2020" that posited three scenarios: the oil in demand, green transformation, and refreeze scenarios. They opened their report with the following core concerns: business opportunities in key sectors such as oil, gas, mining, and fish; relationships between Arctic states and non-Arctic states such as China; global energy trends including oil pricing; and climate change and environmental regulatory structures and their overall impact on business and commerce. The report outlined the scenarios in further detail and argued that the oil in demand scenario would see the maritime Arctic take off as an oil and gas province, especially in the Barents and Kara Seas. China would be a key player in the Russian sector. Under the green transformation scenario, by way of contrast, low-carbon transition policies would diminish the prospects of oil and gas development but might instead focus interest in maritime transport/ trade routes between Europe and Asia and fisheries. Finally, the refreeze scenario addressed the possibility of regionalism rather than globalization and an Arctic where Russia is "isolated" from the West, and the West would increasingly intensify its resource development of Arctic territories and seas. Potential conflict exists over resource access and transportation through the NSR and Northwest Passage and, as we have mentioned, the archipelago of Svalbard might be a potential flashpoint if Russia and Norway clash over understandings of the Svalbard Treaty, including fisheries management in what Norway considers to be its exclusive economic zone.

The report suggested, regardless of which scenario will turn out to be more likely, that there are certain givens that will prevail in the Arctic throughout the 2020s. Energy and resource interest in the Arctic will endure even if the oil and gas sectors remain to be developed, especially in the maritime Arctic. The Arctic will continue to get warmer under conditions of climate change, and that will have implications for infrastructure and community resilience as well as accessibility on land and at sea. The Arctic's diverse regions lack adequate search and rescue facilities, and industry will be mindful of the possible effects of a disaster on the scale of Deep Horizon in the Gulf of Mexico in 2010. Russian economic development will depend on Asian investment (China, Vietnam, and possibly others such as South Korea), and Western interests will be shaped by a combination of political and economic factors, including indigenous and northern community consent and involvement. Technological developments, including drone usage, might either make navigation safer (e.g., drone surveillance of sea ice conditions) or, potentially, riskier if drones (both UAV and USV) are judged to be a security hazard by Arctic states such as Canada and Russia.

A second example of prediction would be the work associated with the Arctic Council's *Arctic Marine Shipping Assessment* (AMSA), which was published in 2009. The starting assumption of the report was that the Arctic is going to be ice-free (in the summer season) by 2040. Ongoing climate change and intensifying resource extraction are assumed to be prevalent but capable of producing different Arctic(s). The report posited four scenarios for Arctic 2040:

- Globalized frontier: The Arctic at 2040 is integrated into the world economy and is no longer a hinterland or periphery (although it is arguably already integrated).
- Adaptive frontier: The Arctic becomes globalized but at a far less intense pace and scale than suggested by the "globalized frontier." Indigenous peoples of the Arctic also demand their right to be consulted and ensure more equitable revenue sharing.
- Fortress frontier: International tension increases as resource exploitation intensifies. Marine and air access are increasingly militarized and securitized.

• Equitable frontier: Arctic governance is viewed as a model for global governance. While resource extraction continues and access to the region widens, the Arctic Council in particular retains its premier position as a forum for the promotion of consensual governance.

The scenario analysis concludes that Arctic 2040 will depend on an array of factors most of which revolve around climate change, resource development, geopolitics, and governance. There are wildcard events and factors, which could also prove decisive in shaping which scenario (or combination of scenarios) is likely to prevail. These include the role and intent of the Arctic Ocean coastal states, and their collective control of the marine Arctic; boundary disputes between Arctic states; the scale and extent of Arctic shipping; and the impact of change on Arctic ecosystems, including invasive species and sea ice loss. Not all these changes are unwelcome per se. While mackerel could be considered an invasive species in the Arctic, it is, as noted, providing the basis for new economic opportunities in Iceland and Greenland—China is investing more in mackerel fishing in east Greenland than in mining projects because of changes in commodity prices and a downturn in global demand.

In his follow-up piece for an academic journal, *Fletcher Forum for World Affairs* in 2015, Lawson Brigham (the chair of the AMSA assessment) extended his scenario analysis to Arctic 2050—another decade. Three key drivers were identified by the author: climate change, globalization, and geopolitics. He argued that by 2038 the last vestige of old and multiyear sea ice will have disappeared from the North American Arctic coastline. The Russian coastline was already sea-ice-free earlier in the current century. The central Arctic Ocean will be covered only by thinner, first-year ice by 2038. The Arctic Ocean would be similar in nature to the Baltic Sea and the Great Lakes in North America. But Arctic marine shipping, while larger in scale and scope, including transits across the central Arctic Ocean, has not revolutionized world trade patterns. Fishing intensifies and other business opportunities will take off, including tourism, and the governance of the Arctic will be fraught as Arctic states, (including a newly independent Greenland), invest heavily (possibly with the help of extra-regional allies such as China) in ensuring that their sovereign interests and rights are protected. As tensions increase elsewhere, Arctic states, non-states, and other actors work harder to ensure that the Arctic does not descend into conflict or even chaos. His conclusion is ultimately optimistic: "The Arctic states will face a more environmentally-challenged, warming globe, and a less stable world to the south. In fact, it is entirely plausible that the Arctic will remain relatively peaceful in the last half of the twenty-first century, while the rest of the world experiences much greater stress and tension."

While not dissenting entirely from that optimistic view, other American observers offer a slightly more jaundiced view of what Arctic 2050 might look like. Laurence Smith, a geographer at the University of California Los Angeles argues in his book, *The New North: The World in 2050*, that by 2050 the marine Arctic will be navigable to moderately ice-strengthened vessels (Polar Class 6) over the North Pole and common open-water (OW) ships via the NSR in the late summer season (i.e., September). Underwritten by climate-modeling work, this assessment does not have to assume anything geopolitical or legal, such as whether the United States becomes a party to the UN Convention on the Law of the Sea (UNCLOS), or whether the United States and Canada manage to resolve their differences over the international legal status of the Northwest Passage. While they acknowledge that trends in Arctic shipping are not just shaped by environmental change, their conclusion is that the International Maritime Organization's (IMO) Polar Code (which entered into force in January 2019) is timely given the prospect of OW vessels traversing the central Arctic Ocean. The Polar Code contains mandatory requirements for crews and ships operating in polar waters and is designed to ensure that shipping remains safe and secure. New shipping routes across the central Arctic Ocean will sail beyond the exclusive economic zones of coastal states, such as Canada and Russia.

Arctic states will, it is thought by informed commenters such as Laurence Smith, be central to future global economic and political affairs primarily because of the region's resource potential; population demographics; trade; and ongoing climate change causing, among other things, mass species migration toward the higher latitudes, including birds, fish, and plants. Across the Arctic, we already have evidence of what some communities, including northern mining towns, are doing to mitigate further climate change. If the mitigation strategies were successful, might we see a reversal of depopulation in some parts of the Arctic and even population growth in the future?

There is a long history of architectural experimentation in the Arctic, some of which may become ever more relevant in the wake of further environmental and geopolitical change. If Smith's view is right that northern territories and peoples will be increasingly central to the future of a warming and more populated world, then we are likely to see further innovation in human settlement and community resilience.

For those who live and work in the Arctic, let alone those who lives will be touched by the Arctic, we have plenty of work to do in trying to understand better the role and scope of feedback loops, direct and indirect effects, contingencies, and interaction effects that will shape the Arctic's relationship with the wider world and beyond. We may not be able (or even wish) to predict as much as we would like, but the Arctic warns us that humanity will need to be ever-more vigilant and anticipatory for what lies ahead of us.

We need to deal with an Arctic undergoing profound state-change. It will require the acquisition of new mental maps and dispositions willing and able to cope with surprise. It is in that spirit that the World Meteorological Organization organized a "Year of Polar Prediction" (2017–2019). As Secretary-General of the WMO Petteri Taalas noted:

> Because of teleconnections, the poles influence weather and climate conditions in lower latitudes where hundreds of millions of people live. Warming Arctic air masses and declining sea ice are believed to affect ocean circulation and the jet stream, and are potentially linked to extreme phenomena such as cold spells, heat waves and droughts in the northern hemisphere.

The implications for planet earth are extraordinary. The Arctic matters more than ever and the comparative isolation of the region is well and truly over. This book has sought to explain why, how, and where.

FURTHER READING

General Readings

Anderson, A. *After the Ice: Life, Death and Geopolitics in the New Arctic* (Washington, DC: Smithsonian Books 2009).

Bravo, M. *North Pole: Nature and Culture* (London: Reaktion 2019).

Chester, S. *The Arctic Guide: Wildlife of the Far North* (Princeton and Oxford: Princeton University Press 2016).

Cone, M. *Silent Snow* (New York: Grove Press 2005).

Dodds, K., and M. Nuttall. *The Scramble for the Poles* (Cambridge: Polity 2016).

Emmerson, C. *The Future History of the Arctic: How Climate, Resources and Geopolitics Are Reshaping the North and Why It Matters to the World* (London: Vintage 2011).

Jensen, L. C., and G. Hønneland, eds. *Handbook of the Politics of the Arctic* (Cheltenham: Edward Elgar 2015).

McCannon, J. *A History of the Arctic: Nature, Exploration and Exploitation* (London: Reaktion 2012).

McGhee, R. *The Last Imaginary Place: A Human History of the Arctic World* (Ottawa: Key Porter Books and Canadian Museum of Civilization 2004).

Nuttall, M., ed. *Encyclopedia of the Arctic* (London: Routledge 2004).

Nuttall, M., T. R. Christensen, and M. J. Seigert, eds. *The Routledge Handbook of the Polar Regions* (London: Routledge 2018).

Pielou, E. C. *A Naturalist's Guide to the Arctic* (Chicago and London: University of Chicago Press 1994).

Vaughan, R. *The Arctic: A History* (London: History Press 2008).

Zellan, B. *Arctic Doom, Arctic Boom: The Geopolitics of Climate Change in the Arctic* (Boulder: Praeger 2009).

Chapter 1. Locating True North

Blum, H. *The News at the End of the Earth* (Durham, NC: Duke University Press 2019).

Bravo, M. 2019. *North Pole: Nature and Culture* Chicago: University of Chicago Press.

Coates, K., and W. Morrison. "The New North in Canadian History and Historiography." *Geography Compass* 6 (2008): 639–658.

Craciun, A. *Writing Arctic Disaster* (Cambridge: Cambridge University Press 2016).

Davidson, P. *The Idea of the North* (London: Reaktion 2005).

Francis, G. *True North: Travels in Arctic Europe* (Edinburgh: Birlinn 2011).

Griffin, D. "Hollow and Habitable Within: Symmes's Theory of Earth's Internal Structure and Polar Geography." *Physical Geography* 25 (2004): 382–397.

Hamelin, L. *Canadian Nordicity: Its Your North Too* (Montreal: Harvest Press 1979).

Kavenna, J. *The Ice Museum: In Search of the Lost Land of Thule* (London: Penguin 2006).

Lewis, M., and K. Wigen. *The Myths of Continents* (Berkeley: University of California Press 1997).

Troubetzkoy, A. *Arctic Obsession: The Lure of the True North* (Toronto: Dundurn 2008).

Chapter 2. Land, Sea, and Ice

ACIA. *Arctic Climate Impact Assessment* (Oslo: AMAP 2005).

AMAP. *Arctic Climate Issues: Changes in Arctic Snow, Water, Ice and Permafrost* (Oslo: AMAP 2011).

Campbell, N. *The Library of Ice: Readings from a Cold Climate* (New York: Simon and Schuster 2018).

Dodds, K. *Ice: Nature and Culture* (Chicago: University of Chicago Press 2018).

Huryn, A., and J. Hobbie. *Land of Extremes: A Natural History of the Arctic North Slope of Alaska* (Fairbanks: University of Alaska Press 2012).

Jouzel, J., C. Lorius, and D. Raynaud. *The White Planet: The Evolution and Future of Our Frozen World* (Princeton: Princeton University Press 2013).

Serreze, M. *Brave New Arctic: The Untold Story of the Melting North* (Princeton: Princeton University Press 2018).

Thomas, D. *Sea Ice* (Chichester: John Wiley 2016).

Wadhams, P. *A Farewell to Ice* (Oxford: Oxford University Press 2017).

Chapter 3. Arctic Homelands

Berry, D., N. Bowles, and H. Jones, eds. *Governing the North American Arctic: Sovereignty, Security, and Institutions* (London: Palgrave 2016).

Bravo, M., and S. Sorlin, eds. *Narrating the Arctic: A Cultural History of Nordic Scientific Practices* (Canton, MA: Science History Publications 2002).

Cruikshank, J. *Do Glaciers Listen? Local Knowledge, Colonial Encounters, and Social Imagination* (Vancouver: University of British Columbia Press 2014).

Friesen, T., and O. Mason, eds. *The Oxford Handbook of the Prehistoric Arctic* (Oxford: Oxford University Press 2016).

McLeish, T. *Narwhals: Arctic Whales in a Melting World* (Seattle: University of Washington Press 2013).

Nuttall, M. *Arctic Homeland: Kinship, Community, and Development in Northwest Greenland* (Toronto: University of Toronto Press 1992).

Petrone, P. ed. *Northern Voices: Inuit Writings in English* (Toronto: University of Toronto Press 1988).

Sorlin, S. ed. *Science, Geopolitics and Culture in the Polar Region: Norden Beyond Borders* (London: Routledge 2016).

Chapter 4. From Colonization to Cooperation

Campbell, N. *Disko Bay* (Edinburgh: Enitharmon Press 2015).

Herzberg, J., C. Kehrt, and F. Torma, eds. *Ice and Snow in the Cold War: Histories of Extreme Climatic Environments* (Oxford: Berghahn Press 2019).

Hønneland, G. *Arctic Euphoria and International High North Politics* (London: Palgrave 2017).

Huggan, G., and L. Jensen, eds. *Postcolonial Perspectives on the European High North: Unscrambling the Arctic* (London: Palgrave 2016).

Jakobson, L., and N. Melvin. *The New Arctic Governance* (Oxford: Oxford University Press 2016).

Kelman, I. ed. *Arcticness: Power and Voice from the North* (London: UCL Press 2017).

Kent, N. *The Sami Peoples of the North: A Social and Cultural History* (London: C Hurst 2018).

McCannon, J. *Red Arctic: Polar Exploration and the Myth of the North in the Soviet Union* (Oxford: Oxford University Press 1998).

McCorristine, S. *The Spectral Arctic: A History of Ghosts and Dreams in Polar Exploration* (London: UCL Press 2018).

Nord, D. *The Changing Arctic: Consensus Building and Governance in the Arctic Council* (London: Palgrave 2016).

Chapter 5. Warming Arctic
Christensen, M., A. Nilsson, and N. Wormbs, eds. *Media and the Politics of Arctic Climate Change* (London: Palgrave 2013).

Kraska, J. ed. *Arctic Security in an Era of Climate Change* (Cambridge: Cambridge University Press 2011).

Lemke, P., and H. Jacobi, eds. *Arctic Climate Change* (Berlin: Springer 2011).

Nuttall, M. *Climate, Society and Subsurface Politics in Greenland: Under the Great Ice* (London: Routledge 2017).

Orttung, R., ed. *Sustaining Russia's Arctic Cities: Resource Politics, Migration, and Climate Change* (Oxford: Berghahn Press 2016).

Sejersen, F. *Rethinking Greenland and the Arctic in an Era of Climate Change* (London: Routledge 2015).

Chapter 6. Resourceful Arctic
Byers, M. *Who Owns the Arctic?* (Toronto: Douglas and McIntyre 2010).

Fondahl, G., and G. Wilson, eds. *Northern Sustainabilities: Understanding and Addressing Change in the Circumpolar World* (Berlin: Springer 2017).

Gad, U., and J. Strandsbjerg, eds. *The Politics of Sustainability in the Arctic: Reconfiguring Identity, Space, and Time* (London: Routledge 2018).

Hønneland, G. *International Politics in the Arctic: Contested Borders, Natural Resources and Russian Foreign Policy* (London: I B Tauris 2017).

Howard, R. *The Arctic Gold Rush* (London: Bloomsbury 2010).

Le Miere, C., and J. Mazo. *Arctic Opening: Insecurity and Opportunity* (London: Routledge 2013).

Nuttall, M. *Pipeline Dreams: People, Environment, and the Arctic Energy Frontier* (Copenhagen: International Work Group for Indigenous Affairs 2010).

Shadian, J. *The Politics of Arctic Sovereignty: Oil, Ice, and Inuit Governance* (London: Routledge 2014).

Southcott, C., F. Abele, D. Natcher, and B. Parlee, eds. *Resources and Sustainable Development in the Arctic* (London: Routledge 2018).

Chapter 7. The Global Arctic
Brady, A.-M. *China as a Polar Great Power* (Cambridge: Cambridge University Press 2017).

Byers, M. *International Law and the Arctic* (Cambridge: Cambridge University Press 2013).

Conde, E., and S. Sánchez, eds. *Global Challenges in the Arctic Region* (London: Routledge 2016).

Evengård, B., J. N. Larsen, and Ø. Paasche, eds. *The New Arctic* (Berlin: Springer 2015).

Finger, M., and L. Heininen, eds. *The Global Arctic Handbook* (Berlin: Springer 2018).

Heininen, L., ed. *Future Security of the Global Arctic* (London: Palgrave 2013).

Keil, K., and S. Knecht, eds. *Governing Arctic Change* (London: Palgrave 2016).

Kristensen, K., and J. Rahbek-Clemmensen, eds. *Greenland and the International Politics of a Changing Arctic* (London: Routledge 2017).

Murray, R. W., and A. Dey Nuttall, eds. *International Relations and the Arctic: Understanding Policy and Governance* (New York: Cambria Press 2014).

Tamnes, R., and K. Offerdal, eds. *Geopolitics and Security in the Arctic: Regional Dynamics in a Global World* (London: Routledge 2014).

Tonami, A. *Asian Foreign Policy in a Changing Arctic* (London: Palgrave 2016).

Wilson Rowe, E. *Arctic Governance* (Manchester: Manchester University Press 2018).

Select web resources on the Arctic

There are a myriad of web-based resources addressing the Arctic region and this list is intended as an sample.

Arctic Circle: http://www.arcticcircle.org

Arctic Council: https://arctic-council.org/index.php/en/

Arctic Economic Council: https://arcticeconomiccouncil.com

Arctic Frontiers: https://www.arcticfrontiers.com

Arctic Portal: https://arcticportal.org

Association of Arctic Expedition Cruise Operators: https://www.aeco.no/resources-and-tools/

Atlas of Community Based Monitoring in a Changing Arctic: https://aoos.org/alaska-community-based-monitoring/what-are-we-observing/atlas-of-cbm/

Canadian Ice Service: https://www.canada.ca/en/environment-climate-change/services/ice-forecasts-observations/latest-conditions.html

Discovering the Arctic: https://discoveringthearctic.org.uk
European Union Arctic Policy: https://eeas.europa.eu/arctic-policy/
    eu-arctic-policy_en
Greenpeace: https://www.greenpeace.org/international/act/
    save-the-arctic/
International Arctic Science Committee: https://iasc.info
Inuit Circumpolar Council: http://www.inuitcircumpolar.com
National Ocean and Atmospheric Administrations's Arctic
    program: https://www.arctic.noaa.gov
National Snow and Ice Data Center: https://nsidc.org
Norwegian Ice Service: http://polarview.met.no
Northern Sea Route Administration (Russia): http://www.nsra.ru/en/
    home.html
Oceans North: https://oceansnorth.org/en/
    canada-arctic-marine-atlas/
Pan-Inuit Trails: http://www.paninuittrails.org/index.
    html?module=module.about
Polar Research Institute of China: http://www.polar.org.cn/en/index/
Sami Council: http://www.saamicouncil.net/en/
Scott Polar Research Institute, University of Cambridge: https://www.
    spri.cam.ac.uk
University of the Arctic: http://www.polar.org.cn/en/index/
Yup'ik Environmental Knowledge Project Atlas: https://eloka-arctic.
    org/communities/yupik/atlas/index.html

INDEX